The Growth Experiment

THE GROWTH EXPERIMENT

How the New Tax Policy is Transforming the U.S. Economy

Lawrence Lindsey

Basic Books, Inc., Publishers

NEW YORK

Library of Congress Cataloging-in-Publication Data
Lindsey, Lawrence.
  The growth experiment: how the new tax policy is
transforming the U.S. economy/Lawrence Lindsey.
    p.   cm.
    Includes bibliographical references (p. 241)
    ISBN 0–465–02750–4
    1. Taxation—United States.   2. Supply-side
economics—United States.   I. Title.
HJ2381.L53   1990
339.5′25—dc20   89-43100

To Susan . . .

Contents

Acknowledgments

Many individuals and organizations helped make this book possible. I would like to thank in particular the National Bureau of Economic Research for access to its TAXSIM model and for a stimulating intellectual environment. Martin Feldstein, president of the bureau and my teacher and thesis adviser at Harvard, taught me much of the economics I know. His learning inspired much of the work that went into this book and his character provides a constant model of intellectual integrity to all who have the good fortune to be associated with him. The Manhattan Institute, under the inspired leadership of William Hammett, provided crucial intellectual, moral, and financial support. Without Bill's initiative and guidance, this book, like so many important works of recent years, might never have seen the light of day. Special recognition should also go to Manhattan Institute Senior Fellow Richard Vigilante for his expert editorial work. Andrew Mitrusi, John Navratil, and Jason Lewis provided indispensable research assistance. The uncompromising standards of Martin Kessler, publisher of Basic Books, elevated and enlarged my own vision of what the book could be. Lydia Lesh, also of Basic, eased the labor pains of an author with his firstborn, and Stephanie Hoppe was an incisive and elegant copy editor. Thanks also to Betty McGrath for providing a quiet place to work.

Although this book was written while the author was a professor at Harvard University, its contents reflect the author's personal views and not those of any employer, past or present.

For all her special support throughout the years and for her patience and encouragement during this project, I dedicate this book to my wife, Susan.

PART I

The Great Experiment

Chapter 1

The Revolution of '81

"To tax and to please, no more than to love and be wise,
is not given to men."
—EDMUND BURKE, 1774

In 1980 the nation was in the grips of the greatest economic crisis it has faced since the Great Depression. The United States had endured a decade of chronic economic disappointment accompanied by a series of acute political shocks, from the defeat in Vietnam to the OPEC oil crises. Not since the Depression had the American economy seemed so fundamentally flawed, or had so many Americans questioned our ability to control our own economic destiny. It was not uncommon to hear economists and political leaders arguing that we were doomed to declining standards of living, that we had entered an Era of Limits, that the new economic order was controlled by OPEC or governed by an ever tightening supply of natural resources.

In January 1980 consumer prices rose 1.4[1] percent. That month's increase exceeded the average *annual* rate of inflation during the 1950s and early 1960s. Had that rate continued for the full year, consumer prices would have risen 18.2[2] percent. Charles Schultze, then chairman of the Council of Economic Advisers, explained to the press that inflation for the year would really be only about 12 percent, but acknowledged that "The Nation has for some time now experienced inflation that would have been unimaginable in earlier days."[3]

Inflation for the year was held down to 12.5[4] percent, largely because output and employment were declining as well. In the second quarter of 1980 the nation experienced one of the fastest economic declines on record, 9.9 percent at an annual rate,[5] exceeding the rate of economic collapse during the Great Depression. It took a major reversal of policy in the third quarter of the year, including another blast of inflationary money creation,[6] to take the economy out of its tailspin. The number of unemployed rose more than 1.3 million in just two months. The unemployment rate climbed from 6.3 percent in March to 7.8 percent in July.[7]

The combination of inflation and unemployment was expressed by a statistic known as the "Misery Index," which sums up the two rates. The index, a rhetorical device invented by the Carter presidential campaign in 1976, stood at 13.5 in that year. By 1980 the Misery Index reached 20.6.[8] The prime interest rate peaked at 21.5 percent just before Carter left office.[9] The real wages of American workers plunged by 9 percent in just the two-year period 1979–81, offsetting nearly two decades of growth and reducing real wages to their 1962 level.[10] With the enormous tax increases accumulated over that period, workers in 1979 were far worse off than their counterparts in 1962. American workers had not taken such giant steps backwards since the 1930s.

Two years later the nation had embarked on the longest and strongest peacetime economic expansion in history, an expansion that would eventually bring more than twenty million new jobs[11] to a once-discouraged American work force and revitalize states and regions of the country that shortly before seemed doomed to years of frustration and decline. The prime force behind this recovery was a revolution in economic policy that was scorned by many orthodox economists. This new direction in economics, though not without its own flaws, revitalized the economy while simultaneously subduing inflation and reducing the burden of government on American businesses and families. This new wave of economic thought is still controversial. But its effects have made the U.S. once again the leader of the world economy and inspired nations throughout the industrialized and developing world to dramatically revise their own economic strategies.

This book is about our most recent cycle of economic decline and economic renewal and the strategy that accomplished the transition from one to the other. It is also more: the story of the clash between an *economic orthodoxy* in decline and a challenger from the fringes of economic thought. Most important, it is a story about limits: the limits of a tax that first revolutionized and then dominated public finance, and to a large extent national politics, for three-quarters of a century.

It is no coincidence that these themes all derive from the same story. In 1981 the income tax, certainly the most powerful force behind the growing size and power of the federal government in this century, had reached its economic and political limits. The national economic crisis was caused in no small part by the constraints the continuous expansion of the tax placed on the economy. The orthodox Keynesian economists who, for philosophical as well as policy reasons had pushed the income tax to and even beyond its limits, were forced by the distortions of the tax they championed into positions that became untenable. The intellectual challengers, who have come to be known as the supply-side school, were, it appears in retrospect, exceptionally clever in selecting the income tax as the issue on which to do political battle. In the presidential election year of 1980, it was the political Achilles' heel of Keynesian orthodoxy.

Among those interested in the study of intellectual revolutions, 1981 will be known as a landmark. The supply-side challenge of that year was the greatest challenge to a reigning economic dogma since the overthrow of classical economics in the 1930s. Throughout the 1970s, Keynesian economics, once the New Economics, but by then the new orthodoxy, had reigned supreme. Like many an orthodoxy, it had never seemed so secure as in the last few years before its demise.

The Keynesians, whose views had been forged in the Great Depression, with its catastrophic contraction in the supply of money and credit, believed that government could most effectively manage the economy by managing the demand for goods and services. The government could do this through fiscal policy, primarily by increasing or diminishing government debt through changes in tax and spending policies. In times of economic contraction the government would spend more, thus increasing demand directly, and take in less taxes, thereby raising the income of consumers and boosting demand indirectly. The increase in demand for goods and services would stimulate new production and employment and the economy would expand. Under the opposite economic conditions the government would reduce spending or raise taxes to keep the economy from overheating and prices from rising.[12]

These policies were followed scrupulously throughout the 1970s. The government repeatedly stimulated the economy through spending increases or tax cuts. The latter did not reduce taxes overall, but did redistribute taxes so as to pump cash into the hands of consumers most likely to spend it. As the decade progressed, however, the inflation that resulted from these initiatives was almost always worse than expected and economic growth less. When the government reined in spending, inflation did not slow as much as it should have, and the anti-inflationary recessions seemed always to be worse than expected.[13] By 1980 this set of policy prescriptions had reached both its practical and theoretical limits.

Contemporary Keynesian theory, based on the Keynesian prescriptions of the 1930s,* simply could not account for the economic facts of the late 1970s. The Keynesians had no solution for the combination of rising prices (which to them indicated excess demand) and a falling economy with high unemployment (which indicated too little demand). The Keynesians were accustomed to using government fiscal policy to smooth out the booms and busts of the business cycle. But by the late seventies the business cycle had twisted into a diabolic double helix, in which unemployment and inflation rose together. The

---

*Though Keynes himself would probably not have been a 1970s–style Keynesian.

new economic malady was called stagflation,[14] and the Keynesians had nothing in their medicine cabinet to cure it.

The challengers, the supply-side school, contradicted contemporary Keynesianism on almost every point. The Keynesians were macroeconomists in their approach. They believed the most effective tools of economic policy were manipulations of broad aggregate phenomena, the most important being aggregate demand. The supply-siders were primarily microeconomists who believed the most important precept of economic policy making was to pay attention to how government policies affected individual decisions to work, save, and invest. Whereas the Keynesians believed in short-run economic management, the supply-siders stressed basic incentives for long-term economic growth. "In the long run we're all dead,"[15] went Keynes's most famous line. To many it seemed that the economy of 1980 had reached the long run.

The Keynesians regarded tax cuts simply as a way to give cash to consumers, or the demand side of the economy, and designed their tax cuts accordingly. The Keynesians did not believe that income taxes did much to discourage either the production of new wealth or the elements of production, such as labor and capital. The supply-siders, on the contrary, focused on the supply-side, or incentive effects of tax policy. For them, tax policy represented the key to the problems of the 1970s and the solution for the 1980s. High tax rates discouraged people from working, saving, and investing and thereby caused the economy to slow and unemployment to rise. Sharp tax cuts aimed at restoring incentives would solve the stagflation dilemma. The right tax cut would work not by stimulating demand alone but supply as well. If the government restored incentives to work, save, and invest, old businesses would be made more efficient and new entrepreneurs would be more willing to take the risks that yield higher rewards. More workers would be hired, and unemployment would fall. Though the supply-siders accepted that tax cuts could stimulate demand, their prescription for economic recovery emphasized not the spending power of the buyer, but the productive power of the seller.

A tax cut, moreover, by lowering the costs of production and increasing volume, would allow the resulting products to sell at a lower price than would be possible with high tax rates. Thus the supply-siders argued that the right type of tax cut would actually restrain inflation. To the Keynesians this seemed the ultimate heresy. Yet many supply-siders went a step further. They also maintained that the right tax cut would substantially pay for itself. High tax rates, they argued, so discouraged productive activity, and so encouraged tax avoidance and even tax evasion, that reducing rates might bring in more revenue.

It is hardly an exaggeration to say the Keynesians as well as most of the media and political establishment were horrified. Carter's treasury secretary, William Miller, argued in 1980, "It would be a great hoax on the American people to promise a tax cut that sets off a new price spiral."[16] Leading Keynesian economist Walter Heller, chairman of Kennedy's Council of Economic Advisers, argued that the huge tax cuts advocated by the supply-siders "would simply overwhelm our existing productive capacity with a tidal wave of increased demand and sweep away all hopes of curbing deficits and containing inflation. Indeed, it would soon generate soaring deficits and roaring inflation."[17]

The Keynesians might not know how to stop stagflation, but they were sure a big tax cut would make inflation worse. They were not sure how safely to restore full employment, but they knew that the high employment and inflation were inexorably linked. Almost no one other than the supply-siders themselves took seriously the claim that reductions in tax rates would pay for themselves. Thus when Ronald Reagan, who throughout his political career had advocated conventional Republican economics (conservative Keynesianism and monetarism), adopted the supply-side program by resting his campaign on a platform of substantial reductions in income tax rates, two great battles were joined: one for the health of the economy and the other

for the future of economics. To most Americans, the first battle
probably seemed more important. The world as most people see
it is not kept spinning by the musings of economists. Yet the
Great Experiment in supply-side economics ushered in by Reagan's decisive victory over an incumbent president in 1980 and
the substantial reductions in income taxes enacted a few
months later yielded insights into economic policy that over the
rest of this century and beyond may be even more valuable than
the record-setting economic expansion that followed.

Though the 1984 and 1988 elections vindicated the Reagan
tax cuts politically, the economic debate over what really happened in the eighties still rages. Keynesians and other representatives of the old economic orthodoxy still insist that Reaganomics was hokum and that the recovery of the 1980s was the
product of standard Keynesian demand stimulus. As careful
research often shows in a dispute of such magnitude, neither
side is entirely correct. Nevertheless, as we shall see in following chapters, the supply-siders proved more right than the
Keynesians on every practical issue in the debate of the early
eighties. While most policy prescriptions are lucky to be just a
little more right than wrong, perhaps earning a "C," the supply-
side experiments of the 1980s deserve at least a "B plus" if not
an "A."[18]

It often happens when an orthodox theory is shaken that the
protests of the true believers take on an air of desperation.
Keynes, himself the subject of orthodox criticisms half a century ago, noted that such protests, "will fluctuate, I expect,
between a belief that I am quite wrong and a belief that I am
saying nothing new."[19] In this case the belief that the challengers are wrong can be subjected to quantitative analysis and the
results will speak for themselves. History is the test of the claim
that the supply-side challengers said nothing new. The true
believers in the old economic orthodoxy need to be reminded
just how vociferous their objections were to the supply-side
challenge.

The 1981 tax cuts represented as clear a test of the Keynesian and supply-side paradigms as anyone could have designed. Some of the more extreme supply-side hypotheses were proven false. But the core supply-side tenet—that tax rates powerfully affect the willingness of taxpayers to work, save, and invest and thereby also affect the health of the economy—won as stunning a vindication as has been seen in at least a half century of economics. The old orthodoxy has retreated from its first line of defense—that the supply-siders were wrong—to the claim that the supply-siders said nothing new. This is the sure sign that an economic orthodoxy has reached its limits.

But the limits discovered in 1981 were more than theoretical. The income tax had reached its practical limits as well. Like any machine, the income tax broke down from overuse and abuse. The job of the income tax, like any tax, is to produce revenue. But for decades it had been used heavily for other purposes as well: income redistribution, macroeconomic management, and social engineering. The engine of income taxation was tinkered with repeatedly in the name of fine-tuning. The tax code had been changed every other year, on average, during the 1970s. In 1980 President Carter's advisers contemplated the addition of yet another gadget: tax-based "income policies"[20] that would control inflationary wage demands at the level of the individual taxpayer. Had the vote come out differently in November 1980, it is likely that the income tax—the engine driving the nation's fiscal machine—would have continued to disintegrate, causing ever more serious economic breakdowns.

Instead, the dramatic reforms of the income tax undertaken by the Reagan administration produced results the Keynesian fine-tuners could not have expected. On the most controversial supply-side claim—that reductions in high rates would bring in more revenue than they lost—the facts are as clear as they are unacknowledged. The reductions in upper-income tax rates produced a net increase in government revenue. Tax cuts for the upper-middle class just about broke even. Only the reductions in the relatively low rates on moderate- and low-income taxpayers caused the tax cut to be a net revenue loser, though not by nearly as much as the critics had predicted and still often claim. These revenue results clearly showed that high income tax rates had passed the limits of their usefulness as revenue producers (see chapter 4).

The income tax had also reached its limit as an income redistributor. The Reagan tax cut, often denounced as a huge favor to the rich, actually reaped a larger share of tax revenue from rich and upper-middle-class taxpayers than the old tax code had and substantially reduced the relative contribution of middle-income taxpayers (see chapter 5).

The Reagan tax cut also devastated the Keynesian view of the causes of inflation. In the first five years in which the tax cuts were in effect, the inflation rate averaged only 3.3 percent,[21] the lowest rate for any five-year period since the early 1960s. To paraphrase Winston Churchill, "Rarely have so many been so wrong about so much." As we will show, inflation dropped in the 1980s not only because of the Federal Reserve's tight money policy, but also in part because of the tax cuts (see chapter 7). The income tax had reached its limits as a macroeconomic stabilizer, at least in the way the Keynesians had been using it.

As to the source of the Reagan boom, the stimulus to consumer demand was, as always, instrumental to recovery, perhaps even more so than the supply-siders expected. But careful analysis of the data shows that it was the renewed incentives to supply that caused the recovery to set peacetime records for length and strength. Recently it has been popular to argue that the Reagan boom was built on debt and consumer spending that we could ill afford. In fact, consumer spending grew at a rate about normal for a recovery, and the Reagan boom was distinguished by an especially rapid growth in business investment.[22] The recovery of the eighties was not launched on a sea of red ink. Americans are not, as Reagan critics claim, in debt up to their ears. Their financial positions improved quite substantially after the tax cut. The same cannot be said of the government. High rates of government borrowing are a long-term problem. But despite persistent claims to the contrary, the

Reagan tax cuts contributed only trivially to the booming deficits of the 1980s. The profligates of the 1980s were not the tax cutters or the consumers but the politicians whose vast spending produced huge deficits they now blame on the tax cuts.

These conclusions are still widely denied by those with a stake in the old orthodoxy. In part the continuing argument is a product of philosophical disagreements about human nature and the role of government and can never be fully resolved by economists no matter how sound their data. But in part the argument has persisted for lack of the data or methods of analysis to settle important disputes of fact. This book will remedy that deficit.

For instance, the job of figuring out whether a tax cut lost or gained revenue turns out to be extremely complex. It is not possible simply to compare the old pre–tax cut revenue estimates with the post–tax cut revenue report. A tax cut changes not only the government's share in the economy but the economy itself. To assess the effects of a tax cut requires a complex and dynamic model of economic decisions and the analysis of large numbers of actual tax returns, totaling tens of millions of bits of data. Practically speaking, the computer technology to do all this has not been available until this decade, and our analytic methods have only recently caught up to the technology.[23] As the data roll in, however, the results of the great Reagan experiment are likely to revolutionize economics and government policy for many decades to come. Crafting incentives for individuals will displace the gross management of economic aggregates as the key to successful economic policy. The creation of wealth will displace its redistribution as the prime concern of government. The scope of state economic power will shrink in the face of mounting evidence that aggressive state intervention, like high tax rates themselves, distorts the natural productive impulses of the people.

In its simplest form the supply-side claim has been, "Taxes matter." In large part this is because the income tax, once a levy on the elite, now profoundly affects the economic lives—and economic behavior—of the vast majority of the population. The nearly universal application of the tax means that federal policies on issues ranging from child care to capital formation to home ownership can be implemented simply by adjusting tax rules. Of course, just because tax policy is a powerful tool for changing behavior does not mean that using it for that purpose is a good idea. President Reagan's underlying policy in cutting tax rates was to reduce the power of taxes over our lives, and in so doing he struck the key blow for a less intrusive government and for more freedom for individual decision making.

Taxes matter because economics is not finally a science of aggregate numbers but a study of human nature. The founders of modern economics in the eighteenth and nineteenth centuries had a high regard for human nature. The intricate mechanisms of the free market model they first developed depend on the assumption that people will react acutely and intelligently to incentives and opportunities, risks and rewards. Those who argue that taxes do not matter are really saying that workers and savers, taxpayers and risk takers are insensitive to the price of government and that citizens will passively allow governments to solve all its problems by writing another invoice to the people.

It is crucial that we learn the right lessons from the great experiment of the 1980s. Not every Reagan tax initiative worked, and those that did work brought costs as well as benefits. Understanding what worked in the 1980s and before will help us make successful tax policy for the 1990s and beyond. The task is an urgent one: now that tax policy has taken center stage in the economic debate we can expect as many foolish tax initiatives as wise ones. The 1981 tax rate reductions took a meat axe to the tax code. Future operations are going to require a scalpel. But to wield the scalpel effectively we must first learn how the meat axe did its job.

The tax policy debate to come will not be over the level of tax rates. Reaganomics has been so successful in practice that only a handful of ideologues advocate a return to dramatically higher tax rates. Future tax policy debates will address the fine-tuning of specific provisions, to reduce inefficiencies in the economy; to hone the nation's competitive edge in a world in which many other nations have learned the lessons of Reaganomics; to encourage investments that help us work smarter, not harder; and, perhaps most pressing of all, to help middle- and working-class families with desperately needed tax relief.

The 1980s tested our willingness to experiment with a radical new approach to economic policy. The 1990s will test our willingness to learn from our mistakes and from our successes. The time has come to set the record straight regarding the great tax-cutting experiments of the 1980s and, in so doing, set the agenda for the tax reforms of the 1990s.

Chapter 2

The Psychic Taxpayer

"In this world nothing can be said to be truly certain except
death and taxes."
— BENJAMIN FRANKLIN in a letter to Jean Baptiste Leroy,
13 November 1789

April 15. No other date on the calendar, save possibly December 25, is as indelibly etched in the national psyche. Yet the proverbial visitor from Mars might wonder what all the hoopla is about. Although income tax returns are due on April 15, most of the taxes people owe were paid during the preceding year and determined by decisions even farther in the past. And though many of us resolve on April 15 to do things differently next year, these resolutions are often forgotten in the wave of relief that comes when the tax form is finally dropped in the mailbox.

The trauma of April 15 symbolizes the cumulative effect of the tax system on our lives. Like the Judgment Day, April 15 settles all accounts. Our sins and our good works are placed in balance and our fiscal fate decided. If we have been good, we sing a chorus of hosannahs and await our reward, the refund check. If we have been bad, we usually wait until the last minute, search deep in our files for that extra deduction, that forgotten act upon which the IRS may smile, hoping that it will mitigate our guilt and our balance due.

April 15 is such a red-letter day because the income tax is designed to change our behavior as well as to collect tax revenue. As such, it is an adjunct to the judicial system. Threats of legal action, fines, or prison are meant to make us obey the explicit dictates of the law. But the tax system goes beyond the simple categories of lawful or unlawful. Within the category of lawful activities, the tax system introduces many shades of gray, ranging from lawful and untaxed to lawful but heavily taxed. The ability of the tax system to change our behavior in this nuanced way, without the cumbersome mechanics of arrest and trial, gives the government a power in some ways far more extensive than that of the legal system.

The tax system influences us in ways that are subtle, often subliminal, and frequently difficult for individuals to measure. Taxes influence us by changing the relative costs of the goods we buy and the rewards we receive for working, saving, and taking risks. We take these tax effects into account just as we take the prices of chicken and beef into account in deciding what to buy at the grocery store, or the salary offered in deciding which job to take. Economists often say that people don't *know* their tax rates but *act* as if they do. Tax-induced changes in behavior may be too small for individuals themselves to recognize and yet result in economic changes worth billions of dollars in the aggregate. Like a psychic in his trance, taxpayers responding to tax rates deliver loud and clear a message they may never hear themselves.

For example, economic studies have established beyond any shadow of a doubt that taxes have a dramatic effect on how much people donate to charitable organizations.[1] When tax rates go up, the value of the deduction a taxpayer receives for making a charitable gift also rises. This causes taxpayers, in the aggregate, to increase the amount they contribute. Yet when people are asked in surveys if taxes influence their charitable giving, they usually deny it, maintaining they are motivated only by their means and the worthiness of the cause.[2] However, these surveys also reveal that most people believe other donors are influenced by the prospect of a tax deduction, particularly those in different economic circumstances.

When Chief Justice John Marshall said, "The power to tax

involves the power to destroy,"[3] he was underscoring the potential of any tax to alter the behavior of the taxpayer. A tax will destroy the taxed activity completely if it is sufficient to eliminate all of the profit in that activity. Typically we think of this as occurring at a very high rate of tax, but this need not be the case. Marshall's famous dictum from *McCulloch* v. *Maryland,* refers to a tax rate of only about 2 percent that the state of Maryland proposed to levy on bank notes issued by non-Maryland banks. Thus a dollar bill issued by a Maryland bank would cost $1.00, but a dollar bill issued by another bank would cost $1.02. It was obvious—indeed it was the intent—that non-Maryland bank notes would soon disappear from Maryland, for no one would use dollar bills that cost $1.02 if dollar bills costing only $1.00 were available.

As the Maryland tax shows, the damage done by a tax depends not only on the rate at which it is levied, but also on the base on which it is being imposed. Non-Maryland bank notes were a fragile and narrow base on which to impose a tax because it would be very easy to substitute Maryland bank notes and pay no tax. Even if the Maryland law had not been struck down it would soon have collected no revenue, for no one in Maryland would have used out-of-state or federal notes. Of course, that would not have bothered Maryland; the state's aim was not to collect revenue but to protect Maryland banks.

The Maryland tax illustrates the two most important consequences of making a tax rate too burdensome for the base on which it is raised. The first consequence is that the base itself—usually some form of economic activity—will shrink. In this case, the base was non-Maryland bank notes, which would have disappeared altogether. The second consequence of excessive tax rates is that revenues will be lower than expected or even, as in this case, the revenue actually would have vanished.

These two costs of excessive taxation are quite distinct, yet they go hand in hand. The shrinking of the base causes the decline in revenues, and the decline in revenues is a sign (though not a one-for-one measurement) of the shrinking of the base. For an example somewhat more realistic than the Maryland case, consider the tariffs and excise taxes on which federal revenues were based until the early twentieth century. The base on which a tariff is levied, say imported steel, is usually much broader and less sensitive than non-Maryland bank notes. Importing steel is a substantial and risky enterprise that will be undertaken only when foreign steel has sufficient advantages in price, quality, or other factors to outsell domestic steel at a profit. A 5 percent tariff on imported steel would probably not destroy the steel import business. Nevertheless, as the tariff rate was raised the amount of imported steel would gradually fall and revenue would shrink by that degree. If a 5 percent tariff raised $50,000 on $1 million worth of imported steel in a year, a 10 percent tariff would probably not raise $100,000. Since somewhat less steel would be imported under the higher tariff, it might raise only $80,000 or $90,000. Push the tariff high enough and revenues will not only be lower than expected, but will fall below the original $50,000. Push the tariff higher still and both imported steel and tariff revenues will disappear.

Shrinking revenue on rising rates is a sure indication that a tax has been pushed too far. But even if revenue does not shrink absolutely, but rises somewhat, the increase may come at too high a price. When we raise the tariff on imported steel, we not only get somewhat less additional revenue than we expected, we lose the economic value of the steel not imported. People were importing that steel for a good economic reason; its loss will have an economic cost. If it was cheaper than domestic steel, steel prices will now rise and fewer projects requiring steel will go forward. If the foreign steel had special qualities, those qualities will be lost to the economy.

It is not my purpose to argue for or against tariffs; these extra economic costs may very well be offset by other benefits. My point is that when tax rates cause the tax base to shrink, that is, diminish some economic activity, the loss of that activity has a cost over and above the revenue produced by the tax. These additional costs, beyond the tax payment itself, imposed on society by a tax are called the "excess burden" of a tax.[4] We must have taxes, and all taxes impose some excess burden. The key to sensible pro-growth tax design is to raise the needed revenue with the least excess burden on the economy.

The broader and more durable the tax base, the higher tax rates can rise before taxpayers change their behavior enough to narrow the base and reduce revenue significantly. Even a modest tax on Ford automobiles would considerably change taxpayer behavior: Ford customers would buy Chevys. Because there is not much cost to the individual in switching from a Ford to a Chevy, Fords alone (like non-Maryland bank notes) make a narrow and fragile tax base. By contrast, even a rather stiff tax on all automobiles would not bring back the horse and buggy.

For many years most economists believed that personal income, the tax base for the income tax, was so strong and broad a tax base that it was not very sensitive to tax rates.[5] They reasoned that choosing to earn income is not like choosing between a Chevy or a Ford: Income is not optional. Everyone needs it no matter how high it is taxed.

Within limits these economists were right. The income tax base is less sensitive to rate charges than many other taxes. Nevertheless our seventy-five years of experience with the income tax in the United States, the dramatic results of the Reagan tax cut after the similar results of the Kennedy tax cut twenty years before, along with mounting evidence from abroad suggests that the income tax base is far more fragile than most economists believed even a few years ago.[6] There are numerous alternatives to earning taxable income. Wealthy investors can switch from high-yield, risky, and productive but taxable investments into municipal bonds, real estate, or tax shelters. Very high tax rates make a life of leisure look even more attractive to such people than it might otherwise. At the lower end of the economic scale, even middle-class taxpayers will discover the advantages of leisure when their overtime pay is taxed at 40 and 50 percent. Union negotiators understand full well the advantages of pay settlements that substitute untaxed fringe benefits for taxable cash.[7]

All these tax-driven decisions burden not only the treasury, which receives less revenue than expected, but the economy as a whole. Under excessive tax rates taxpayers may be driven as much by the desire to hide production as by the need to produce. A decade ago, the top U.S. rate of 70 percent was about average for the developed countries. At that rate, a taxpayer benefited as much by avoiding 30 cents in taxes as by earning an additional dollar.

The observation that high income tax rates may discourage the activities that produce income seems so commonsensical that we may wonder why governments would ever let taxes get so high. Of course, they need the money. Moreover the counterargument—that people must have income and so will produce even when tax rates are high—seems commonsensical as well. The trick of tax policy is to find where one principle leaves off and the other takes charge. Is it at 20 percent, 50 percent, or 70 percent that taxes cause too much pain to taxpayers and damage to the economy for the additional revenue they produce? Through most of the history of the income tax it has been impossible precisely to measure taxpayers' responses to rates. Only now with computer analysis of detailed tax return data can we accurately measure the true effect of tax rate changes.

Nevertheless, our first fifty years' experience with the income tax offers circumstantial evidence of the levels to which income taxes rates can safely be raised. Those lessons did not take hold with many economists or most politicians in part because for many years the income tax did not have nearly as much power over the lives and work of Americans as it has today. When the tax was first established in 1913, it applied only to rich or upper-middle-class taxpayers. Though the reach of the tax has since broadened continuously, only since World War II has it been a permanent and powerful force in the lives of nearly all Americans. Only in recent decades have most Americans faced for extended periods tax rates high enough to profoundly influence their behavior. It is hardly surprising that many economists have denied the power of high income tax rates over the economy when our experience of their broad application has been so brief.

In its infancy the income tax searched for limits, political and economic. In recent years it has found them. When high rates applied only to the rich, they brought few political consequences and their economic consequences were more easily ignored, even as the economic consequences of a tariff may be ignored when only a few people are directly involved in paying the bill. Income taxes can be raised to a much higher level than most tariffs before they do noticeable damage, but we have long since passed the point when they can be raised with impunity. Today every working American pays a significant tariff on his or her labor. The contemporary income tax places a tollgate at every workplace, savings institution, or investment house. Raise the tolls too high and the entire economy suffers directly and rapidly. Perhaps even more important, raise the toll too high and voters will rebel. In very large part the political limits of the income tax have forced us to learn its economic limits.

At the birth of the income tax in 1913, over 98 percent of American families were exempt from its levies. The standard tax rate was 1 percent on the first $20,000 of taxable income, but single taxpayers earning under $3,000 and married taxpayers earning under $4,000 (which included almost everyone) were exempt.[8] The 1913 income tax also included various "surtax" brackets which could add as much as six percentage points to the tax rate. The combined top rate of 7 percent began at a taxable income of $500,000. Today this income would be equal to $5 million in purchasing power and $15 million in relative position in the income distribution.[9]

Taxes rose moderately in 1916, but the increase left nearly all American families still altogether exempt. World War I brought the first real tax increase and began transforming the income tax from a class tax into a mass tax. The exemption for low-income earners was slashed to $1,000 for singles and $2,000 for married couples. The number of taxpayers increased more than tenfold, and the surtaxes were applied to lower income levels. The standard rate was raised to 6 percent and the top rate reached 77 percent. It was wartime, and patriotic zeal for the boys over there greatly muted opposition to the new rates.

This wartime expansion permanently changed both the public image and the political character of the income tax. It established that income taxes would ordinarily be paid by the moderately prosperous as well as the rich and that truly confiscatory rates were politically feasible. Levying confiscatory rates on the rich probably made it easier to convince the middle class that rates of 5 to 10 or 15 percent were reasonable. Moreover, the flood of revenue produced by Wilson's wartime rates revealed resources previously undreamt of by politicians or the public and permanently changed the political agenda of this country. Never again would the number of income taxpayers shrink to a small minority of the population. Though Progressives still spoke of the income tax as a "rich man's tax," most of the additional revenue did not come from the relative handful of wealthy taxpayers exposed to high rates but from the vastly increased ranks of citizens paying the 6 percent tax rate. In 1916, with a top rate of 15 percent, the income tax produced $173 million in revenue, 73 percent of which came from taxpayers earning over $100,000. By 1918, with the top rate at 77 percent, the income tax was producing $1,127 million in revenue. Only 42 percent of that money came from taxpayers earning over $100,000. While the revenues collected from the very rich jumped fourfold, taxpayers earning under $10,000 upped their contribution thirty-four–fold, from $7 million to $238 million.

In 1918 4.4 million Americans filed tax returns, eleven times the number that had done so in 1916. It was this much broader tax base, not the rise in rates, that produced the extra revenue. In fact, in spite of record wartime prosperity, and an enormous inflation of incomes between 1916 and 1918, the number of taxpayers reporting incomes over $100,000 dropped by nearly one-third between 1916 and 1918. The amount of income reported by these upper-bracket taxpayers fell by nearly half. Though most of these taxpayers had seen their tax rates rise eight or nine times 1916 levels, tax *revenues* from these taxpayers were only 3.7 times higher.[10] World War I thus brought the first demonstration in the United States of high income tax rates dramatically shrinking the tax base.

When peace came in 1919, taxes were barely reduced. In the wake of a postwar recession, Republican Warren Harding promised a "Return to Normalcy," including a return to previously normal rates of tax, and won election to the White House in a landslide. Harding delivered only a modest tax cut, more by fiddling with the exemption than by cutting rates, which stayed quite high. An increase in the amount of income exempt from taxes lowers taxes on the first dollars a taxpayer earns but not the additional dollars he earns. Such a reduction provides no incentive to earn more and thus no extra incentives for economic growth. The results were predictable—a major decline in tax revenue with minimal economic improvement.*

Harding's death brought Calvin Coolidge to office. Coolidge, with his secretary of the treasury, Andrew Mellon, engineered the first dramatic tax rate reduction in American history, and justified his decision by what we might today call supply-side arguments. In his 1924 state of the union address Coolidge argued that "the larger incomes of the country would actually yield more revenue to the Government if the basis of taxation were scientifically revised downward. . . . There is no escaping the fact that when the taxation of large incomes is excessive they tend to disappear."[11] Coolidge's proposal reduced the top rate from 73 percent to 25 percent (to start at a taxable income

---

*The tax rate that has the most effect on a taxpayer's behavior is the marginal rate, the rate on the next dollar he will earn. Take a fairly typical four-person family of today with an income of $35,000. On their first $13,000 of income, they pay no taxes. They pay 15 percent on the remainder for a total tax payment of $3,300. Though on average they give the government only 9 percent of their total income, their marginal rate is the 15 percent they pay on their next dollar earned. That is the tax rate a wage earner in the household considers in deciding whether to work overtime.

of $100,000), with similarly dramatic cuts for most other brackets. The lowest tax rate was cut from 4 percent to only 1.5 percent, and special exemptions for labor income reduced that rate even further, to 1.125 percent for most taxpayers. These reductions, together with an increase in the standard exemption, eliminated tax liability altogether for 2.5 million Americans.

Though the total tax package lost revenue at first, the results clearly vindicated Coolidge's supply-side intuition. Total tax receipts did decline from $861 million in 1922 to $734 million in 1925, a loss of $127 million. But this overall loss obscures more important events. The loss resulted entirely from cuts in the lower brackets, where rates had already been fairly low, and so had little effect on taxpayer behavior. A reduction in rates from 4 percent to 1 percent is a nice gift for the middle-class worker, but hardly changes his incentives. The higher exemptions and lower rates cost the government $340 million in revenue from taxpayers earning less than $10,000 a year. But families earning over $100,000 paid more in income tax than they had previously: $359 million in 1925, up from $300 million in 1922. By 1928 taxpayers earning over $100,000 per year were paying $714 million in income taxes, or 61 percent of the total. Taxpayers earning under $10,000 were paying only $36 million, or less than 4 percent of the total.

The tax rate reductions of the Coolidge era turned the income tax from a mass tax back into a class tax, and did so by sharply cutting the tax rates on the rich. Moreover, after the initial drop, total revenue growth continued strong for the next several years. In effect rich taxpayers had paid for a tax cut for the middle class, and had done so by having their own rates cut dramatically.

The Hoover administration started off with a dramatic tax increase, the Hawley-Smoot Tariff Act, which fueled a worldwide trade war. Along with inappropriate Federal Reserve policies, the tariff helped trigger the financial collapse that eventually became the Great Depression. Government revenues collapsed along with the economy. In short order the political establishment agreed that income taxes should be raised. They were, drastically. The government more than doubled all tax rates to two and a half times their previous level. (The bottom tax rate rose from 1.5 percent to 4 percent and the top tax rate went from 25 percent to 63 percent.) This increase in rates was coupled with a $1,000 reduction in the exemption for married couples and a $500 reduction for single taxpayers. Whatever the reasoning behind this draconian increase, it has been judged by history a blunder of the highest magnitude. Keynesians and supply-siders alike now argue that the tax rate increase of 1932 helped turn what was a deep recession into the Great Depression.

Though the tax increase was a disaster for the economy, it could claim modest success as a budgetary measure. Income tax revenue rose from $246 million in fiscal 1931 to $330 million in 1932 and $374 million in 1933, when the tax increases were fully effective. Though this represents a 52 percent increase in income tax revenues, a closer look at the data undercuts even this modest success. Though incomes were falling rapidly as a result of the depression, the reduction in the standard exemption was so great as to increase the number of taxpayers. This increase in the base offset the decline in incomes[12] and should have produced a revenue increase even if rates had not been increased. Even so the 150 percent tax rate increase produced only a 52 percent increase in revenue. Once again high incomes disappeared, causing revenue to be lower than expected.[13] Though some of the reduction in high incomes can be explained by the economic collapse, most cannot.

Over the ensuing decade, as the economy emerged from the Great Depression, income tax revenue never fully recovered. By 1939 the economy had substantially recovered but reported personal income remained below the 1928 level. The tax base had broadened substantially, the number of taxpayers nearly doubling from 4.1 million to 7.7 million, and tax rates had been increased yet again in 1936. Still, in 1939 tax revenue lagged 20 percent behind its 1928 level. Taxpayers earning over $100,000 paid 58 percent less in taxes than they had in 1928, in spite of the higher rates. By contrast, the reduction of the standard exemption sharply increased taxes paid by taxpayers earning under $10,000. In 1928 these taxpayers paid $36 million, by 1939 they paid $174 million. Their share of the total income tax revenues rose from 4 percent to 19 percent while the government was supposedly trying to soak the rich and make life better for the common man.

Each major adjustment in the income tax code up through the late 1930s produced similar effects: very high income tax rates on high incomes caused that portion of the tax base to shrink, in most cases sufficiently to reduce revenues. Tax cuts on the upper brackets actually raised revenues. Clearly income tax rates can be raised higher than the rates of other taxes without rendering the tax ineffective or dangerous to the economy, but there are definite limits.

World War II further changed the character of the income tax. The base was broadened until income taxation became a nearly universal requirement for the working population. Tax rates at the lower end of the scale were hiked roughly fivefold. For the first time top rates were pushed over 90 percent. Nor did the end of the war bring back peacetime taxes. Tax rates were slightly reduced in 1946 and 1948, but then raised again for the Korean War. After Korea, rates settled at 91 percent at the top and 20 percent at the bottom and stayed that way until 1963. Inflation gradually eroded the personal exemption. By 1963 the bottom rate of 20 percent was producing 85 percent of all revenue, and if all rates above 50 percent had been abolished only 2 percent of revenue would have been lost. The top rates served not to produce revenue but as political camouflage, kept to reassure middle-class taxpayers that they were not paying rich people's rates. Very high top rates shifted the whole structure upwards, justifying middle-class levies that might otherwise have provoked political revolt. As incomes rose, partly as a result of real growth and partly because of inflation, the number of middle-class Americans encountering marginal rates in the 30, 40, and even 50 percent range increased every year.

In 1963 at age fifty, the income tax was clearly so overbearing in both scope and reach that it was damaging the economy. The class tax had decisively and permanently become a mass tax. Tax rates that ratcheted up in a series of national emergencies never came all the way back down after the emergencies passed. Rates first intended for the rich were soon applied to the less affluent, and justified by ever higher rates on the rich. By the 1960s the "psychic" responses of taxpayers to tax rates had become one of the most powerful forces in the economy as millions of taxpayers adjusted their behavior in the face of tax rates once confronted only by the rich and their accountants.

Not all taxpayer reactions were "psychic." As the burden of taxation became apparent the nation underwent a political transformation. The income tax, regarded benignly by the generality of voters when it applied primarily to the rich, threatened to become a liability to every politician as ever more taxpayers felt its burden.

Chapter 3

Camelot Capitalism and Keynesian Crisis

> "I am convinced that the enactment this year of tax reductions and tax reform overshadows all other domestic problems in this Congress. For we cannot lead for long the cause of peace and freedom if we ever cease to set the pace at home . . . I am not talking about giving the economy a mere shot in the arm to ease some temporary complaint. This [tax cut] will increase the purchasing power of American families and business enterprises . . . It will, in addition, encourage the initiative and risk-taking on which our free system depends; induce more investments, production, and capacity use; help provide the two million jobs we need every year; and reinforce the American principle of additional reward for additional effort."
>
> —JOHN F. KENNEDY,
> State of the Union Address, 1963

The Kennedy Tax Cut proposed in 1963, passed in 1964, and named after the martyred president, is the real starting point of the supply-side–Keynesian debate about the effect of tax rate reductions. For the Keynesians, then in ascendency as the purveyors of the New Economics, the 1964 tax bill represents a masterstroke in economic demand management. For the supply-side school, unborn in 1964, the Kennedy tax cuts exemplify the power of microeconomic incentives. Most important, the fight over the Kennedy tax cuts set the tone for the next fifteen years of tax policy. Though the cuts were successful in themselves, a misreading of their results prompted policies that brought the postwar income tax to endgame and precipitated a crisis for the economy, the taxpayer, the treasury, and the electorate that would only be resolved in the Reagan Revolution.

The year preceding Kennedy's 1963 state of the union address was not the best of years. The Cuban missile crisis gave our competition with the Soviet Union a new urgency and, against glowing reports of Soviet economic growth, the recent mediocre performance of our economy seemed all the worse. In the nine-year period 1947 to 1956, the American economy had grown at a 4 percent annual rate, but in the six following years, growth of the real U.S. GNP dropped to less than 2.3 percent, less than half the alleged Soviet rate. The year 1958 brought a steep recession, with a milder one following in 1960. Unemployment rose to 6.5 percent in 1961, from an average 4.4 percent during the previous decade. Something clearly was wrong, and very worrisome for the generation that had lived through the Great Depression.

The political news was no cheerier. When in the summer of 1962 the economy appeared to be experiencing some difficulty just two years after the 1960 recession,[1] it seemed the administration would face the 1964 elections with a recession on its hands. The Republicans had turned over the White House to the Democrats by the narrowest of margins in the recession year of 1960, and the Democrats had no wish to return the favor. Towards the close of the year, the president and his advisers decided to try to revive the economy with a major tax cut. Announcing his plan in the state of the union address a few months later, the young president proclaimed, "We cannot lead for long the cause of peace and freedom if we ever cease to set the pace at home," thus putting the flag on the side of the largest tax cut in American history.

In 1963 nearly all working families paid income tax. Tax rates were quite high, starting at 20 percent and topping out at a confiscatory 91 percent. The 50-percent tax bracket started at $36,000 of taxable income for married couples and only $18,000 for single persons. Of course, a lot of inflation has passed under the bridge since then. In 1963 dollars, $18,000 would be worth about $63,000 today. Nevertheless, even in 1963 there was certainly room to "reinforce the American principle of additional reward for additional effort," as Kennedy put it.

The tax cuts President Kennedy proposed in 1963 were the most dramatic since the Coolidge-Mellon tax cuts of the 1920s. But in the 1920s, before the Mellon cuts, only 7 million people paid any income tax at all. By 1963 the number of taxpayers had grown to 64 million. Though the earlier tax cuts affected only the top quarter of American society, the Kennedy tax proposal would put more money in the pockets of virtually every American family. That fact had a profound effect on the structure of the Kennedy tax reductions.

Kennedy proposed to cut taxes most steeply at the top and bottom of the income distribution, and relatively modestly in the middle (See table 3.1). In dollar terms some 70 percent of the apparent reduction, or $5.5 billion, would go to taxpayers making $10,000 or less. In 1963 these taxpayers comprised 84 percent of the total taxpaying population and paid 48 percent of the income tax. Thus the vast majority of the tax cut was focused on persons of relatively modest means.

On the other hand, the largest percentage point reductions in

TABLE 3.1

The Kennedy Tax Cut Proposal*

Taxable Income	Old Tax	Proposed Tax	Proposed Cut
$2,000	$400	$300	25%
4,000	800	660	18
8,000	1,680	1,452	14
12,000	2,720	2,388	12
20,000	5,280	4,692	11
50,000	20,300	18,210	10
100,000	53,640	47,028	12
200,000	134,640	105,528	22
500,000	404,640	281,028	31

*Reduction as reported in *Newsweek*, 14 January 1963, 18.

tax rates came at the top of the scale: Kennedy's proposal to lower the top personal income tax rate a whopping twenty-one points from 91 percent to 70 percent meant that the largest individual tax reductions would go to a relatively small number of high-income taxpayers. Assuming the tax cut did not otherwise affect their earning behavior, taxpayers earning $500,000 would get a $123,000 tax cut while those making $20,000 would get only $600. To offset the political indelicacy, the Kennedy people put great stress on the aggregate volume of the tax cut for those of modest means.

The political motive for adding deep cuts in the bottom rates to sharp reductions on top is obvious. But there was also an economic motive for this two-track approach, or rather two very different motives. What we might call the demand-side objective was to stimulate the economy by putting more money in the pockets of consumers so that they would spend more. This strategy was particularly popular with the president's economic advisers, Keynesians all, who believed the economy was underperforming because not enough goods were being purchased by consumers. The development of Keynesian theory and practice over the previous three decades had taught the Kennedy men to target the majority of the tax-cut dollars toward lower- and moderate-income taxpayers for maximum effect. They believed these people were the most likely to spend any windfall, thus increasing demand and stimulating production. Taxpayers who already had ample resources might save more of the extra money. Thus a family with taxable income of $2,000 would get a 25 percent reduction but a family earning $20,000 only 11 percent.

The second or supply-side objective of the tax cut proposal was to increase the incentives to work, save, and invest, especially for high-bracket taxpayers. Taxpayers at the 91 percent bracket who earned but 9 cents for a dollar's worth of work might easily find a better way to spend their time. For them, an investment producing a 10 percent return would yield but 1 percent after taxes, hardly enough to justify any risk at all, not to mention the sort of high-risk investments that fuel real economic advance. A substantial reduction in these rates, restoring incentives to work, save, and invest, would increase the *supply* of the economic factors of production: labor, capital, and entrepreneurship.

Kennedy clearly believed in the importance of the supply-side initiative, as his 1963 address made clear. In 1963, however, neither the supply- nor the demand-side strategies won much support. *Business Week* and other free market voices argued that the upper-bracket reduction was too little and too late. As *Business Week* editorialized, "The stultifying effects of the present tax system have been demonstrated again and again in the past five years. . . . The net reductions [the Kennedy bill] proposes are too small and too slow to give a substantial lift to production and employment."[2]

On Capitol Hill most of the critics argued that the tax cut was too large. Congressional leaders such as Wilbur Mills, the Democratic chairman of the House Ways and Means Committee, were not at all comfortable with what was still called the New Economics and feared that the Keynesian plan for stimulating demand would only worsen the existing federal deficit. As it was, the federal deficit in 1962 was 1.3 percent of GNP, the equivalent of a $65 billion deficit today.[3] Kennedy was proposing a tax cut that would apparently reduce revenues by an additional 2 percent of GNP[4] or, in today's terms, another $100 billion. Even today, we do not take $165 billion deficits lightly. Kennedy's Keynesian advisers believed that the right deficit (as determined by Keynesian theory and new mathematical models for economic forecasting) could stimulate an economy suffering from "tired blood,"[5] as Walter Heller, Kennedy's chairman of the Council of Economic Advisers put it. Heller considered unwavering opposition to deficits a vestige of our colonial heritage. "It's remarkable," he wrote in 1963, "how our basic Puritan ethic convinces people that they should deny themselves a tax cut."[6]

On Capitol Hill, the Puritans stood fast[7] and the tax cut

stalled. Kennedy opposed either broadening the tax base or cutting spending to minimize the deficit effect of the tax cut, and the Congress was unwilling to give him a tax cut unless he did one or the other. On 22 November 1963, without seeing the enactment of the massive tax cut he proposed, Kennedy was assassinated.

Kennedy's martyrdom won the day for many of his programs, including the tax cuts, passed by both houses and signed by President Johnson in March 1964. Taxes would be cut in stages, in 1964 and 1965, the top marginal rate dropping from 91 to 70 percent and the bottom rate falling from 20 to 14 percent, with less dramatic cuts in between (see table 3.2).

On the supply side, the tax bill was everything that Kennedy had asked for. The sharp reductions in the upper rates were augmented with new incentives for corporate investment and capital formation. The situation on the demand side was not so clear. By itself, the tax bill provided a significant stimulus to consumer demand, providing a total apparent tax reduction of $11.5 billion, or 1.8 percent of GNP. But because of deficit worries, budget outlays for fiscal 1965 were cut below their level in fiscal 1964. Overall, federal spending declined by 1.2 percent of GNP between 1964 and 1965, offsetting two-thirds of the demand-side stimulus of the tax cut.

At the time the bill passed, Treasury Secretary Douglas Dillon proclaimed that it would "help launch a brilliant new chapter in the economic history of the United States."[8] Even treasury secretaries can succumb to hyperbole. But with the benefit of hindsight it is difficult to argue with Dillon's assessment. Real GNP grew 5.3 percent between 1963 and 1964 and a further 5.8 percent between 1964 and 1965. The civilian unemployment rate fell from 5.7 percent to 4.5 percent between 1963 and 1965 as 4.1 million new jobs were created. Productivity in the business sector jumped 4.3 percent and 3.5 percent in 1964 and 1965, respectively. The effect on personal income tax receipts was even more impressive. Though rates were cut between 17 and 30 percent between 1963 and 1965, receipts rose

TABLE 3.2

The Kennedy Tax Cut As Enacted

Taxable Income	1963 Tax Rate	1964 Tax Rate	1965 Tax Rate
$0–1,000	20%	16 %	14%
1,000–2,000	20	16.5	15
2,000–3,000	20	17.5	16
3,000–4,000	20	18	17
4,000–8,000	22	20	19
8,000–12,000	26	23.5	22
12,000–16,000	30	27	25
16,000–20,000	34	30.5	28
20,000–24,000	38	34	32
24,000–28,000	43	37.5	36
28,000–32,000	47	41	39
32,000–36,000	50	44.5	42
36,000–40,000	53	47.5	45
40,000–44,000	56	50.5	48
44,000–52,000	59	53.5	50
52,000–64,000	62	56	53
64,000–76,000	65	58.5	55
76,000–88,000	69	61	58
88,000–100,000	72	63.5	60
100,000–120,000	75	66	62
120,000–140,000	78	68.5	64
140,000–160,000	81	71	66
160,000–180,000	84	73.5	68
180,000–200,000	87	75	70
200,000–300,000	89	76.5	70
300,000–400,000	90	76.5	70
over 400,000	91	77	70

SOURCE: *Statistics of Income* for 1963, 1964, and 1965. Data is provided for married couples filing jointly.

$1.2 billion, or 2.5 percent. The federal deficit declined from $4.8 billion in 1963 to $1.4 billion in 1965. By any economic measure, the tax cut was a solid success.

With such a success, naturally there was quite a spat over who deserved the credit: the Keynesians or the supply-siders (though no one used that term at the time). The argument intensified as the income tax was driven to its limits over the next fifteen years, and was a key part of the tax cut debates of the late 1970s and early 1980s. Walter Heller, an ardent demand-sider, wrote of the Kennedy tax cut in 1978, "the record is crystal clear that it was its stimulus to *demand* [emphasis his], the multiplied impact of its release of over $10 billion of consumer purchasing power and $2 billion of corporate funds, that powered the 1964–65 expansion and restored a good part of the initial revenue loss."[9] On the other hand, supply-siders used the Kennedy tax cuts as exhibit A in arguing for the Reagan tax cuts and other supply-side tax initiatives.

The truth is that both supply-side and demand-side influences contributed to the economic recovery and the very favorable revenue results. It is important, nevertheless, to assess the relative strengths of the two effects. As we shall see, the failure of the Keynesians to properly credit the supply-side effects of the Kennedy cuts was a major cause of the confused and ineffective policies of the late 1960s and the 1970s, policies that finally brought the income tax, and the economy, to crisis.

To assess the relative merits of the competing theories, let us consider two tests, one macroeconomic, using Keynesian tools, and one microeconomic, examining the effects of various incentives on taxpayers. The macroeconomic test looks at the causes of economic growth after the tax cut. To do so scientifically we must first determine how much extra economic growth the tax cut caused. Between 1947 and 1963, the American economy averaged a 3.4 percent annual rate of real economic growth. Had this "normal" rate of growth continued during 1964 and 1965 (the two years of the tax cut), real GNP would have been $667 billion in 1965. Instead, real GNP was $705 billion. So it would be reasonable to estimate that the tax cut was worth an extra $28 billion in GNP, or 4.4 percent, by 1965. This means that about 40 percent of the economic growth between 1963 and 1965 could be attributed due to the tax cut, and about 60 percent due to normal factors.[10]

The next step is to divide this $28 billion between its supply-side and demand-side causes. The demand-side stimulus is easiest to quantify: It results from the government putting extra money in the pockets of taxpayers by cutting taxes or increasing its spending. The combination of these two effects is known as the fiscal stimulus.

On the tax side, this fiscal stimulus amounted to some $11.5 billion in 1965. But, as was already noted earlier, the Congress took back some of this fiscal stimulus by cutting federal spending in 1965 instead of letting it continue to grow at its previous rate of 6 percent. The reduction in fiscal stimulus due to lower spending is $7.3 billion. Thus the net increase in fiscal stimulus in 1965 amounted to only $4.2 billion.[11]

According to demand-side analysis, each dollar of fiscal stimulus creates more than a dollar of extra GNP. This is the multiplier effect of which Heller spoke. In a 1978 report on the Kennedy tax cut, Donald Kiefer of the Congressional Research Service wrote, "The major econometric models of the U.S. economy all have multiplier effects for various fiscal policies which range from 1.3 to 2."[12] Thus the $3.4 billion of net fiscal stimulus which occurred in 1965 could only account for a rise in GNP of at most $7 billion out of the $28 billion of extra GNP, leaving $21 billion, or three-quarters of the extra economic growth, unaccounted for by the demand-side explanation.

Taking Keynesian reasoning a bit further, consider the effect of the tax-cut on the composition of the economy. If the demand-side story were correct, the extra spending power in the economy should have mostly found its way into things people buy: consumer spending and housing. But these items grew only 10.5 percent between 1963 and 1965, compared to a 13.3 percent rise in total private demand. The fastest expansion of demand between 1963 and 1965 was in business spending, not consumer spending. Total business investment grew some 29 percent, and business spending on equipment, which was the target of the investment incentives in the 1964 tax bill, jumped 32 percent. Thus the composition of GNP suggests that the change in tax incentives powerfully increased the supply of financial and physical capital to the economy, a supply-side effect, and that this increase explains much of the GNP growth.

Our microeconomic test proceeds by a close examination of tax return data.[13] Though tax rates were dramatically reduced between 1963 and 1965, total tax liabilities rose from $49.2 billion to $50.6 billion. By itself, this fact is consistent with both the demand-side and the supply-side arguments. After all, GNP grew rapidly between 1963 and 1965, which would cause an expansion of the tax base, and thus in tax revenue. What tips the balance in favor of the supply-side explanation is that most of the growth in the tax base occurred among upper-income taxpayers, who we expect to respond primarily to more powerful incentives to supply labor and capital to the economy. If the demand-side explanation were correct, most of the expansion in the tax base would have been focused on the bottom of the income distribution as unemployed workers (an existing supply of labor) entered the labor force as a result of new demand for their services.

To see more clearly how various taxpayers responded to the tax cuts assume for a moment that the economic growth that occurred between 1963 and 1965 increased the incomes of all taxpayers proportionally, which is roughly what we would expect if neither supply- nor demand-side effects dominated. This even distribution can then be contrasted with what actually happened to see if one effect actually was dominant. Table 3.3 presents the results. The data support the supply-side explanation. Upper-income groups, which saw a dramatic reduction in their marginal tax rates, reported substantially more income than could be accounted for if economic growth had been spread evenly across the population. On the other hand, lower-income groups reported slightly less income than we would expect if the economic growth between 1963 and 1965 had been evenly distributed. It is important to note that this does not mean that the "rich get richer while the poor get poorer." Incomes rose substantially for both upper-income taxpayers and for lower-income taxpayers. But reported taxable incomes rose substantially more for upper-income taxpayers than for lower-income taxpayers.

High-income taxpayers reported so much more taxable in-

TABLE 3.3

Allocation of Income Reported on Tax Returns for 1965*

Income Class	Assuming Even Growth (millions of dollars)	Actual Distribution (millions of dollars)	Difference
under $10,000	$246,490	$245,864	−0.3 %
10,000–20,000	123,110	121,398	−1.4
20,000–50,000	38,911	39,524	+1.6
50,000–100,000	10,676	12,400	+16.1
100,000–500,000	5,611	7,115	+26.8
over 500,000	1,569	2,308	+47.0

*The actual distribution was taken from the *Statistics of Income* for 1965. The even growth distribution was computed by taking the distribution reported in the 1963 *Statistics of Income* and increasing the total dollars in each income bracket by the growth in total income. This had the effect of shifting some taxpayers into a higher income bracket. As the data in the SOI is more detailed than that presented here, this was easily calculated. At higher income levels some interpolation was needed to calculate the new income brackets. While interpolating any function, especially a non-linear function such as the income distribution is necessarily imprecise, the results clearly overwhelm any imprecision.

come that more revenue was collected under the lower rates than would have been collected under the higher tax rates prevailing before the tax cut. Taxpayers earning over $100,000, who had been subject to rates ranging from 75 to 91 percent, saw those rates reduced to a range of 62 to 70 percent yet actually paid more in taxes as a result. Taxpayers earning between $50,000 and $100,000, who saw their rates cut from 59 to 72 percent to 50 to 60 percent, paid essentially the same amount in taxes. This happened because these taxpayers reported more income, either because they actually did work harder or because they shuffled their money out of consumption or tax-sheltered investments into more productive but taxable investments, or because of some similar adjustment. Some of them may have just stopped fudging their returns as the rewards for evasion were reduced.

To show this, we first calculated the amount of tax that would have been collected in 1965 if there were no tax cut and therefore no special supply-side response. To make the claim even stronger, we assume that the economic growth that occurred between 1963 and 1965 would have happened anyway and, as earlier, that the growth was spread evenly across the popula-

TABLE 3.4

*Effect of Tax Cuts on Tax Revenue: Upper-Income Taxpayers**

	Taxpayers Earning $50,000–$100,000	Taxpayers Earning $100,000–$500,000	Taxpayers Earning over $500,000
Tax Paid Old Law	$3,622 million	$2,405 million	$701 million
Tax Paid New Law	$3,693 million	$2,780 million	$1,020 million

*These tables are compiled by taking the income distribution calculated for table 3.3 and applying the income tax bracket tables. We assumed no change in the ratio of taxable income to AGI in making the transition. The tax paid under old law was computed by taking the old high rates and applying them to the "Even Growth" income distribution. Tax paid under new law was the actual tax paid.

tion. Thus, the revenue response we are measuring is in addition to the extra revenue which was collected because of the more rapid economic growth of the period.[14] Table 3.4 presents the results.

If the battle between supply-siders and demand-siders over the effectiveness of tax cuts were limited to the Kennedy experiment, the data show that the supply-siders win hands down. Not only were supply-side responses, particularly to investment incentives, the major cause of the economic expansion after the tax cuts, but the behavioral response of taxpayers at the very highest income tax brackets proved to be sufficient to cause tax revenue to rise even as tax rates declined. These findings indicate that the economic effect was three parts supply-side for every one part of demand-side stimulus. This does not mean that there were no demand-side effects or that they were unimportant, but they would have been greater had the Congress not reduced the net fiscal stimulus of the tax cut by slashing federal spending. Taking back some two-thirds of the net fiscal stimulus substantially reduced the Keynesian potential of the tax change.

In retrospect this may have been sound macroeconomic policy. Had demand-driven economic growth been even faster, it is possible that inflation would have accelerated. The rapid growth of federal spending after 1965, caused by both the Vietnam War and the Great Society, was accompanied by much higher inflation. The Kennedy cuts, with the combination of demand-side and supply-side effects that characterizes most successful tax cuts, were just what was required to reinvigorate the tax system and the nation's economy. The Coolidge-Mellon cuts of the 1920s similarly both stimulated demand and unleashed an increased drive to work, invest, and take risks. The 1932 tax increase, on the other hand, collapsed demand and punished effort and risk taking. If a close analysis of the Kennedy cut provides any specific lesson, it is that tax policy should stimulate both demand- and supply-side effects in a balanced fashion.

The tax cuts of 1964 were a major cause of the longest economic expansion then on record, which continued until 1970.[15] Unfortunately, economists seem to have benefited less than the economy. Most policy makers credited the tax cut's success exclusively to its demand-side features, and in attempts to recapture the successes of the Kennedy cuts, the government launched repeated demand-side experiments throughout the 1970s. The Congress established a new ritual: a tax cut for every even-numbered year, which by pure happenstance coincided with congressional elections. These tax cuts were aimed purely at stimulating demand. The Congress left rates essentially the same and focused relief at the bottom of the scale by raising personal exemptions and the standard deduction. In addition to cutting taxes the Congress repeatedly raised spending levels, usually to fund new social programs but also with the intention of stimulating demand. The results, almost always disappointing, culminated by the end of the 1970s in a crisis for which the Keynesians had no cure: chronic and serious stagflation, a paradoxical (for the Keynesians) combination of high inflation and high unemployment.

The orthodox Keynesians of the post–World War II period held that unemployment and inflation were contrary, not complementary economic conditions. High unemployment and slow economic growth were thought to be caused by too little demand in the economy and curable by increasing government spending or reducing taxes. High inflation was caused by too much demand in the economy and could be cured by reducing government spending and increasing taxes. There was no orthodox economic prescription for simultaneous high unemployment and high inflation, in part because the Keynesians considered them cures for each other.

The key to the stagflation paradox is that the repeated inflations of the 1970s in themselves dramatically increased taxes over the course of the decade, since in a progressive tax system inflation raises taxes automatically. In the absence of a tax cut powerful inflation raises rates brutally. Never during the 1970s did the Congress cut upper- or even upper-middle bracket rates, even though millions of taxpayers of relatively modest means were gradually being forced to pay tax rates once meant for the upper-middle class and the rich. Years of demand-side tax cuts were thus accompanied by years of unlegislated supply-side tax increases, erecting ever greater disincentives to supply capital or labor to the economy.

To see how this happens, imagine a tax system with only two rates: 10 percent on income below $10,000 per year and 20 percent on any additional income. Further suppose that ten years ago Fred earned $10,000 dollars and thus paid 10 percent of his income in tax. If over the course of the ten years inflation had doubled his nominal income to $20,000, he would now be paying the 20 percent tax rate on the top half of his income. His average tax rate would be 15 percent, and his marginal rate 20 percent, even though he had not become one dollar richer in real terms. In fact, this "bracket creep" left him poorer in real terms after taxes, and the government richer.

That is exactly what happened in the 1970s and early 1980s. By the late seventies, ordinary taxpayers were paying "rich people's taxes." In 1980 the median-income four-person family earned about $30,000. After deductions and exemptions they found themselves at the top of the 28 percent tax bracket, fast approaching a 32 percent marginal rate. By contrast, in 1965 a family in the same relative position had been in the 19 percent tax bracket. In 1965 the 28 and 32 percent income tax brackets were reserved for people who were doing quite well. A family of four would not have hit the 32 percent tax bracket until they made 3.8 times the median family income, the equivalent of $114,000 in 1980. The rise in tax rates was even more dramatic for families who, though not rich, were doing a bit better than average. For example, a four-person family earning $60,000 in 1980, or about twice the median income, faced a top rate of 49 percent. Just fifteen years earlier, a family in the same relative economic position faced a 22 percent top rate. Figures 3.1 and 3.2 show the upward path of tax rates over this fifteen-year period.

The dramatic tax increase on the middle and upper-middle classes extended the behavioral controls of the income tax

FIGURE 3.1

Tax Rates for Four-Person Family
Earning the Median Income
1965 to 1980

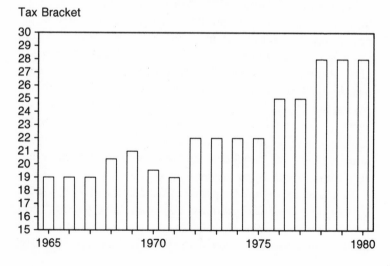

Tax Bracket

FIGURE 3.2

Tax Rates for Four-Person Family
Earning Twice the Median Income
1965 to 1980

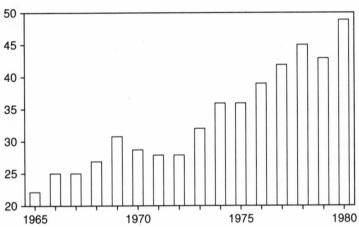

much farther down the income distribution, exposing a much larger share of the nation's earning, spending, saving, and investing decisions to destructive tax distortions. In 1963 the major problem with tax rates had been the nearly confiscatory level of taxes imposed on a few taxpayers. By 1980 very high but not quite confiscatory rates were distorting the behavior of a broad section, perhaps a majority of the taxpaying population. The income tax had been pushed beyond its limits both politically and economically. This time the excesses applied not just to a few elite taxpayers but to the vast majority. The resulting perversities and distortions gradually became a pervasive force in the behavior of both individual taxpayers and the economy as well as in national politics.

As inflation steadily increased taxes, taxpayers who never before spent much on tax avoidance began to do so. Tax shelters, once the preserve of the very rich, were advertised in periodicals with mass circulation such as the *New York Times* and

Money magazine. Lawful tax avoidance became one of the great growth industries of the nation. Middle-class taxpayers facing upper-class tax rates hit upon shelters of their own, such as taking more of their pay in tax-free fringe benefits. In 1965 fringe benefits represented only 4.9 percent of wage and salary payments. By 1980 this figure had risen to 10.1 percent, and in itself, by reducing the 1980 tax base by $72 billion, cost the government between $20 and $25 billion in tax revenue, or between 8 and 10 percent of the revenue collected that year. Other tax revenue figures confirm the seriousness of the problem. In 1965 personal income taxes took 10.3 percent of personal income. By 1980, though typical taxpayers had seen their marginal tax rates rise by 50 to 100 percent, income taxes still took only 11.4 percent of personal income. A drastic increase in tax rates, combined with but a modest increase in revenues, proves beyond doubt that the tax base was shrinking.

A shrinking tax base may seem an abstract peril. It is not. To say that the tax base is shrinking is to say people are doing less of all those things—working, saving, and investing—by which we maintain prosperity. The shrinking of the tax base in turn makes traditional Keynesian demand management obsolete. Under the traditional prescriptions, raising taxes is supposed to cure inflation by cutting purchasing power, thus reducing the *demand* for goods and services in the economy. But if tax rates are already high enough to distort taxpayer behavior and discourage work, savings, and investment, any further tax increase will also reduce the *supply* of goods and services to the economy. Supply and demand will remain out of balance and the inflation rate will stay stubbornly high. The economy, suffering from cuts in both demand and supply, will shrink. The result is stagflation.

Nor will Keynesian strategies for stimulating the economy help in these conditions. Traditional Keynesians focus their demand-side stimuli (either tax cuts or higher spending) on lower-income taxpayers, who can be relied on to spend the money and raise demand. But if excessive upper-bracket rates continue to discourage effort and risk, there will be no commensurate increase in the supply of goods and services to the economy. Higher demand coupled with stagnant supply will produce only higher inflation, not economic growth: again, stagflation. The nation scrupulously followed Keynesian advice[16] between 1965 and 1980. Fifteen years of faithfully stimulating demand and ignoring the growing penalties on supply increased the inflation rate from 1.9 percent to 12.4 percent and the unemployment rate from 4.4 percent to 7.0 percent.

By 1980 tax rates were clearly damaging the incentives to supply both labor and capital to the economy, though the disincentives for capital were particularly obvious. Consider, for example, the case of the middle-income family and its savings account, an important source of investment capital. The account earned 5.5 percent interest, but after taxes the family kept only 3.7 percent. Moreover, consumer prices rose 13.5 percent between 1979 and 1980. The real purchasing power of the money left in the savings account after taxes actually fell nearly 10 percent that year, leaving little incentive to save.

Much the same story could be told of the typical stock portfolio. A couple earning $60,000 who invested $10,000 in the stocks which comprised the NYSE Composite Index in 1974, when the stock market hit its low for the decade, would have seen their investment grow to $15,500 in 1980. Assuming they sold out and took their profit, federal capital gains taxes, which are lower than ordinary income taxes, would have left them $14,400. Unfortunately, consumer prices rose 67 percent in that same time, leaving our couple $1,400 poorer in purchasing power, though they had timed their stock purchases perfectly. Most investors did worse.

The combination of high taxes and high inflation also encouraged borrowing (dis-saving) for current consumption. Since consumer interest such as the 18 percent rate on credit card purchases was deductible, the effective interest rate dropped to 9.2 percent for a family in the 49 percent tax bracket. With inflation pushing up prices by 13.5 percent per year, it was cheaper to buy now on credit than to wait a year, save the money, and pay cash.

High taxes and high inflation directly discouraged business investment in new plant and equipment. The tax code allows businesses to deduct from their taxable profits, over time, the costs of the gradual wearing out of their plant and equipment. This deduction quickly loses its value in times of persistent inflation, because it is based on the original purchase price of the tools, not the inflated cost at which they will have to be replaced. The erosion of this depreciation deduction causes business profits to be overstated and overtaxed, discouraging business investment, particularly for capital-intensive businesses.

By the late 1970s the tax penalties on the suppliers of capital were so severe that there was strong sentiment on Capitol Hill for reducing them. The 1978 Steiger amendment reduced by nearly half the top effective rate of the capital gains tax, the tax on the increase in the value of an investment, such as stock shares, paid only after the investor chooses to cash in his or her investment. After this reduction the government actually took in more capital gains tax than before; 45 percent more in 1979 than in 1978, new confirmation that high tax rates had been shrinking the tax base, penalizing supply, and punishing the economy.

The results of the Steiger amendment certainly strengthened the growing supply-side movement as well as making some converts to tax cutting on Capitol Hill. But the Carter administration, believing that high and rising taxes would slow inflation and help to cure the nation's economic ills, remained firmly opposed to any broad, significant change in tax policy. In the 1980 *Economic Report of the President,* Carter's economic advisers argued,

> Fighting inflation continues to be the top priority of economic policy, and hence the President has not recommended any legislated changes in tax rates in the 1981 budget. Since individuals will be

moving into higher tax brackets as their incomes increase, the share of personal income taken by Federal income taxes will rise. Social security tax liabilities are scheduled to increase in January 1981 by $18 billion. The resulting rise in effective tax rates, combined with limited growth of Federal outlays, will cause the Federal budget to move significantly toward restraint in the next fiscal year.[17]

In the midst of an economic and political crisis, the president sought refuge in the bosom of orthodoxy. He would fight fire with more fire, deliberately using bracket creep to raise taxes yet higher so as to brake the rise in prices.

Carter's stand-pat approach did not sell. Ronald Reagan was a relative newcomer to supply-side ideas, but as he would show repeatedly in the years to come, he had a fine sense of the ripening of a crisis and the opportunities thereof. He ran for president largely on a promise of dramatic reductions in personal tax rates, which he promised would revive first the American spirit of enterprise and then the American economy. And it was largely for those promises that he was elected.

The campaign called for a reduction in rates and in rates alone. Reagan's speeches included no complicated lists of minor adjustments; exemptions; loopholes; or subsidies for the poor, the powerful, the rich, or the well connected. Yet by the time the Economic Recovery Tax Act of 1981 (ERTA) became law, it seemed to address nearly every social wrong or economic woe known to the nation. The final bill not only cut tax rates but extended the tax incentives for charitable deductions to all taxpayers, increased the subsidy for child care, provided a deduction for adoption expenses, increased the tax-free profit a retired couple could realize from the sale of their home, and made dozens of other major and minor adjustments to the tax code. These included numerous special tax favors for businesses or individuals represented by key members of Congress. The Joint Committee on Taxation estimated that by 1986 fully half of the revenue cost of the bill would come from provisions other than the personal tax rate reductions.[18]

Not all of the additional changes were unrelated to the central crisis of the tax system. The Accelerated Cost Recovery System (ACRS), the Individual Retirement Account (IRA), and the Two Earner Deduction, each of which we examine fully in the coming chapters, directly addressed the dilemmas of the late 1970s and powerfully contributed to the recovery and expansion of the 1980s. In brief, ACRS reduced the impact of inflation on the depreciation deduction for business plant and equipment, curbing the overtaxing of business profits and encouraging business investment. The IRA, aimed at increasing national savings, allowed taxpayers to deduct from their taxable income up to $2,000 in annual contributions to a retirement account and to accumulate earnings tax free until withdrawal. The Two Earner Deduction reduced the marriage penalty, under which the earnings of married working women effectively were taxed at a rate much higher than the earnings of single working women. The deduction was intended to give working women equitable tax treatment, to provide tax relief for families, and to raise the labor force participation of married women, who have been shown by economic research to be very sensitive to tax rates in deciding whether to work.[19]

All these provisions, as we shall see, were relatively successful. But the most important additional change of ERTA was the indexing of the tax code for inflation, ending the bracket creep that had drastically raised federal tax rates over the previous fifteen years even while the Congress "cut" taxes five times.

As the congressional staff noted in its *General Explanation* of ERTA,

> The Congress believed that "automatic" tax increases resulting from the effects of inflation were unfair to taxpayers, since their tax burden as a percentage of income could increase. . . . In addition, the Federal Government was provided with an automatic increase in its aggregate revenue, which in turn created pressure for further spending. . . . Indexing will prevent inflation from increasing that percentage and thus will avoid the past pattern of inequitable, unlegislated tax increases and induced spending.[20]

No words could better express why the introduction of indexing was such an important change in tax policy. Bracket creep
is the twentieth-century version of "taxation without represen-
tation." Not only does it raise taxes without a vote of the
Congress, it generally raises them most fiercely for people of
modest means. In almost any progressive income tax schedule,
rates climb most steeply at the bottom of the scale; typically a
few thousand dollars of additional income will move a taxpayer
from the 15 to the 20 percent bracket, while it may take tens
or hundreds of thousands of dollars to move a taxpayer from
the 60 to the 70 percent bracket. Of course, taxpayers in the
very top bracket can go no higher. Inevitably brackets creep
fastest at the bottom.

Indexing leaves tax rates unchanged, but in case of inflation
adjusts the income levels to which each tax rate applies, effectively eliminating bracket creep. Indexing not only compensates for inflation, it removes a clear incentive for a government
to pursue it. Without indexing a government in fiscal difficulty
may be tempted to inflate its way out of the crisis. This was
essentially the fiscal strategy tried by the Carter administration.
The Carter administration reduced the budget deficit of the late
1970s not by cutting spending, which increased faster than
inflation, but through an enormous unlegislated tax increase,
courtesy of bracket creep.[21] Indexing shifted power back from
the government to taxpayers and voters. Its passage, probably
only possible at a time of political crisis, was perhaps the most
powerful symbol of the revolt against the postwar tax system.

There is no such thing as a free lunch. The cost of the various
special provisions of ERTA, good and bad, was smaller tax rate
reductions than those the president had endorsed during his
campaign. Nevertheless, rate reduction remained the center-
piece, however diminished, of the Reagan strategy and the
Great Experiment.

The Reagan tax cut really got its start in 1977 when Senator
William Roth and Representative Jack Kemp proposed the "Tax
Rate Reduction Act," calling for income tax rate reductions of
33 percent over a three-year period. Candidate Ronald Reagan

endorsed the Kemp-Roth legislation during his campaign in 1980, but the proposal President Reagan sent to the Congress was more modest. It called for three consecutive 10 percent tax rate reductions, the first to be retroactive to January 1981. In the political shorthand of the time, this came to be known as ten-ten-ten. To most people, three reductions of 10 percent add up to a 30 percent reduction, quite close to the Kemp-Roth scheme. In the arithmetic of tax experts, it does not work out that way. The first 10 percent cut is worth 10 percent. But the second 10 percent cut is applied to tax rates already reduced to 90 percent of their original level. So the second 10 percent cut is really only a 9 percent reduction in the original tax rates, and the third cuts rates by only 8.1 percent. Ten-ten-ten adds up not to 30 but 27 percent.

Not even the 27 percent cut survived. Despite a convincing Reagan victory in November and a stunning twelve-seat turn-around in the Senate—giving the Republicans control of that body for the first time in a generation—the Reagan proposal ran into stiff opposition. Congressional hearings dragged on until Memorial Day, and the entire package came closer to defeat than is now generally remembered. Finally in early August the House and Senate approved the bill, but only after the rate cuts had been trimmed further to five-ten-ten. And just as ten-ten-ten did not add up to 30, five-ten-ten did not add up to 25 but 23 percent. Nor were the reductions retroactive to January 1981 as the president had hoped; the first cut would not go into effect until 1 October 1981.

Reagan had wanted to move more quickly because he feared, rightly as it turned out, that the country was headed for a full-scale recession. The signs of economic decline were every-where as he took office. Unemployment remained at 7.5 percent and real GNP declined in the second quarter of 1981. The econ-omy was clearly headed for trouble. But since the first 5 percent cut would be in place for only a quarter of the year, the net effect of ERTA in 1981 was to reduce income tax rates by a derisory 1.25 percent. The first 10 percent cut was scheduled to take effect 1 July 1982. On average 1982 taxes would be only about 10 percent lower than 1980 rates. The second 10 percent rate reduction was scheduled to take effect 1 July 1983, making 1983 rates, on average, still only 19 percent lower than those of 1980. Not until 1984 would tax rates drop fully 23 percent below those of 1980.

There was one encouraging break in all these delays: At the initiative of some congressional Democrats who seemed to accept supply-side arguments about the hazards of very high rates, rates were capped at 50 percent as of January 1982.[22] All rates in excess of 50 percent, including the former top rate of 70 percent, were immediately reduced to 50 percent, with additional reductions to follow on the established schedule. The top effective tax rate on capital gains was also reduced from 28 to 20 percent, a reduction of just over 28 percent. (The schedule of reductions is shown in table 3.5.)

TABLE 3.5

Tax Rate Schedules Under Prior Law and the Act for 1982, 1983, and 1984 (Joint Returns)

Taxable Income Bracket	Under Prior Law	Under the Act		
		1982	1983	1984
0 to $3,400	0%	0%	0%	0%
$3,400–$5,500	14	12	11	11
$5,500–$7,600	16	14	13	12
$7,600–$11,900	18	16	15	14
$11,900–$16,000	21	19	17	16
$16,000–$20,200	24	22	19	18
$20,200–$24,600	28	25	23	22
$24,600–$29,900	32	29	26	25
$29,900–$35,200	37	33	30	28
$35,200–$45,800	43	39	35	33
$45,800–$60,000	49	44	40	38
$60,000–$85,600	54	49	44	42
$85,600–$109,400	59	50	48	45
$109,400–$162,400	64	50	50	49
$162,400–$215,400	68	50	50	50
$215,400 and over	70	50	50	50

SOURCE: *General Explanation of the Economic Recovery Tax Act of 1981* (Joint Committee on Taxation. Washington, D.C.: U.S. Government Printing Office), 405–11.

Delaying the tax cuts almost certainly contributed to the very severe recession of 1981-82. The economy declined most precipitously in the fourth quarter of 1981 and the first two quarters of 1982. As soon as the first big tax cut hit workers' paychecks in the third quarter of 1982, consumer demand began to rebound. The economy as a whole began to expand in the next quarter.

In sum, the president got smaller tax rate reductions than he asked for, and got them too late to forestall the 1982 recession. Nevertheless, the Great Experiment was in place. Over the next five years the economic paradigms and policies, the fiscal strategies, and the public finance principles of a generation would be weighed in the balance.

Chapter 4

The Great Experiment

"It is increasingly clear—to those in government, business and labor who are responsible for our economy's success—that our obsolete tax system exerts too heavy a drag on private purchasing power, profits, and employment. Designed to check inflation in earlier years, it now checks growth instead. It discourages extra effort and risk. It distorts the use of resources. It invites recurrent recessions, depresses federal revenues, and causes chronic budget deficits."

—A presidential state of the union message

"It is not credible that the more Reagan cuts taxes the sooner we reach budget balance. Here is an easy way to call Arthur Laffer's bluff: cut tax rates and don't cut spending programs. Conservatives will not like the result."

—PAUL A. SAMUELSON, *Newsweek,* 2 March 1981

This state of the union address was delivered not by Ronald Reagan but by John F. Kennedy, who numbered among his principal economic advisers Paul Samuelson. Eighteen years later Samuelson found himself a vigorous opponent of the Reagan tax cut proposal, though it was inspired in large part by Kennedy's great success. Samuelson was joined in his opposition to the Reagan proposal by Kennedy economic advisers Walter Heller and John Kenneth Galbraith as well as most of the Democratic political and intellectual establishment.

Why the change? Politics, like the heart, has its own reasons. Politics aside, the Kennedy and Reagan tax cuts were made in very different economic circumstances. When Jack Kennedy argued that high marginal tax rates were destroying incentives to work and invest, injuring the economy, and depressing tax revenues he could point to a top tax rate of 91 percent as exhibit A. Though the dominant view among economists was that tax rates could go quite high without serious consequences, few economists could argue that 9 cents on the dollar would incite anyone to work weekends or pry any family fortunes out of cozy tax shelters.

At the time of the Reagan proposal the top marginal rate was 70 percent. Though fairly stiff, it nevertheless gave top-bracket taxpayers more than three times the incentives they had in 1963 to work an extra hour or make an extra investment. It was harder to argue that top tax rates were a significant drag on productive activity, and it was much harder to argue that the top rates might actually be losing revenue.

Moreover, despite the recessions of 1958 and 1960 and some worrisome employment figures, the Kennedy tax cuts had come at a time of relatively favorable economic conditions. The tax cuts of 1981, by contrast, were proposed in an era of stagflation: low or negative growth paradoxically combined with a steep inflation. Under these circumstances, the Keynesians believed an expansion of demand (which they regarded as the only significant likely result of the proposed tax cut) would increase inflationary pressure while producing little or no additional real growth. The result would be a big drop in revenues, a deepening deficit, and more pressure on prices. Under this scenario the potential inflationary impact of the tax cut would make the Federal Reserve's job more difficult and dangerous. The Fed, which was already tightening money to fight inflation, would have to tighten still further, sending interest rates up yet higher and crowding out business investment. If on the other hand the Fed failed to act, inflation, already in the double-digit range, would spiral out of control. Though the Keynesian view provided no clear path out of stagflation, it did suggest that tax cuts would get us deeper into trouble. The Keynesian's assumption that tax rates in roughly the 40 to 70 percent range have only a modest effect on taxpayer behavior led them to believe that the only significant economic effect of a reduction in tax rates would be an untimely expansion of demand.

On these premises, the Reagan tax cuts were a bad idea. But the supply-siders believed that cutting tax rates would also increase the productive activities of taxpayers and thus the supply of labor and capital. If the supply-siders were right, the tax cuts might be the way out of stagflation. An increase in productive activity would put downward pressure on prices by increasing the supply of goods and services available for purchase. This might offset the upward pressure on prices caused by increased demand. The right tax cut would increase overall economic activity by increasing supply and demand simultaneously, and avoid an increase in prices. As taxpayers increased—or exposed—their productive activities, tax revenues would increase, decreasing the cost of the tax cut and perhaps paying for it outright.

As often happens in politics, the argument between the supply-siders and Keynesians soon narrowed to a single point: Would the Reagan tax cuts be big revenue losers, or would the tax cuts largely or entirely pay for themselves? Although this emphasis on revenue led to distortion and hyperbole in debate, it was not without use in concentrating discussion on a key fiscal issue: Could we afford a tax cut? However much economists may seem to bicker, they agree about quite a number of things. Most recognize that to some degree taxes are a drag on economic activity and a burden on the happiness of the people, an evil we tolerate only to obtain necessary government services. (Most also regard taxes as a necessary tool for redistributing income.) If it were true that the tax cuts would largely pay for themselves, the Keynesians, though not sharing the enthusiasm of the supply-siders, could have few objections. Without a big revenue loss, the deficit would not get significantly worse, and the pressure on the monetary policy of the Federal Reserve would be minimal. If the supply-siders were correct about revenues, the argument that we ought to have the lowest tax rates we can afford would carry the day. To this day, economists and politicians who criticize the 1981 tax cuts claim that the Reagan policy cost the government a great deal of revenue. When, in the 1988 vice-presidential campaign debate, Senator Lloyd Bentsen argued the Reagan recovery was built on "hot checks," or debt, he was depending ultimately on the claim that the tax cuts lost lots of money.

There was, however, another and deeper motivation for this focus on revenue, for more was at stake than a single tax bill. The supply-siders were challenging a paradigm that had dominated economic thought for nearly a half century. The revenue effects of the tax bill would show to what extent taxpayers change their behavior in response to tax cuts. Whoever turned out to be right about the effect of taxes on taxpayer behavior would gain a big advantage in the overall debate about the effect of tax rates on the economy and the proper course of economic policy. Most positive revenue effects would indicate that taxpayers had changed their behavior in ways that would be good for the economy (or at worst neutral) over the long term as well as the short. Positive revenue effects would indicate that taxpayers were working either harder or smarter and investing more or making their current investments more efficiently.

By a "positive revenue effect" we do not mean that the tax cut necessarily would be fully self-financing, but merely that some of the anticipated revenue loss was recovered by the treasury. The extent to which the tax cut cost less than anticipated would be the true measure of how much taxpayer behavior was affected: The larger the revenue feedback, the more the point would be proved that taxes affect taxpayer behavior and are a decisive policy tool.

Nearly a decade after the tax cuts were passed, public perceptions over the revenue results vary considerably, in part because so many people have a political stake in showing that the numbers support different positions. But the disagreement rages for another reason as well: Until quite recently we simply lacked the technological and analytical tools to assess the precise ef-

fects of tax law changes. Absent good data analysis, the debate
on the tax cuts produced more heat than light.

Only very detailed computer modeling can pin down the
behavioral effects of tax cuts. Such detailed analyses of tax
changes were simply impractical in the 1920s, 1930s, and even
the 1960s. Economic research, like politics, is an art of the
possible: Without the technological tools for detailed analysis
there was little point in developing analytic method. Only since
the technology has been generally available have we begun to
develop analytic methods to take advantage of it.

The method used here, developed for the express purpose of
evaluating the effects of the Reagan tax cut, is based on the
actual tax returns of more than 34,000 taxpayers in each of six
tax years.[1] The actual analysis was done using the National
Bureau of Economic research TAXSIM model, developed by
economists including Daniel Feenberg, Martin Feldstein, Daniel
Frisch, Lawrence Lindsey, and Andrew Mitrusi. This computer-
ized model, like the tax models used by the Treasury Department and the Joint Committee on Taxation, relies on the Individual Tax Model developed by the Internal Revenue Service.
With nearly one hundred items of information about each taxpayer, computers enabled us to employ some twenty million
items of tax data. By contrast, the analysis of the 1964 tax cuts
had to be done using only a few pages of published data from
the period.

Although modern computers are great at generating answers,
we humans still have to frame the questions. Much of the
confusion regarding the effect of the 1981 cuts on tax revenue
is the result of critics considering only *some* of the effects of the
tax cut, neglecting others that failed to fit their preconceived
notions. To get a useful answer, we must carefully think
through what happens to the overall economy as well as to
individual taxpayers when tax rates are cut.

The numerous responses to tax rate changes seem to fall
into four interacting and occasionally conflicting sets, which
we will term "effects." The first and simplest—though it is in

some ways misleading—is what we will call the "direct effect."

The direct effect of a tax cut is the revenue change that would result if nothing else changed. The direct effect assumes that if everyone were taxed at, say, a 40 percent rate, and that rate was cut to 30 percent, revenues would decline by exactly 10 cents on the dollar. In figuring the direct effect, both taxpayer behavior and the economy are assumed not to change as a result of even a substantial tax cut. The direct effect provides a ballpark estimate of the revenue effects of tax changes. It can be useful in the case of small tax changes but is not very accurate for changes of any significant size. Whether by changing taxpayer behavior, the level of economic activity, or both, tax changes almost always do change the size of the tax base. These changes are summarized by the three indirect effects, in combination with which the direct effect does yield an estimate of the true amount of revenue lost or gained in a tax cut.

The first indirect effect, is the "demand-side effect." The demand-side effect is based on the assumption that, at least in the short run, a tax cut will increase consumer demand and thus economic activity. After a tax cut, taxpayers have more money to spend and demand more goods; with more demand for goods, more people are employed and those already employed work more hours. As a result of this increased economic activity, the government collects higher tax revenue. This is hardly a new idea, and Keynesian economists, quite rightly, have argued it for many years. In fact, the demand-side effect might be called the Keynesian indirect effect.[2]

The next indirect effect is the "supply-side effect." The supply-side effect measures revenue changes that result from a change in the supply of factors of production (capital and labor) as a result of tax changes. At lower tax rates, each taxpayer keeps more of each additional dollar earned. This tends to make him more willing to work longer hours, to work harder and more efficiently in hope of a raise, to save or invest more, or—if he is an entrepreneurial type—to take greater risks in pursuit of now higher after-tax rewards. These extra efforts and investments yield more economic activity, more income, and thus more tax revenue. These are considered supply-side effects because they are due to an increase in the resources *supplied* to the economy rather than to increased demand for the economy's output.

Consider a single self-employed electrician, Fred, earning $20 per hour. Prior to the 1981 tax cut, he was taxed at the 44 percent rate on his last hour of earnings, leaving him $11.20 after taxes. After the tax cut was in place, his tax rate fell to just 34 percent, leaving him $13.20; the tax cut gave him a $2.00 per hour "raise." Common sense suggests that his raise will make Fred more willing to make a house call on Saturday or work longer hours.[3]

Married women exemplify a supply-side response backed by particularly strong economic evidence. Consider an $18,000 per year secretary, Jane, who gets our electrician to the altar. In 1980 the new bride would have discovered that after her federal and state payroll taxes she would henceforth keep but 45 percent of her income. This was because of the "marriage penalty" rule which combines the income of married persons for tax purposes, in effect stacking her income on top of his to determine her tax bracket. Rather than work full time for $8,100 per year after taxes, Jane might well have decided it would be more worthwhile to stay home and renovate the house or take care of the children, activities which, while valuable, produce no taxable income.

By the 1980s married couples in which both spouses worked formed the core of the nation's middle and upper-middle class. In 1984 two-thirds of the married couples earning between $30,000 and $75,000 were two-income couples. The unlegislated tax increases of the 1970s were particularly hard on these people. As brackets crept upwards, the marriage penalty levied a very stiff tax on the lower earner. The evidence suggests that the most common reaction to the growing marriage penalty was for married women to work less than they otherwise would have. No other group in the population reduces its labor force participation more in the face of high taxes than married women.

The Two Earner Deduction of the Economic Recovery Tax Act substantially reduced the marriage penalty by allowing Jane and Fred to deduct 10 percent of Jane's earnings, up to $30,000. This change, combined with the general reduction in tax rates, gave married working women a substantial after-tax "raise," in Jane's case more than $2,300 a year. The results were impressive: With sharply increased incentives to work, married women not only increased their labor force participation, but also took on jobs that, on average, paid more than those they had previously held. In 1982, the year the Two Earner Deduction began, the adult female unemployment rate fell below the adult male unemployment rate for the first time since 1949. In the eight years preceding the passage of ERTA, the earnings of year-around full-time female workers were only 60 percent of those of year-around full-time male workers. In 1982, the first year during which ERTA was in effect, this figure jumped to 63 percent, and averaged 64 percent in the five years during which ERTA was the tax law of the land.

If Jane's "raise" were to convince her to keep working, the government would continue to collect taxes on her $18,000 salary, all of which it would otherwise have lost. As with Fred's willingness to work longer hours after his tax cut, the extra tax revenue produced by Jane's extra work would be a supply-side effect, since it would come from a taxpayer supplying more labor to the economy. Supply-side responses by investors work much the same way: When a tax cut raises the after-tax reward of investment, people move capital out of consumption (a bigger house, a faster car, a longer vacation) and into investment, increasing the capital available to the economy and, ultimately, the revenue available to the treasury.

Our final entry, the pecuniary effect, measures changes in taxpayer behavior that change tax revenue but do not change the amount taxpayers work or invest or the supply of any factor of production. The pecuniary effect is the result of taxpayers' tax-driven decisions about how to arrange their given financial condition, such as choosing taxable or tax-exempt bonds, or one stock over another, or more cash over fringes in salary negotiation, or how much to contribute to charity. Unlike supply-side effects, such decisions have neither clear or direct impacts on the size of the economy. These are known as pecuniary changes because they change the allocation of money without necessarily increasing or decreasing production.

Consider the decision to buy a bond. Suppose a taxable bond yields 10 percent and a tax-exempt bond, issued by a state or municipal government, yields only 4 percent. For a taxpayer in the 70 percent tax bracket, the taxable bond yields only 3 percent after taxes. The tax-exempt bond is the better investment. On the other hand, if this taxpayer's tax rate is cut to 50 percent, the after-tax yield on the taxable bond rises to 5 percent, more than the tax-exempt bond. Thus one pecuniary effect of tax cuts is to cause investors to hold more taxable securities and fewer tax-exempt securities, producing more tax revenue.

Another example would be a shift away from non-taxable fringe benefits and towards taxable money payments in employee compensation. After a tax cut, the effective bonus from taking income as tax-free benefits drops. Workers are likely to ask for more in regular wages, which they can spend as they see fit. This shift will show up as an increase in national taxable income and will increase revenues without evoking significantly more labor supply.[4]

It is worth noting that while the pecuniary effect does not assume any increase in factors of production, certain pecuniary responses are likely to be beneficial to the economy. In the first example, lower taxes allowed the investor to move capital around more freely and efficiently (that is, in response to genuine market forces rather than tax rules). Over the long term the more efficient use of capital certainly helps the economy. On the other hand, such increases in efficiency cannot be quantified reliably and play no role in a study of the revenue effects of a tax cut over a four-year period. The economic impact of other pecuniary responses, such as shifting income from tax-free fringe benefits to taxable income, are even harder to assess.

To summarize these four responses to tax changes: the supply-side effect is produced by changes in both the behavior of the taxpayer and the size of the economy; the demand-side effect is produced by changes in the size of the economy but not taxpayer behavior; the pecuniary effect is a product of taxpayer behavior alone; and the direct effect ignores both the size of the economy and taxpayer behavior. (See figure 4.1.) Estimating the total impact of these various effects of the tax change is a bit like solving a puzzle. It must be done piece by piece. Only when we have all of the various pieces in place will we be able to tell what the true revenue results of ERTA were and, just as important, how those results were produced.

It sounds complicated. In some ways it is. Even though we

FIGURE 4.1

Taxpayer Responses to Tax Rate Changes

	Static Economy	Dynamic Economy
No Taxpayer Behavior	Direct Effect	Demand-side Effect
Taxpayer Behavior	Pecuniary Effect	Supply-side Effect

present here only a summary of the actual calculations used in the full model, the next few pages are certainly the most difficult in this book. There is no getting around that. But I can offer two encouraging thoughts. First this section lasts for only a few pages and the rest of the book can be read independently of those pages. Second, these next few pages will be less difficult if the reader remembers that we are doing something that in concept at least, is fairly simple and quite straightforward. We are separating the effects of ERTA on taxpayer behavior and economic growth from all other economic events of 1981–85. Only after we do that can we tell how much revenue the government really would have reaped in the absence of the tax cuts, and thus how much the tax cuts cost.

We start with the assumption that the tax cut had no effect on the economy (whether by boosting demand or changing taxpayer behavior): We assume that everything that happened between 1981 and 1985 would have happened even without the tax cuts. This assumption allows us to estimate the direct effect of the tax cut.

To obtain a base for comparison, we apply the old tax rates and rules to the actual events of 1981–85 by means of the 34,000 sample tax returns employed in the computer model.[5] The computer takes actual tax returns from 1979, before the tax cut was in place, and extrapolates the income and deduction items on each tax return to reflect the size of the economy in the years 1981–85, in effect completing tax returns for each of these taxpayers in each year, but using the old tax law. This yields a figure for the income tax revenue the government would have received in each year if it could have had both the old tax code and the new economy (as produced by both expansion of demand and changes in taxpayers' willingness to supply factors of production). These figures are shown on the "Old Law, New Economy" line of figure 4.2.

The second step in estimating the direct effect of the tax cut is to run the same sample tax returns (still adjusted for the economy of 1981–85) through the computer, this time applying

FIGURE 4.2
Direct Effect of Tax Law

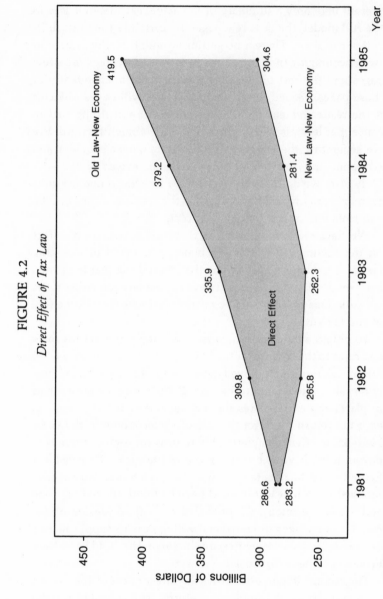

SOURCE: Based on author's calculations. See note 1, chapter 4.

the new tax rates and the rest of the changes included in the new tax law. This procedure yields projected revenues from the new tax law under the actual economy of 1981–85. (See the "New Law, New Economy" line on figure 4.2.) The difference between the "Old Law, New Economy" figures and the "New Law, New Economy" figures is the direct effect of the tax cut: it is the result you get by pretending that a change in tax rates and rules will not effect the economy. In figure 4.2, the direct effect of the tax cut from 1981 through 1985 is the region between the upper ("Old Law, New Economy") and lower ("New Law, New Economy") lines. Note that the direct effect of ERTA is quite large, rising from $44 billion in 1982 to $115 billion in 1985.

You may feel that estimating revenues from the old law under the new law's economy has a certain never-never land quality, and so it does. This estimate is something called a counterfactual, an economic scenario that runs counter to the events that actually took place. Counterfactuals are used to isolate specific economic effects. But this direct effect estimate, or a set of similar numbers, is what many ERTA opponents use when they criticize the alleged high cost of the tax bill. They are using assumptions from never-never land.

We use those assumptions also, but only as a starting point in the process of isolating the real effects of the tax changes on tax revenues. Our job is to calculate the extent to which this direct effect is an exaggeration of the true cost of the tax bill. Step by step, we will correct our estimate downward from how much revenue the government would have collected under the counterfactual "Old Law, New Economy" assumption. We will do this by separating out the revenue effects of the tax-induced changes to the New Economy. Our goal is a reliable estimate of the revenue the government would have reaped under the old law and the old economy, the revenue the government would have collected had the tax cuts never happened. Then we will be but a few short steps away from estimating the true revenue cost of the tax cut.

The old economy that we will use for our "Old Law, Old Economy" revenue estimate is also a counterfactual construct. Building it is a matter of some educated guesswork. We can estimate what the old economy (the economy absent the tax changes) would have looked like by examining the effects of other, smaller tax changes made in other years and studied by other economists, extrapolating those effects to the tax changes enacted in 1981 and then subtracting those extrapolations from the new economy.

The demand-side, or Keynesian, effect is the least controversial aspect, because both Keynesians and supply-siders agree that it occurs. To estimate the demand-side effect we first estimated the additional funds ERTA made available to taxpayers (assuming no change in their behavior). We then apply to that figure the estimates of the multiplier effect used by the DRI model of the U.S. economy, among the oldest and most respected of all economic forecasting models.[6] As noted in the previous chapter, the multiplier accounts for the fact that each dollar of a tax cut produces more than a dollar of demand-induced GNP growth. Since there is a consensus that the multiplier tends to be large when there are many unemployed workers available to the economy, and since the ERTA tax cuts came at a time of very high unemployment, the figures were adjusted accordingly. Economists agree that over time, as there remain fewer additional workers to be hired, the multiplier effect tends to diminish toward zero. We employed that assumption. Thus, although the tax cuts may have contributed significantly to the demand-induced growth in the early 1980s, the DRI model assumes that the effect of the tax cuts on demand have been largely dissipated by now.

The results indicate that had these demand-side effects not occurred, the economy would have been 2.1 percent smaller in 1982, 3.2 percent smaller in 1983 and 1984, and 2.7 percent smaller in 1985. The recession of the early 1980s would have continued past the last quarter of 1982 into the middle of 1983. This smaller economy was then incorporated into the computer model of the taxpayer population. Had the economy been smaller, taxpayers would have received smaller incomes. Some would have been unemployed, others would have worked shorter hours. Small businesses would have seen lower profits, and taxpayers who receive corporate dividends would have gotten smaller dividend checks. It is impossible to allocate precisely these various effects among each of the 34,000 representative taxpayers in our sample, but because these taxpayers are representative of the whole population, we can safely assume that the 2 to 3 percent reduction in the nation's GNP would have translated into a 2 to 3 percent reduction in their incomes as well. After adjusting for these demand-side changes, we find that income tax collections under the old law would have been $14.1 billion lower in 1982 and $40.1 billion lower in 1985. Those figures represent the extent to which the "Old Law, New Economy" line overestimated tax revenues by incorporating demand-side changes in the economy that would not have occurred without the tax cut.

Subtracting this demand-side effect from the "Old Law, New Economy" line, we get an "Old Law, New Economy, Minus Demand Effects" line. This line shows that after taking demand-side revenue increases into account, the revenue cost of ERTA falls sharply (see figure 4.3). Instead of costing $44 billion in 1982, the tax cut cost only $29.9 billion. Instead of costing $115 billion in 1985, the actual revenue forgone was only $74.8 billion. Over the early 1980s roughly one-third of the direct effect revenue loss was recaptured by the demand-side response to the tax cuts.

The second effect of the tax cut on GNP was the supply-side effect. As in the case of the hypothetical electrician and secretary, the reduction in marginal tax rates had the effect of giving a raise to most workers in the economy. Previous economic studies have estimated the effects of such tax cut–induced raises on labor supply.[7] These studies suggest that males in their prime earning years tend to be quite unresponsive to wage changes, while the response of married females is quite high.

FIGURE 4.3
The Demand-Side Effect

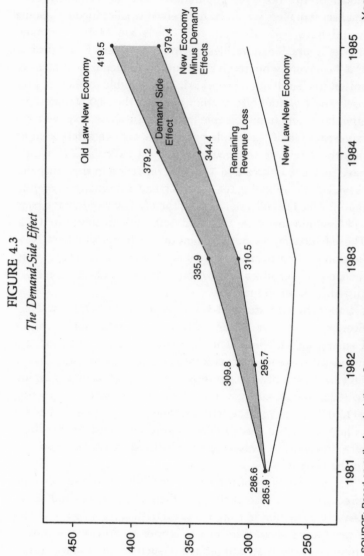

SOURCE: Based on author's calculations. See note 1, chapter 4.

This different response of men and women is important because ERTA provided an extra marginal rate reduction for the lower-earning spouse in a two-earner family, the worker in the family likely to be most responsive to a tax rate change.

To estimate the effect on labor supply, we assumed that a 10 percent rise in after-tax wages would cause the primary earner in the family to work 1 percent more while a 10 percent rise in the secondary earner's wages would cause that earner to work 10 percent more. We then tested whether these responses seemed plausible in light of the actual results of the tax change; they appeared to be on the cautious side of the estimates.[8]

Of course, how much any particular taxpayer responded to the tax rate changes depends on how much of a raise he or she received. We estimated the after-tax income of each of the taxpayers and their spouses covered by our 34,000 tax returns and used the above response estimates to estimate how much less they would have worked had they not received a tax cut. The value of the extra work effort from the tax cut amounted to $38 billion, or about 2.5 percent additional labor supply from 1981–85. Of this figure, about three-fifths, or $23 billion, was due to the response of secondary earners in two-earner families. We performed the same type of calculation for entrepreneurial income to see how much more self-employed people chose to earn as a result of the tax rate reduction and found it to be around $6 billion.

In addition we calculated the effect the tax cuts would have on how much of their compensation workers take in the form of tax-free fringe benefits. A leading estimate of the responsiveness of workers' choice of fringe benefits to tax rates was performed by Professor Robert Turner at Colgate University, who found that each percentage point rise in the tax rate causes workers to increase the fringe share of their total compensation by 0.18 percent.[9] Applying this estimate to the actual tax rates faced by our representative 34,000 taxpayers yielded an increase of about $30 billion in taxable wage income. Technically this fringe benefit response is part of the pecuniary effect rather than the supply-side effect, because the taxpayers did not work any more as a result of the compensation change. However, it does have an effect on the amount of taxable income reported by taxpayers after tax rates were cut. We include it among the supply-side effects because it appears so directly in the labor-supply response, though, as we shall see, most pecuniary effects show up much more indirectly.

All this extra taxable income produced extra tax revenue. Falsely assuming that this extra income and extra revenue would have appeared even in the absence of the tax cut caused the direct effect estimate of the cost of the tax cut to be too high by about $20 billion in 1985. Subtracting that $20 billion from the "Old Law, New Economy Minus Demand Effects Line," produces the "Old Law, Old Economy Line" in figure 4.4.

With the construction of this line we have achieved most of what we set out to do. We have created an Old Law, Old Economy revenue estimate. This new revenue estimate gives us an internally consistent picture of how much income tax revenue the government would have collected had it not passed ERTA. A comparison of the "Old Law, Old Economy" line with the "New Law, New Economy" line shows just how powerful the economic effects of a tax cut can be. The difference between these two lines is only $17.9 billion in 1982, less than half the direct effect revenue estimate of $44 billion. In 1985, the difference is $54.1 billion, again less than half of the direct effect of $115 billion.

One final step remains. We have not yet estimated the pecuniary effect of the tax cut, that which results not from any change in the size of the economy but merely from taxpayers reshuffling their assets. The pecuniary effect played no part in producing our "Old Law, Old Economy" line: we could not back pecuniary effects out of the new economy to get the old economy, because they did not significantly affect the size of the new economy in the first place. Since we have already computed all the ERTA-induced revenue effects that we can account for by examining observable changes in the economy,

FIGURE 4.4
The Supply-Side Effect

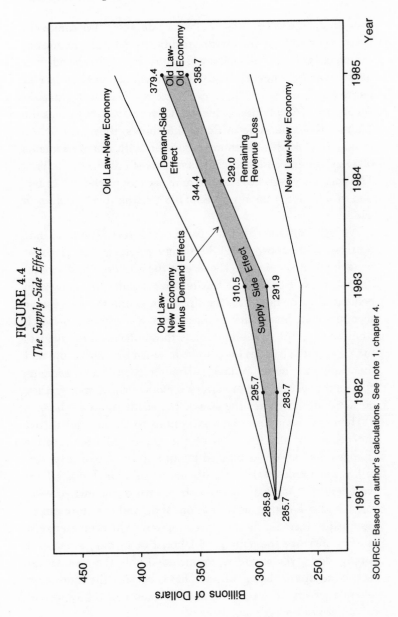

everything else is a pecuniary effect by default.[10] We can calculate the pencuniary effect with a reality check by comparing our estimates for how much money "should" be collected under the new law and the new economy with actual revenue results (see figure 4.5). Our "New Law, New Economy" line shows taxpayers paying $265.8 billion of income taxes in 1982. In fact, as the "Actual Revenue" line in figure 4.5 shows, they paid $277.6 billion. In 1985 this difference is greater, with actual payments of $325.7 billion and predicted payments of only $304.6 billion. The pecuniary responses to the new tax law provided $12 billion of additional tax revenue in 1982, rising to $21 billion in 1985.

Why the difference? The "New Law, New Economy" line reflects, for the most part, ERTA-induced changes in taxpayer behavior that show up in the size of the economy. It does not, for the most part, reflect the revenue results of changes in behavior that do not affect the size of the economy. As we have seen, there are many such changes, from the decision to switch from tax-exempt to taxable bonds to the decision to give less to tax-exempt charities (as people do when tax rates drop) and therefore pay more in taxes. Though such rearrangements change the relative size of various sectors of the economy, they do not materially alter the size of the economy as a whole.

There are some important exceptions to the statement that the pecuniary effect section of the graph indicates revenue changes that are not explained by an improved economy. Recall, for example, that in our discussion of supply-side effects we noted that tax cuts increase the return on savings, investment, and risk taking, as well as on labor, and therefore can be assumed to increase the supply of capital to the economy even as they increase the supply of labor. But in our estimate of supply-side revenue effects we included only the revenue effects of additional labor supply. That is because the short-term revenue effects of even quite large increases in the supply of capital are often very small.

Suppose, for instance, that in 1985, with all the tax cuts in

FIGURE 4.5
The Pecuniary Effect

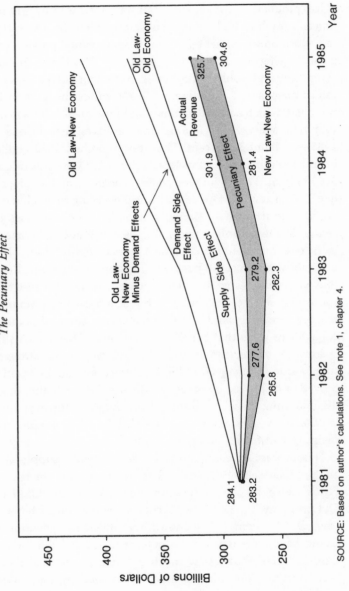

SOURCE: Based on author's calculations. See note 1, chapter 4.

place, productive investment of all sorts increased by $20 billion as a result of ERTA's very substantial increase of the after-tax return on investment. Such an increase would provide very great long-term benefits to the economy. Yet the short-term revenue effects would be negligible. Assuming a 10 percent real return on business investment,[11] a $20 billion increase in investment, which national income would rise by $2 billion in one year. The average marginal tax rate on investment income in 1985 was about 30 percent. Thus, our hypothetical $20 billion increase in capital would yield additional 1985 revenue of only $600 million. That is just too small a needle to find among our haystack of revenue figures, so instead of trying to break it out, we include it and any similarly small revenue responses increases in the pecuniary effect. This is worth noting because it is the one important case in which revenue figures do not help us establish the tax cut's positive effects on the economy. Recall that we are interested in revenue figures not only because they show how much the tax cut cost, but also because certain positive revenue effects indicate that the tax cut changed taxpayer behavior in ways that benefit the economy. That tax cuts increase risk taking and investment was one of the strongest supply-side arguments for ERTA, yet the claim cannot be either proved or disproved by revenue evidence. Intellectually, this is disappointing. As we shall see in later chapters, however, there is other very substantial evidence that ERTA was a boon to savings, investment, and risk taking.

This process of eliminating the demand-side, supply-side, and pecuniary effects leaves us with the true cost of the tax cut. Figure 4.6 shows this as the difference between the "Old Law, Old Economy" line and the "Actual Revenue" line. The "Old Law, Old Economy" line shows how much the government would have collected had we not cut taxes, and the "Actual Revenue" line shows how much it actually collected. ERTA cost less than one-third as much as implied by the naively calculated direct effect estimate, which is roughly the figure that most political and media critics of ERTA cite. In 1982 this true

FIGURE 4.6
The Actual Revenue Effect

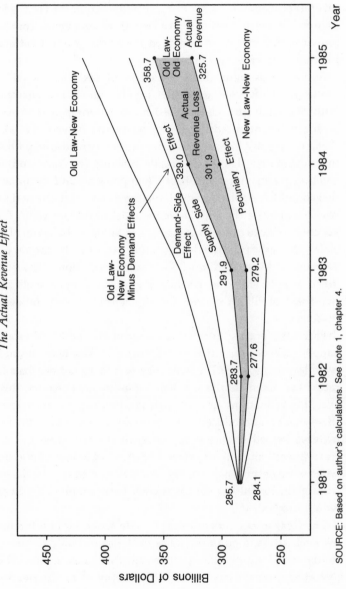

SOURCE: Based on author's calculations. See note 1, chapter 4.

revenue cost amounted to only $6.1 billion, compared to the $44 billion direct effect estimate. By 1985 the true revenue cost had grown to $33 billion as compared to the direct effect estimate for that year of $114.9 billion.

So who was right about the effect of tax changes on the economy, the Keynesians or the supply-siders? The answer is both, at least in part. The Keynesians were right in claiming that such a substantial reduction in rates would powerfully boost demand, a point the supply-siders never denied but perhaps underestimated. The demand-side revenue feedback and the combined behavioral feedbacks (supply-side and pecuniary) turned out to be roughly equal. On the other hand, the revenue results vindicate the supply-siders' most important claim: The tax cut produced quite large changes in taxpayer behavior. That claim, strongly confirmed by results, ran directly contrary to Keynesian theory and most Keynesian predictions. The combined supply-side and pecuniary effects recouped well over one-third of ERTA's estimated direct cost, a very powerful response.

ERTA did not pay for itself as some of the most enthusiastic supply-siders claimed it would. Personal income tax collections were lower under ERTA than they would have been had tax rates never been cut. As we shall see in the next chapter, however, the reductions in very high tax brackets easily paid for themselves and produced a rather sizable increase besides. This increase helped finance a large part of the reduction in taxes from lower- and middle-class taxpayers. Though this is not what some enthusiastic supply-siders predicted during the political fight for the tax cuts, it is what basic supply-side theory would predict.

The Reagan tax cuts put supply-side economics on the map intellectually and politically. The evidence certainly favors the fundamental supply-side proposition that taxes matter: they distort taxpayer behavior, limit the supply of productive factors, and hold the economy below its potential. The effects of the 1981 tax changes shift the burden of proof to those who claim government can raise taxes with impunity.

Putting theory to one side for a moment, were the Reagan tax cuts a good idea? More specifically, could the country afford them? By 1985, at a revenue cost in that year of $33 billion, economic output was between 2 and 3 percent higher than it would have been without the tax cut. That extra growth stands for millions of new jobs and a higher standard of living. Moreover, as we shall see in the next few chapters, the tax cuts had salutary effects on inflation, investment, and savings and contributed only marginally to the deficit. By the standards of government programs this one would have to be judged a bargain.

Critics persist in arguing that the 1981 tax cut lost huge amounts of revenue and brought few benefits. This is not surprising. The analysis we have used here can be difficult to accept for the simple reason that nearly all the numbers involved are hypothetical and relative. The only real number on any of our figures is the actual revenue amount. The supply- and demand-side effects, which "reduce" the revenue shortfall, do not make the actual revenue any larger; they simply correct downward the direct effect estimate of how much more revenue could have been reaped without the tax cut. However, the direct effect numbers on which the critics rely actually involve the most drastically counterfactual assumptions.

All these counterfactual calculations do give the enterprise an unreal quality. One yearns for down-to-earth numbers. There are none to be had. By any method for determining the effect of the tax cuts, there will be only one real number: actual revenue. All others will be estimates derived from events that did not happen.

To see more clearly the problems with apparently more straightforward ways of figuring the loss in tax revenue, let us imagine that the direct effect estimate really does represent the revenue the government ought to have received, as critics of the tax cuts maintain. This would mean that the 1985 actual income tax revenue figure of $325 billion dollars really should have been $94 billion dollars higher, or $419 billion. Remember you can get this figure only by assuming that the tax cut had absolutely no effect on anything, either the size of the economy or the behavior of taxpayers.

A $419 billion income tax take for 1985 would mean that income taxes that year would have taken more than 26 percent of the tax base (that is, of the income on which taxes are paid after deductions and exemptions), instead of just the 21 percent actually absorbed by taxes. It would also mean that the average marginal tax rate on the base would have been roughly 44 percent instead of just 34 percent. To be consistent, the critics of ERTA or of the analysis presented in this chapter must believe that we could have imposed a 44 percent marginal tax rate on the tax base, instead of a 34 percent rate, without affecting the size of the base.

For the government to have actually collected $419 billion in tax revenue, consider what would have had to happen, for example in consumer spending. In 1985 disposable personal income, or income after taxes, was $2,841 billion. Of this, consumers spent $2,629 billion on purchases and paid $85 billion in installment interest and transfers to foreigners, which left them $127 billion in personal savings, or 4.5 percent of their income. If we really believe that the tax cuts had no demand-side effect, then we would have to assume that the extra $84 billion the government would have collected in taxes would have left consumer spending unaffected. Stated differently, consumers would have only been able to save $43 billion, or 1.3 percent of their incomes. To believe that the government actually would have collected $419 billion in tax revenue if the tax cuts had not taken place, we have to believe that households would have cut their savings rate by 70 percent.

That is implausible, to say the least. And nearly all economic analysts accept that there would be a demand-side feedback from the tax cuts. Some critics accept the demand-side argument but reject all alleged supply-side or pecuniary effects. Consider some of the assumptions these "pure" demand-siders must make. In 1981, just before the tax rates were cut, roughly four million taxpayers were in the 49 percent or higher brackets of the income tax. By 1985, absent the tax rate cuts, that figure would have grown to more than seven million taxpayers. In order to assume that we really would have collected $94 billion more tax revenue had we not cut taxes, the demand-siders must assume that the three million taxpayers who would have become eligible to share half their income with the government would have done so cheerfully, without increasing their tax avoidance behavior at all. They must also assume that a 10 point rise in the nation's average marginal tax rate, from 34 percent to 44 percent, would have had no effect on taxpayer behavior. They must assume, contrary to all existing empirical evidence, that taxpayers would have contributed no more to charitable organizations, realized the same amount of capital gains, and refrained from switching from taxable investments into tax-exempt bonds. They must assume that labor-force participation rates would have moved strongly upward, as happened throughout the 1980s, even if workers had been taking home steadily less after-tax income rather than steadily more. They would have to believe, contrary to common sense and the empirical evidence, that lower wages cause people to work more while higher wages cause them to work less. They would have to believe that the sudden jump in the labor-force participation and taxable income of married women, which occurred in the 1980s, would have happened without ERTA's quite dramatic reduction in tax rates for working spouses. They would have to believe that the sudden halt in the decade-long trend towards more fringe benefits and less taxable cash in pay settlements would have occurred even if the taxes on that cash had continued to rise instead of being dramatically decreased. In short, they would have to assume away most of the microeconomic research on the effects of taxes over the past ten years.

The real never-never land is the one of revenue projections that do not take behavioral and macroeconomic repercussions into account. The direct effect estimates used by those who maintain that ERTA cost "hundreds of billions of dollars" presume that the world would have been the same regardless of the level of taxes. Their world is also a counterfactual one. To decide who to believe, one must decide which counterfactual assumption is more plausible. Does it make sense to believe that taxes have no effect on behavior or that they have the kind of effect demonstrated by various economic studies? Clearly the latter. The challenge to policy makers for the coming years is to remain true to the principles that common sense suggests and the evidence has now established: taxes matter. When they are too high, they impair not only the happiness of the people, but the wealth of the nation, and the resources of the treasury.

Chapter 5

Did the Rich Get Richer?

"Mr. Reagan's individual tax cuts were skewed to the rich
and Congress added more goodies for corporations."
—*The New Republic*, 4 July 1983

We often hear that "under Ronald Reagan the rich got richer
and the poor got poorer," and that the 1981 tax cuts were a big
windfall for the rich and only for the rich. It would seem to be
common knowledge. But what everyone knows isn't always
true, and in this bit of common knowledge there is no more
than a tiny kernel of truth.

During the early part of Reagan's first term, the rich[1] did get
richer while most of the rest of the country stayed even. Some
lost ground. The causes were not the tax cuts but record high
interest rates and the back-to-back recessions of 1980–82.
When interest rates go up, lenders get richer and borrowers get
poorer. Since the lenders tend to have more money than the
borrowers in the first place, high interest rates do make the rich
richer. Recessions reinforce this process because recessions are
costliest to middle- and working-class people who lose their
jobs, while the rich rarely become unemployed.

Common knowledge stumbles at this point because rising
interest rates and higher unemployment began well before Reagan became president. For example, a common bit of evidence
used by Reagan critics is that the poverty rate rose after the tax
cuts. Actually, the poverty[2] rate bottomed out at 11.4 percent
in 1978. It hit 13 percent in 1980 and 14 percent in 1981, the year
Reagan took office but before his economic program was in

place. The poverty rate peaked at 15.2 percent in 1983, by which time the tax cut was still only three-quarters in place. In short, two-thirds of the rise in the poverty rate occurred before Reagan's tax and budget policies could take hold, and all the rise occurred before ERTA was fully in place. By 1985 the poverty rate was back down to the level it was at when Reagan took office. It dropped even further during his last three years in office. Thus, though the poverty rate rose in three of Carter's four years as president, it fell in six of Reagan's eight years.

Consider the "rich got richer" critique.

When interest income rises as a share of national income the rich get richer compared to everyone else. This is because the rich derive more of their income from investments than most people. Interest income did increase its share of national income during Reagan's first term. Again, however, the trend had started under Carter. In 1976, the year before Jimmy Carter took office, interest income was 9.2 percent of personal income. By 1981, when Ronald Reagan entered the White House, it was up to 13.3 percent. The interest share of personal income peaked in 1985 at 14.4 percent of income. Thus three-quarters of this windfall to the rich occurred before Reagan took office. Like the poverty rate, interest income as a share of personal income fell in the latter half of the Reagan presidency.

Who got richer under Reagan? Taking into consideration data from both Reagan terms, the answer is that, on average, everyone did. The real income of the median family rose over $3,000 under Reagan, after falling that same amount between 1973 and 1981 (the largest such retreat since the Great Depression). Continuing the trend of the late 1970s, families above the median did best early in the administration, with everyone else catching up later as the economic recovery continued apace. This situation had more to do with macroeconomic trends than with the direct effect of the tax cuts however.

The phrase "tax cuts for the rich" has become a staple of the rhetoric of anti-Reagan politicians. Even the most cursory look at the evidence, however, shows ERTA raised the share of the

FIGURE 5.1

Share of Taxes Paid by the Rich
1979–1986

Top .1%   Top .5%   Top 1%

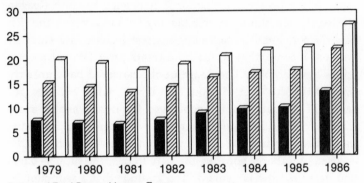

Percent of Total Personal Income Taxes

tax burden borne by the rich. As figure 5.1 shows, the top 0.1 percent of all taxpayers (roughly speaking those making over $200,000 a year) saw their share of income tax payments rise from 7 percent in 1981 to 14 percent in 1986. The share of taxes borne by the top 2 percent of taxpayers (roughly those making over $60,000) rose from 26 percent in 1981 to 34 percent in 1986. By contrast, taxpayers on the bottom half of the income scale saw their share of tax payments fall from 7 percent at the start of the decade to only 6 percent by 1986. The great American middle class, people earning between $20,000 and $60,000 in the early 1980s saw their tax share fall from 67 percent to 60 percent between 1981 and 1986. It was they who received the vast bulk of the Reagan tax cuts. The rules of arithmetic dictate that if the rich ended up paying a bigger share of taxes, everyone else must have taken a bigger tax cut than the rich. So much for common knowledge.

This simple demonstration does not settle the argument. Presented with these facts, the Reagan critics switch gears. They point out that the rich, having had a tax rate cut, could only be paying more in taxes if they had gotten a lot richer compared to everyone else. This is true by definition. The rich will pay more taxes at lower rates only if their *reported taxable* income goes up, which it did. This conclusion, however, is not very interesting in itself. The more important question is: Why did the rich report more taxable income? If it happened because Reagan shifted the nation's economic playing field in favor of the rich (say by permanently increasing interest income as a share of national income, that is, favoring capital over labor) then the critics have a point: The Reagan policies would have unfairly favored the rich over the poor. But if the change occurred because the tax cuts simply encouraged the rich to expose more income to taxation or, even better, to work harder at producing more income, then the Reagan administration can hardly be accused of unfairly boosting the rich. In fact, the supply-siders had defended the tax cuts on the grounds that a reduction in rates would cause the rich to shift from tax-free to taxable activity and to work harder. Before the tax cuts the critics had agreed this would be a good thing; they simply denied it would happen.

If the rich got richer mostly because of underlying economic currents, and not because they worked harder or rearranged their finances, that would imply that the Reagan tax cuts failed to change taxpayer behavior. But if underlying economic currents cannot explain the rising share of taxable income reported by the rich, then the changes in the taxable income must be the result of the kind of behavioral responses to tax rate cuts that supply-siders predicted.

The question can be resolved by the analysis described in the last chapter because it takes account of underlying economic currents, assuming changes in the share of interest and other capital income in national income to have occurred under all scenarios. What is left is the changes in tax revenue from the various effects of the Reagan tax cuts. To the extent that the higher tax payments (and, implicitly, higher reported taxable income) result from behavioral responses to the tax cut, the supply-side case is vindicated: The rich paid more because their behavior changed, not because the economy was shifted in their favor.

Rerunning the model used in the last chapter, this time only for taxpayers earning more than $200,000, gives the results shown in figure 5.2. As before, the "Old Law-New Economy" line represents estimated revenues, assuming that the pre-ERTA tax rates had stayed in place but the economy still boomed as if rates had been cut. The "Old Law-Old Economy" line shows this revenue if that growth never happened. The difference between these two lines is the demand- and supply-side effect of the tax change. The "New Law-New Revenue" line estimates tax revenues with the ERTA tax rates but with no behavioral response by taxpayers. The "Actual Revenue" line shows how much was actually collected.

As figure 5.2 indicates, the supply- and demand-side effects combine to recoup about one-fourth of the supposed direct revenue loss from high income taxpayers. This is much less than for the general taxpayer population. The benefits of the demand-side stimulus to employment went almost entirely to the non-rich. And the increase in the labor supply to the economy, mostly from ERTA's after-tax "raise" for married women, also was disproportionately large among the non-rich. But what is most striking about figure 5.2 is the huge "pecuniary" effect (the region between the "New Law-New Economy" line and the "Actual Revenue" Line). The pecuniary effect is so large for the rich that it drives the "Actual Revenue" line above the "Old Law" line. From the rich, ERTA reaped not only a relative increase in the share of the tax burden but an absolute increase in tax revenues, derived almost entirely from the pecuniary and other effect.

Recall that the pecuniary effect, is the result of taxpayers rearranging their finances in response to tax changes, but not always in ways that clearly increase the supply of labor or capital to the economy. Here these pecuniary changes were so

FIGURE 5.2

Effect of Tax Cuts on Taxes Paid by the Rich

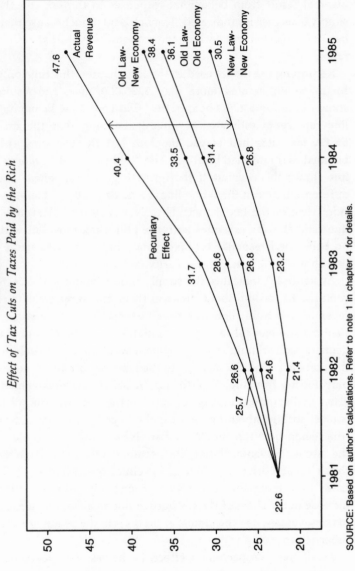

SOURCE: Based on author's calculations. Refer to note 1 in chapter 4 for details.

large that the government collected more tax revenue from upper-income taxpayers at a 50 percent top rate than it would have at 70 percent. The model also indicates that upper-middle-class taxpayers, with incomes ranging from $75,000 to $200,000, whose rates were cut from a range of 54–69 percent to a range of 38–50 percent, paid about 92 percent of what they would have paid under the old law. For these taxpayers also, the pecuniary effect plays a larger than average role. Only middle-class and working-class taxpayers paid substantially less taxes (about 18 percent less for taxpayers earning $20,000 or less and 14 percent less for taxpayers earning between $20,000 and $50,000) under the new law. These latter groups were almost entirely responsible for ERTA's revenue losses.

These results show that high tax rates do affect taxpayer behavior dramatically. This increased taxable income represents a behavioral response by taxpayers above and beyond any underlying macroeconomic trends that might have caused the rich to get richer. The data are quite clear: The principal reason the rich paid a bigger share of taxes was not underlying economic trends, but a behavioral response by the rich to lower marginal tax rates. The Congressional Budget Office, which has not generally supported supply-side theories, reached essentially the same conclusion:

> The data show considerable evidence of a very significant revenue response among taxpayers at the very highest income levels. This finding of a strong revenue response in the top income groups holds true for both projection methods and all target years.[3]

The implications of these findings are enormous. Tax rates over 50 percent are counterproductive from the view of collecting tax revenue. The old high rates were purely punitive; they discouraged taxpayers from earning or reporting high incomes while simultaneously lowering government tax revenues.

The very large pecuniary effect for upper-income taxpayers thus drives home an essential lesson: Upper-income taxpayers have enormous discretion over how and when they receive income, and over whether it will be exposed to taxation. Tax cuts that prompt them to take more income in taxable form will improve government revenues. But such changes may also make the rich appear much richer statistically without considerably increasing their share of the nation's wealth.

Consider the owner of a very successful business consulting firm in the 70 percent tax bracket. How should he take his compensation? His twelve-hour a day job requires extensive travel around town. His company could buy a red Maserati for his use for sixty thousand dollars, a fully justified deductible business expense: It is important to impress those clients. The consultant also gets some non-taxable satisfaction from his business-owned toy, but at a 70 percent tax rate, his company would have had to pay him $200,000 in salary in order for him to buy the same car for himself. Cut this fellow's tax rate to 50 percent and things change a bit. The after-tax cost of the Maserati will be lower in terms of foregone salary, but so will the after-tax costs of a lot of items that he could not have justified as business expenses: mink coats, backyard swimming pools, etc. He might very well decide that the company should spend only $30,000 on a car, a Cadillac say, and pay him $30,000 more in cash. The government takes $15,000, which is brand-new revenue because he would not have exposed that $30,000 to taxes at the 70 percent rate. With the $15,000 he has left after taxes, he buys a mink coat for his wife or a swimming pool for the whole family. He might make other adjustments as well, such as redecorating the office less frequently and less lavishly—paying himself still more cash.

After these adjustments, the government is richer, and the businessman and his family are happier. But are they richer? In an absolute sense the answer is yes: he has more choice over how to use the resources under his control over his money. His well-being has increased because he has more control, but the rise in his income greatly exaggerates the rise in his well-being. The rise in his well-being is measured by the increased happiness gained from having the mink and Cadillac instead of the Maserati. That is clearly less than the rise in his income—the equivalent of the mink by itself.

Most important, he has made no one poorer in the process. In fact, he has made his less prosperous fellow citizens somewhat better off by helping to finance a reduction in their taxes or an increase in their government services. Yes, we might call him "richer," but this is not the sort of picture people usually have in mind when they angrily complaint that "the rich get richer and the poor get poorer."

This example shows a classic pecuniary response because there is no clear benefit to the economy when our businessman switches from Maseratis to minks and Cadillacs. However, as noted in chapter 4, in many other versions of this story the economy does benefit. If, for instance, the tax cuts also prompted our businessman to rearrange his personal investments in ways that increased both their exposure to taxation and their productivity for the economy, not only the government and the businessman would be happier, but so would future generations. The businessman's reported taxable income would rise quite a bit, but it would seem even more unreasonable to say he was substantially richer, especially in the short term.

The greater after-tax reward of entrepreneurship would probably cause more people to emulate the businessman of our example and to put in the enormous personal investment required to strike out on their own, or to really excel at a high-paying job. In other words, some of the not-so-rich will get rich, though national income statistics won't distinguish them from the rich who get richer.

High tax rates not only harm the economy, they fail to soak the rich. They neither net appreciably more tax revenue from the rich nor redistribute wealth. Indeed, the evidence suggests that high tax rates help ossify the class structure rather than break it down. In 1960, when the top rate was 91 percent, the income of the rich was drawn disproportionately from interest

and dividends. The top 2 percent of taxpayers received 48 percent of interest and dividends but only 8.7 percent of wage,
salary, and entrepreneurial income. By 1985, with a 50 percent
top rate, the share of interest and dividends received by this
group was cut in half while the share of wage and entrepreneurial income had risen 28 percent. The real losers from
soak-the-rich taxation aren't the presently rich, but the would-
be rich. High income tax rates bar access to the upper class. At
a 91 percent rate it is hard to accumulate enough after taxes to
make the upper-class club. As the rates come down, so do the
barriers to entry.

The data from the early 1980s show conclusively that governments that play soak-the-rich to win votes do so at the
treasury's expense. Politicians of both political parties now
favor tax rates much lower than those of the late 1970s. One
still sees the politics of envy, but it seems much more common
in campaign speeches than in legislation. Instead of trying to
soak the rich, politicians now more commonly seek something
they call the "revenue-maximizing tax rate." Just their use of
that phrase is a triumph for supply-side reasoning. Conceptu-
ally, the revenue-maximizing rate is the peak of the once-de-
rided "Laffer Curve."

Nevertheless, the revenue-maximizing rate, like the Laffer
Curve itself, is a poor guide to tax policy. Consider taxpayers
with incomes slightly below $200,000. Taxpayers earning be-
tween $75,000 and $200,000 did not produce more revenue
under ERTA than they would have under the old law. The
government cut their tax rates by 25 percent and their tax
payments fell by about 8 percent. Their new tax rates, ranging
from 38 percent to 50 percent, seem to be generally below the
revenue-maximizing rate.

Does that mean we cut their taxes too much? To answer that
question, let's rephrase it. Would it be wise to increase tax rates
25 percent to gain 8 percent more tax revenue? An 8 percent
revenue increase after a 25 percent rate increase suggests the tax
base shrank by 14 percent. Is it worthwhile reducing overall

economic activity by 14 percent in order to transfer 8 percent more money from taxpayers to the treasury? Remember, the 8 percent is no increase in national wealth but only a transfer from citizens to the government, while the 14 percent shrinkage is a real reduction in the tax base.

We can show this trade-off more graphically by considering an economy worth $10. The government currently collects a 40 percent tax on the economy, or $4. Wanting more revenue, it increases the tax rate to 50 percent, the equivalent of a 25 percent income tax rate increase. The economy shrinks by nearly 14 percent to $8.64. The government now has 8 percent more revenue, a total of $4.32. The people are left with $4.32. The government is 32 cents better off, but the private sector is $1.68 poorer, having paid both the cost of the tax—32 cents— and the cost of the shrunken economy, $1.36.

If it were true that the revenue-maximizing rate is always the correct rate, then it would always be correct to make the trade-off described here, charging the private sector $1.36 to make 32 cents for the public sector. In fact, it would always be right to charge the private sector $10 to make the public sector a penny. Tax rates could only be considered too high when the government actually started losing money. Unfortunately the revenue-maximizing rate is now often referred to as the "optimal" tax rate. This is a misuse of a basic economic concept. Optimal means the best possible trade-off. The truly optimal tax rate depends on how high a surcharge or excess burden society is willing to pay in transferring resources from the private sector to the public sector. Except in times of dire emergency, few people aside from revenue-hungry politicians would consider it a good bargain to charge the private sector $1.68 to get 32 cents more in government revenue. Yet the present revenue maximizers want to do even worse.

Today, tax rates on very high income taxpayers stand at 28 percent, well below the revenue-maximizing rate. The revenue maximizers want a raise, often suggesting a new higher rate of 33 percent, the special bracket rate that now applies to some upper-middle-income taxpayers.[4] The data suggest this would shrink the tax base by at least 10 percent. The government would then collect 33 percent of a 95 cent tax base or 31.5 cents, instead of the 28 cents it now collects. The cost to the affected taxpayers totals 8.5 cents, a five-cent loss of income and 3.5 cents more in taxes. In other words, the government would shrink the after-tax income of upper-income taxpayers by almost $2.50 in order to produce $1.00 more in tax revenue. Does a 2.5 for 1 trade-off, with all its implications for blunted incentives and shrunken demand, really make sense?

It is encouraging to see that politicians realize high tax rates can cost the government money. But the willingness of some to propose that $1 in government revenue is worth making the private sector $2.50 poorer indicates how far the debate still has to go.

Chapter 6

Who Made the Deficit?

"I think it would not be a favor to the people to send them
a tax refund written in red ink that's going to add to their
interest rates and add to inflation."
—Senator Lawton Chiles, in the Democratic response to
a Reagan television address[1]

"All in all, I believe it is feasible to attain President Reagan's original goal of (budget) balance in fiscal 1983, and
relatively easy to do so by fiscal 1984."
—Professor Milton Friedman[2]

From the time the Reagan tax cuts were proposed, they have
been linked to the problem of the federal deficit. Critics like
Senator Chiles argued the tax cuts would substantially increase
the deficit and add to inflation. Proponents such as Nobel Lau-
reate Milton Friedman, no fan of deficits, maintained that the
deficit could be reduced and inflation avoided by the rest of
President Reagan's programs: spending cuts and monetary restraint. Now the facts are in. The deficit did increase dramatically in the wake of the tax cut. Yet, as with the revenue effects
of the tax cut, what seem to be the bare facts don't tell the story
very well. By reasonable standards of measurement the tax cut
contributed only minimally to the deficit.

Before addressing the various did-the-tax-cuts-cause-the-
deficit questions, we have to answer a semantic question. There
is a big difference between contributing to a problem and causing it, and a big difference between being a minor and a major
contributor. To the question Was the deficit larger with the tax
changes than it would have been without them? there is only

one answer: Yes. Even with the offsetting indirect effects of the tax rate reduction on taxpayer behavior and the size of the economy, the rate reductions still caused government revenue to decline. Yet even the most cursory examination of the revenue cost of the tax cuts which ignores these indirect effects and shows a revenue loss of between $30 billion and $60 billion per year and the size of the federal deficit during the 1980s between $150 and $200 billion per year. Thus, even ignoring all we have learned about tax rates and tax revenue, the rate cuts can not alone account for the deficit.

That rather simple observation does not end the argument but shows we were asking the wrong question. The really interesting question is not whether the tax cuts caused the deficit—after all, the deficit was substantial already in 1980—but how much of the *increase* in the deficit can be blamed on the tax cuts rather than the many other major changes in fiscal and monetary policy in the eighties. To untangle the causes of the deficit growth we must measure the effects of these various changes, starting in the era before the tax cuts and the other policy changes took effect.

In 1980 the federal government ran a deficit of $61.3 billion, or 2.2 percent of GNP. By 1983 the deficit had grown to $176 billion, or 5.2 percent of GNP.[3] It is the increase, 3.0 percent of GNP, that we are concerned with here: we must measure the *change* in tax policy against the *change* in the deficit.

This analysis requires some basis for comparison, or "baseline." The fiscal policy mix in the last full year of the Carter administration offers such a baseline. The impact of Reagan policies, including the tax cut, can be measured by comparing what actually happened during the 1980s with this 1980 baseline. For example, the change caused by Reagan tax policies in 1983 is the difference between the actual taxes collected that year and the amount of taxes which would have been collected if taxes took the same share of GNP in 1983 as they did in 1980. By applying the same analysis to spending, the contribution of tax changes to the change in the deficit can be determined.[4]

First it is important to put our 1980 baseline into perspective. All the tax and spending numbers were very high to begin with. In 1980 federal receipts took 20.3 percent of GNP, the second highest level of any year up to that time, peacetime or wartime.[5] From the end of World War II to the start of the Carter administration, federal receipts averaged 18.6 percent of GNP, 1.7 percent of GNP below their 1980 level. The Reagan tax cuts reduced taxes from an historic high to a level still slightly above the postwar average, 19.3 percent at their lowest.

Non-defense spending, at 17.3 percent of GNP, was also at a record level in 1980. During the Great Society years of the Johnson administration (1965–68), non-defense spending was 11.1 percent of GNP. From 1965 to 1979, the year before our baseline, non-defense spending averaged 13.9 percent of GNP. On the other hand, defense spending in 1980 was at a record low level of 5.2 percent of GNP, compared to the post–World War II average of 7.5 percent.[6] Despite the parsimonious defense spending of 1980, total government expenditures reached 22.5 percent of GNP, the second highest level since the end of World War II.

Relative to 1980, most years in the last decade saw the tax share of GNP decline slightly, but increases in both defense and non-defense spending raised the government-spending share of GNP to new records. Figure 6.1 shows the effect of these changes with a tax bar and a spending bar for each year, which give the tax and spending contributions to the deficit as percentages of GNP. The tax bar is positive for years in which tax changes added to the deficit by taking a lower share of GNP than in 1980, negative for years in which taxes took a higher share of GNP than in 1980. Similarly, the spending bar is positive for years in which spending took a greater share of GNP than in 1980 and negative otherwise.

The delay in passing the tax bill and the postponement of the tax cuts until October 1981 increased the tax share of GNP for that year, reducing the deficit by $20.7 billion, or two-thirds of 1 percent of GNP. With the start of the recession that year,

FIGURE 6.1

Contributions to the Deficit
1981–1987

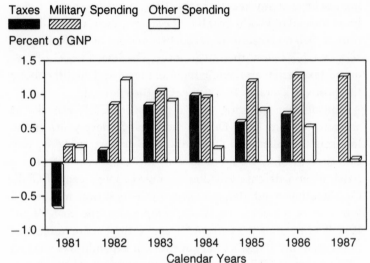

Relative to 1980 shares of GNP

SOURCE: Historical Tables of the Budget of the United States Government.

spending rose (to meet both added unemployment and welfare costs and higher defense spending) by $16 billion, or about one-half of 1 percent of GNP. Overall, the 1981 deficit was therefore slightly smaller than it would have been had 1980 fiscal policies continued in place.

The first major tax cut occurred in July 1982, dropping the tax share of GNP below the 1980 level, and increasing the deficit by $6.3 billion relative to 1980. Spending continued to skyrocket, adding $68.4 billion to the deficit, again largely due to anti-recession spending. The 1982 deficit took twice the share of GNP as the 1980 deficit. Taxes were cut again in July 1983, lowering the tax share of GNP to 19.4 percent and adding $30.3 billion to the deficit. The spending share of GNP was 24.5 percent, the 2 percent of GNP excess over 1980 levels contributing $68 billion to the deficit. In total, the 1983 deficit hit a peacetime record 5.2 percent of GNP, nearly $100 billion above the level it would have been if 1980 fiscal policies had stayed in place. Yet only 30 percent of this increase was due to lower taxes. Seventy percent was due to higher spending.

The final phase of the tax cut took effect in July 1984, shrinking the tax share of GNP to 19.2 percent of GNP, the lowest level in the 1980s. This further tax cut contributed $38.5 billion to the increase in the deficit that year. Yet the tax share of GNP was still higher than in any peacetime year of American history except those of the Carter administration. Spending was trimmed to 23.7 percent of GNP that year, but the extra spending above 1980 levels still amounted to $46.4 billion. By 1985 the tax share of GNP started to rise again, reducing the contribution of the tax cuts to the deficit. Spending also rose and contributed $81.9 billion to the deficit. There was little change in 1986, but in 1987 the Tax Reform Act of 1986 increased taxes, pushing the tax share of GNP up to their 1980 level. Taxes thus made no net contribution to the deficit that year. By 1987 the *entire* cause of the increase in the budget deficit since 1980 was added spending, not lower taxes.

Between 1980 and 1987 the national debt rose $529 billion more than would have been the case had 1980 fiscal policies stayed in place. Of this $529 billion, only $112 billion, or 21 percent, was due to the tax reduction. The remaining $417 billion, or 79 percent, was caused by the spending increases. And though the tax cuts no longer contribute to the national debt, the spending problem remains unsolved. This may seem surprising given all the talk about budget cuts in the Reagan years. Some specific programs were cut. But overall spending not only increased, it increased even faster than the economy expanded.

By far the major reason for this increase was defense spending.[7] In the late 1970s, a bipartisan consensus held that defense spending had been cut too far. President Carter agreed in 1978 with the leaders of the other NATO nations that each would increase defense spending by 3 percent in real terms each year.

During the 1980 campaign, President Carter committed himself to a 5 percent annual real increase in defense spending. Between 1980 and 1987 real defense spending increased by an average of 6.3 percent per year, or 55 percent total. This added defense spending increased government spending by 1.3 percent of GNP. By 1987 the cumulative increase amounted to $275 billion of the $417 billion added to the national debt by higher spending, or 52 percent of the total increase in the debt. These proportions result from the choice of 1980 as a baseline—by historic standards, the 6.5 percent of GNP spent in 1987 on defense is relatively low. Had other years besides 1980 been used as a baseline, the change in defense spending would have appeared as a *decrease* in the deficit.

The second biggest increase in expenditure during the 1980s was for interest payments on the national debt, an increase caused in part by the increase in the national debt due to the tax cuts or added defense spending. From 1981 to 1987 the tax cuts cost about $17.5 billion in extra interest and increased defense spending cost an extra $53.6 billion in interest.[8]

After accounting for defense increases, tax cuts, and the extra interest payments due to each, $71 billion of extra spending remains on non-defense programs. Although the 17.3 percent of GNP spent in 1980 on non-defense programs set a record, non-defense spending continued to grow during much of the 1980s.

In sum, all types of spending increased during the 1980s, not only in real terms, but as a percent of GNP. About 13 percent of the increase in the deficit was due to an increase in non-defense spending, although the 1980 baseline represents a record high for non-defense spending and a historically low level of defense spending. Even including the extra interest payments ascribable to the tax changes, only 24 percent of the rise in the deficit during the 1980s was tax induced. The remaining 76 percent was caused by increases in spending. The overall reduction in the tax burden was thus neither the *cause* of the deficit increase, nor the major *contributor* to it.

TABLE 6.1

Change in Taxes Relative to Constant 1980 Share
(figures in billions of dollars)

Year	Personal Taxes	Other Taxes	Total Taxes
1981	+10.7	+10.1	+20.8
1982	+5.4	−12.1	−6.3
1983	−26.9	−3.4	−30.3
1984	−45.7	+7.2	−38.5
1985	−32.5	+7.2	−25.3
1986	−38.6	+5.2	−31.4
1987	−21.7	+21.8	+0.1

Though personal income taxes were generally lower during the decade, other taxes increased. As table 6.1 shows, this increase in other taxes significantly reduced the tax contribution to the deficit. Personal tax cuts added $149 billion to the cumulative deficit increase during the period 1981–87, while other taxes reduced the cumulative deficit by $37 billion. In 1980 all taxes were at or near historic highs. The tax changes of the 1980s successfully lowered personal taxes toward normal levels, but other taxes continued to rise dramatically.

In its early days the Reagan administration confidently predicted a balanced budget by 1983 or 1984. The administration missed the mark so badly not because of the tax cuts, which contributed only one dollar out of every five to the deficit increase, but largely because administration officials were wildly optimistic about their ability to cut overall spending, even while increasing defense spending.

Shortly after taking office the Reagan administration, in *A Program for Economic Recovery*,[9] outlined its economic and fiscal strategy, including numerous specific proposals for reducing the federal deficit. But the administration quickly learned it could exert little influence over the fiscal 1982 budget, initially submitted by President Carter on 1 January 1981. Though the final vote on the 1982 budget did not come until summer of 1981, six months isn't enough time for a new administration to get control of the budget process, begun in the bureaucracy a year earlier.

The first true Reagan budget was the fiscal 1983 budget, submitted in January 1982 and scheduled to run from October 1982 through September 1983. The 1983 Budget proposal detailed domestic spending cuts which would have pared spending $43 billion in 1983, $80.5 billion in 1985, and $105[10] billion by 1987. The administration lost the ensuing political struggle. Few of its reductions were enacted by the Congress. Had the administration prevailed, the picture might have been quite different. In fiscal 1983 non-defense spending came to 3.9[11] percent of GNP more than proposed by the administration when it first came to office, exactly the amount by which the deficit increased. Of course, the recession contributed to the deficit in that year, somewhat muddying the water.

By fiscal 1985, a year of healthy economic growth, the picture was quite clear. The 1983 administration proposal requested defense spending of 7.0 percent of GNP and non-defense spending of 13.8 percent of GNP, for a total level of spending of 20.8 percent of GNP. After the Congress finished with the budget, non-defense spending that year hit 17.5 percent of GNP, raising total spending to 23.9 percent of GNP. The result was a dramatically higher deficit than would have occurred under Reagan's 1983 budget.

The administration also seriously underestimated both the effectiveness and the cost of its anti-inflation policy. It underestimated the rate at which inflation would drop and, probably because of that first error, failed to allow for the 1982 recession, which also partly resulted from anti-inflationary monetary policies. Table 6.2 shows how far off the administration was in forecasting inflation and real GNP growth. Administration officials made the "First Forecast" immediately upon coming to office; the "Second Forecast," incorporated in the fiscal 1983 budget, was made late in 1982. A joke around Washington at the time had it that these forecasts were made by an administration employee named Rosie Scenario. But though the predic-

TABLE 6.2

Reagan Administration Forecasts of Inflation and Growth*

	Inflation			Real Economic Growth		
Year	First Forecast	Second Forecast	Actual Level	First Forecast	Second Forecast	Actual Level
1981	9.9 %	9.1 %	9.7 %	1.1 %	2.0 %	1.9 %
1982	8.3	7.9	6.4	4.2	0.2	−2.5
1983	7.0	6.0	3.9	5.0	5.2	3.6
1984	6.0	5.0	3.7	4.5	5.0	6.8
1985	5.4	4.7	3.0	4.2	4.7	3.4
1986	4.9	4.6	2.7	4.2	4.4	2.8

*These data are calculated assuming an inflation elasticity of revenues of 1.6 with respect to inflation and an elasticity of 1.36 with respect to real economic growth.
SOURCES: *A Program for Economic Recovery* and *1983 Budget of the United States Government.*

tions for growth were definitely rosy, those about inflation were pessimistic. The 1982 rate of inflation was only about half what was expected, and cumulative inflation from 1983 to 1986 was just over half the predicted level.

Inflation raises taxes through bracket creep. Typically, 10 percent inflation causes personal income tax collections to rise 16 percent, for a 6 percent real increase. The dramatic reduction in the inflation rate and the corresponding slowdown in real economic growth during the early 1980s therefore caused tax collections to be lower than they would have been had inflation stayed high. Lower inflation not only causes lower revenue, it also reduces both real (that is, adjusted for inflation) tax revenue and the tax share of GNP. Thus, until tax indexing began in 1985, lower-than-expected inflation caused tax revenues also to be lower than expected.

A much larger share of GNP would have been taken in taxes for each year from 1982 through 1987 had the administration forecasts been correct. Under the administration's original economic assumptions, the income tax share of GNP would have been 0.55 percent higher in 1983, 0.58 percent higher in 1984, 0.75 percent higher in 1985, 0.78 percent higher in 1986. In a typical year, about 30 percent of the overestimation of revenue was due to overoptimism in the real-GNP forecast (Rosie Scenario), while about 70 percent was attributable to administration pessimism about the decline in the rate of inflation. Total income tax collections over the period 1983–87 would have been $73 billion higher had the administration's 1982 forecasts come true. The total value of the personal income tax cuts between 1983 and 1987 was $145 billion relative to their 1980 share of GNP. Thus it can be argued that the administration expected to reduce the personal tax share of GNP by only half the actual figure.

On average, the difference between what the administration expected to collect and what it actually collected was about $14 billion, about 10 percent of our current deficit and about 14 percent of the total deficit increase during the 1980s. The bottom line is clear. The great deficit increase of the 1980s was overwhelmingly the result of higher spending, not lower taxes. Even with the personal tax cuts, taxes remained high by historic standards. Though in 1980 overall spending hit a then record high as a share of GNP, spending continued to climb throughout the Reagan years and was responsible for at least three quarters of the increase in the deficit.

There is, however, one way in which the tax cuts contributed more to the deficit than anyone expected. For contrary to nearly all predictions, the evidence shows the tax cuts were one of the reasons inflation dropped so much more quickly than expected. But that is our next story.

Chapter 7

Why No Inflation?

"Reagan's task of winning credibility is made more difficult by widespread skepticism among economists and
other opinion makers who fear that his unconventional
program—by traditional economic standards—could
worsen inflation rather than cure it."
—*Business Week*, 1 December 1980

Jimmy Carter presided over the first sustained double-digit inflation since official U.S. records have been kept.[1] In the fierce
debate over Reagan's Great Experiment no issue caused more
concern than the possibility the tax cuts might send inflation
even higher, with devastating effects to the economy and the
nation. Carter's treasury secretary, William Miller, argued in
1980, "Hasty tax cutting now could be counterproductive. It
would be a great hoax on the American people to promise a tax
cut that sets off a new price spiral."[2] Walter Heller warned that
"a $114 billion tax cut in three years would simply overwhelm
our existing productive capacity with a tidal wave of increased
demand and sweep away all hopes of curbing deficits and containing inflation. Indeed, it would soon generate soaring deficits
and roaring inflation."[3] Charles Schultze, chairman of Carter's
Council of Economic Advisers argued, "We want to take a
careful, deliberate approach and develop tax cuts that will address both short- and long-run problems, rather than come in
with some quickie program that seeks immediate stimulus,

without long-term benefits."[4] These men reflected what had become the Keynesian orthodoxy: Because the prime cause of inflation is too much demand, or spending power, in the economy, tax cuts, which give consumers more money to spend, would exacerbate inflation.

Yet the record is clear as to the contrary. Consumer prices, which had risen at a double-digit pace in 1979 and 1980, increased only 8.9 percent in 1981, the year the tax cut was passed. In 1982, the year that the tax cuts first hit the spending stream, prices rose only 3.8 percent. After additional tax rate reductions in 1983 and 1984, the rate of inflation dropped below 4 percent. From 1982 through 1987[5] the inflation rate averaged only 3.3 percent, the lowest rate for any five-year period since the early 1960s. The Reagan experiment devastated the contemporary Keynesian's view of inflation. Not since the Great Depression itself has the prevailing economic orthodoxy been proven so decisively wrong.

The fault was not that of Keynes, but of his latter-day disciples. *The General Theory* was written in the 1930s, when inadequate demand was clearly a problem and prices were actually falling, not rising. Keynes focused on solving the problem of inadequate demand, not excess demand, or inflation, neither of which were pressing problems in the midst of the Great Depression. The early postwar Keynesian model of the economy thus did not consider inflation, assuming for the sake of analysis that prices were stable. It was only much later that the disciples of Keynes tried to extend his theory to the problem of inflation. Their reasoning went like this: Keynes showed that when demand is too low, unemployment rises and prices fall. Therefore, they concluded, when prices rise it must be because unemployment is falling and demand is too high. But this inverse reasoning, which seems commonsensical, does not work as symmetrically as one might expect. Reducing inflation by raising unemployment through demand management is a slow, painful process.

To fully understand why the modern Keynesian paradigm

failed we need a new paradigm that can account for the unexpected events of 1982–86. In short, we must answer the question, Why no inflation?

We start with a clear and widely accepted model of the mechanisms of inflation, developed not by the supply-siders but by the monetarist school of economic thought and rooted in a simple observation. The amount of money in the economy, multiplied by the rate at which money is spent must equal the total amount of spending which takes place:

$$\text{Money} \times \text{Rate Spent} = \text{Spending}$$

If this doesn't seem controversial to you, it's because it isn't. The observation is true by definition. It is complemented by another observation: the amount of spending which takes place equals the price of each good sold times the number of units of the good which are sold.

$$\text{Spending} = \text{Price} \times \text{Quantity Sold}$$

Taken together, these statements produce the conclusion that the amount of money times the rate it is spent equals the level of prices times the amount of goods sold.

Of course, economists have their own jargon. The amount of money is called the money supply, "M." The rate at which money is spent is called velocity, "V." The quantity of goods sold is called real output or real GNP, "Y." And the price at which these goods are sold is called the price level, "P." The money supply times velocity equals the price level times real GNP. In economists' shorthand this is:

$$M \times V = P \times Y[6]$$

The nice thing about an equation like this is that it can easily express changes in the economy. Any change in one side of the equation must be matched by a change in the other side. If one side goes up by 10 percent, then the other side must also rise by 10 percent. In other words:

$$\% \text{ change } M + \% \text{ change } V = \% \text{ change } P + \% \text{ change } Y$$

To translate, "% change M" is the growth rate of the money supply, "% change V" is the change in the velocity or rate of spending, and "% change Y" is the real growth in the economy. That leaves "% change P," the change in the price level, or what we call inflation.

Now we have a formula for figuring out the rate of inflation. Inflation equals how fast money is created, plus how much faster each dollar is spent, minus how fast the real output of the economy is expanding. Our formula is just a mathematical version of the old saw that inflation is caused by too much money chasing too few goods.

Start with money. If either the money supply or the velocity increases by 1 percent (and the other remains the same), total demand (the left side of the equation) will increase by 1 percent. But that increase must be matched by a change on the right side. If the rate at which goods are produced by the economy (Y, or real growth) goes up 1 percent, then P can stay unchanged and there will be no additional inflation. But if production does not rise, the price level must rise, adding 1 percent to the inflation rate. By the same token, if real growth goes up, and (M+V) growth stays the same, inflation must go down.

Thus, other things being equal, an increase in the rate of real growth will lead to a decline in inflation, because the same amount of money will be chasing more goods. And a decrease in the rate of real economic growth will lead to an increase in inflation—again, other things being equal—because the same amount of money will be chasing fewer goods.

With this model of inflation, we can analyze the acceleration of inflation in the late 1970s and its decline in the early 1980s. Table 7.1 presents the data for the four variables of our equation for the periods just before and just after the passage of

TABLE 7.1

Money, Inflation, and Real Growth 1978–1985

Year	Percent Money Growth	Percent Velocity Change	Percent Inflation	Percent Real Growth
1978	8.0	6.3	8.0	6.3
1979	8.0	1.5	8.9	0.6
1980	8.9	0.9	9.9	−0.1
1981	10.0	−0.7	8.7	0.6
1982	8.8	−5.5	5.2	−1.9
1983	11.8	−1.7	3.6	6.5
1984	8.3	0.2	3.4	5.1
1985	8.5	−2.0	2.9	3.6
1986	9.5	−4.7	2.8	2.0

NOTE: Money growth rates are calculated on a December to December basis. As GNP and the price level (the GNP deflator) are not calculated monthly, fourth quarter to fourth quarter growth rates are used. Velocity is calculated as an arithmetic residual for exposition, although it should more properly be calculated as a logarithmic residual; the difference however is small.
SOURCE: *1989 Economic Report of the President*, and author's calculations.

ERTA. Again, the sum of the changes in money and velocity minus the rate of real growth will give us the rate of inflation in the economy.

The most striking fact in these numbers is that the rate of money growth, in this case measured by M2 (a measurement of money supply that includes money in cash, checking and NOW accounts, money market funds for individuals, savings accounts, and small value certificates of deposit, all of which individuals could spend fairly readily), hardly changed over the period in question, though the inflation rate (as measured by the GNP deflator) increased in the years up to 1980 and fell sharply thereafter. This strongly suggests that the Federal Reserve's effort to control the money supply during this period cannot by itself explain the drop in inflation. In 1985, for instance, money growth was slightly faster than it had been in 1979, yet inflation was less than half as severe. The big changes were not in money supply but in velocity, which moved from a positive to a negative number, and in real growth. Both the slowdown in velocity and the rise in real economic activity were helped along by the tax cuts.

Velocity is the speed at which the money supply is spent on final goods and services. Over long periods of time, the velocity of the M2 money supply is relatively stable. Between 1960 and 1980, for example, M2 velocity grew at an average annual rate of only 0.1 percent. The dramatic velocity swings of the late 1970s and early 1980s are a bit of a puzzle. Why did people spend their money so much faster in the late 1970s and then slow their spending so rapidly in the early 1980s?

To solve this riddle, we must realize that money not only serves as a means of carrying on transactions, but also as a store of value. Most of our personal wealth is stored in long-term investments, whether stocks or office buildings or the family home. But for security and convenience we all store a certain amount of our worth in ready money, cash or its near equivalents. We may prefer to keep a chunk of cash sitting in our wallets so as not to use the credit card. We tend to put enough cash in the checking account to cover a few months' bills without having to draw upon savings.

The portion of the national money supply we allow to "sit" as a store of wealth in our checking accounts and in our wallets is the key to the velocity of money. If a large share is sitting, the *average* velocity of money in the economy will be low. Those dollars that stay put have a velocity of zero and pull down the average velocity for all the dollars in the economy. On the other hand, if the share of dollars which is sitting in cash or in checking accounts falls, then the average velocity of dollars in the economy rises. Over the long term there is little reason for the share of the money in the economy which is kept sitting to change much. That is why, over a long period of time, velocity is fairly stable. But velocity can change dramatically, as in the late 1970s and early 1980s, when changes in the economy changed people's attitudes toward holding money as a store of wealth.

Keeping money idle has costs. When these costs go up, the amount of idle money goes down and velocity increases. The most obvious cost is the profit we lose by failing to invest our cash. Keeping money in cash or in a checking account means sacrificing the interest one might earn by holding a bond or other interest-bearing security.[7] When interest rates rise, the cost of keeping money idle rises. People then keep less money in checking accounts and more in securities. The issuer of the securities, who gets the money, keeps some of it idle but puts most of the money to use to earn more money to pay interest to his investors and bondholders. Thus, during periods of rising interest rates, velocity tends to increase.

Individual consumers may say they do not fine-tune their finances in this way. In fact, there is evidence that the proportion of money put into money market funds instead of checking accounts does vary with interest rates.[8] The bulk of this fine-tuning, however, is done by firms, not individuals. The financial officers of major corporations manage millions of dollars in cash assets. They must balance the desire for a good return on those assets against the risk the company will be caught short of cash if too much of its money is tied up in interest-bearing investments. The higher the return from lending, the more willing they are to squeeze their cash balances to the minimum.[9] This nationwide balancing act has a significant effect on velocity.

From 1978 to 1985 interest rates closely followed velocity. Interest rates rose until 1981 and then fell, as did velocity. But why did interest rates fall? According to the opponents of the tax cuts, interest rates should have risen as the government was forced to borrow more and as consumers got more spending power. In part interest rates may have fallen because the Federal Reserve convinced people it was serious about controlling inflation. But as the data indicate, money supply creation increased in 1982. Changes in money alone simply cannot explain the changes in inflation. There is an alternative explanation: the effect of tax cuts on the velocity of money.

Before the tax cuts a taxpayer in the top 70 percent tax bracket who invested in a 10 percent bond would earn only a 3 percent return after tax. The tax cut, by reducing the top rate to 50 percent, nearly doubled this net return to 5 percent. Logic suggests that this increase in return would make more money available for investment and lower its price, that is, the interest rate. And that is just what happened. In the high inflation pre–tax cut years of 1978–81, net purchases of financial assets by households grew at an annual rate of only 3.7 percent even though personal income was rising at an annual rate of 11.5 percent and interest rates were very high. People put less and less of their earnings into financial assets despite record high interest rates. Instead, the money went to spending. After the tax cuts were passed, this trend reversed. Between 1981 and 1984, net purchases of financial assets by households grew at an astounding 19 percent annual rate while personal income grew at only 7.2 percent. The share of personal income being committed to financial assets rose from 12.7 percent in 1981 to 17.4 percent in 1984 after falling in the years leading up to 1981.[10] Because most of this increase came from increased income and decreased spending rather than a reduction in idle cash, it did not increase velocity significantly.

The increase in the funds flowing into financial assets did put downward pressure on the before-tax interest rate. Since corporate tax rates were left essentially unchanged, this decline in interest rates reduced the incentives for corporations to stretch their idle cash to the limit, and they began to keep more on hand to meet day-to-day needs. The consequent increase in idle cash reduced velocity.[11]

Tax rate reduction reduced velocity in another way as well. As we explained in chapter 3, high tax rates can encourage consumer borrowing and spending, especially in an inflationary environment. Because of the tax deduction for interest payments, a 19 percent credit card loan effectively cost a taxpayer in the 49 percent bracket only 9.2 percent. With inflation at double-digit rates, that taxpayer had a big incentive to borrow and buy now rather than wait till next year when the price might be 12 percent higher. In that environment, it was very much to people's advantage not only to spend all the money they had, but to borrow money as well. By cutting tax rates, the government cut the incentive to spend and to borrow to finance spending. Our 49 percent bracket family, for instance, saw its marginal tax rate reduced to 37 percent. That tax cut raised the after-tax cost of the same 18 percent credit card loan to 11.5 percent, a bit more than the prevailing inflation rate. The bonus for borrowing and spending had disappeared. This reduction in spending helped slow velocity somewhat. And the reduction in consumer borrowing[12] contributed to the drop in pre-tax interest rates, further reducing the velocity of corporate funds. This helps explain why interest rates and velocity fell after the tax cut was passed. It also explains why the inflation rate started to fall so rapidly: Changes in velocity, caused by a significant change in individual behavior, helped reduce inflation independent of, but in addition to, the effects of monetary policy.

In sum, cutting tax rates on the return to savings allowed before-tax interest rates to fall. The falling interest rate led to a fall in velocity which acted as a brake on inflation (and on the economy). The tax cut also reduced the incentives to borrow to finance consumption purchases. This led to a further reduction in the demand for goods and services, thus putting even more downward pressure on the inflation rate. Instead of inflation accelerating, which opponents of the tax cuts had expected, the exact opposite occurred.

The tax cuts slowed velocity and reduced inflation in another way as well. The tax cut clearly helped raise the value of the dollar as compared to other currencies. This increase meant each dollar could buy more overseas. Moreover, a rising dollar makes foreigners more willing to hold idle dollar balances: with the dollar going up, idle dollars grow in value every day. The tax bill raised the foreign exchange value of the dollar by making the United States the most profitable place in the world to invest. The next chapter details how ERTA's increased depreciation allowances and reduced tax rate on interest, dividends, and capital gains drew capital from all over the world to America in search of a profitable rate of return.

In order for foreigners to invest in the United States, they first had to purchase U.S. dollars. After all, American investments, from factories to treasury bonds, are priced in dollars, not yen, marks, or pounds. The rush to invest in the United States thus increased the demand for dollars, which increased their price. The U.S. dollar rose from 1.8 German marks in 1980 to 2.9 marks in 1985. Between 1980 and 1985 the value of the dollar rose 64 percent compared to the currencies of our major trading partners. As a result, each U.S. dollar bought more foreign goods in 1985 than it did in 1980.[13] In 1985 imports from abroad comprised about 11 percent of our total purchases. Since 11 percent of our purchases were 64 percent cheaper than they would have been had the dollar not risen, by 1985 the rise in the value of the dollar probably had reduced U.S. prices by about 7 percent, or 1.4 percent per year.[14] The reduced cost of imported goods also restrained price increases on those American goods that competed with imports.

The tax cuts also reduced inflation by increasing real growth. Recall that the inflation rate equals the rate of money creation plus the change in velocity minus real growth. If inflation is more money chasing fewer goods, it can be reduced by increasing the amount of goods as well as by reducing the amount of money. In the eight years[15] leading up to the passage of the tax cut, real economic growth averaged only 2.1 percent. In the eight years following the passage of the tax cut in 1981, real economic growth averaged 3.0 percent per year, even including the deep recession year of 1982. The rate of real economic growth seems to have accelerated. It is too early to tell if this is a permanent phenomenon. But, as the discussion of the supply-side effects of tax policy in chapter 4 indicate, the tax cut does explain an increase in the rate of real growth of at least 0.5 percent per year from 1982 to 1985.

One of the key ways the tax cuts add real growth is by increasing the labor force the economy has to work with. Real after-tax wages rise, making work more attractive or making it cheaper to hire workers at the same after-tax wage. Since the first reduction in withholding in July 1982, over 20 million new jobs have been created in America, twice the new jobs created in Europe and Japan combined. This record expansion in employment is a major reason real output increased and inflation declined.

The modern Keynesians failed to see that the tax cuts might restrain inflation for the same reason they failed to see that the tax cuts would earn back much of the revenue they apparently lost. They focused almost exclusively on the tax cuts' impact on aggregate demand, the increase in the amount of money in consumers' pockets, and they largely ignored the profound effect high tax rates have on taxpayer behavior. High taxes had been encouraging people to buy more, borrow more, and produce less. As inflation redoubled these bad incentives and steadily raised tax rates through bracket creep, inflation continued to get worse even as the economy declined.

The key to breaking this vicious cycle was not gross manipulation of aggregate demand, but subtle changes in individual incentives. The key, to breaking the vicious double helix of stagflation was, to a very large extent, cutting taxes.

Chapter 8

A Deluge of Debt?

"Something quite bad is going to happen to the U.S. economy fairly soon. Politically, the big question is whether it will happen before or after the 1984 election."
—The Editors, *The New Republic,* 9 July 1984

The conventional wisdom holds that the 1981 tax cuts ushered in a period of profligate borrowing and consumption in America, a binge that diminished savings and investment, impoverishing future American generations and hampering the economy. The specter of looming catastrophe was raised by the critics in the 1984 election and again in 1988. It will no doubt be raised again in 1992. Yet now that the catastrophe has been postponed for nearly a decade, perhaps we should examine the great sea of red ink on which the Reagan economic recovery supposedly floats.

It is not surprising that the Keynesians believe the recovery of the 1980s was built on debt and consumer spending. Keynesian theory maintains that stimulating consumer spending is one of the most effective ways of stimulating the economy and that too much savings can actually hurt economic performance. Moreover, as we saw in chapter 4, the 1981 tax cut did stimulate spending by putting more money into the hands of taxpayers. But this is a far cry from the claim that the Reagan *recovery* was good old-fashioned Keynesianism.

The data indicate that the record-setting expansion of the 1980s was exceptional not for a binge of consumption, but for a rapid rise in investment spending.[1] It is important to note that this economic expansion, which began in the final quarter of 1982, is one of the strongest as well as one of the longest on record. During the first two years of the expansion, real GNP expanded at a 5.8 percent annual rate, compared to a 4.8 percent annual rate in the other five continuous expansions of the preceding quarter century. Typically an economic expansion lasts about three years. The present expansion is entering its eighth year as this book goes to press.

Consumption spending played a role in the current recovery, but consumption spending is an important part of any economic recovery. In the expansion of the 1980s, real consumption grew at a 5.4 percent annual rate in the first year and a 4.8 percent annual rate during the first two years. This is the evidence cited by the Keynesians. But this consumption pattern is almost identical to that of previous expansions. The five preceding expansions averaged an identical 5.4 percent increase in consumption during the first year and a slightly higher 4.9 percent increase during the first two years. In this regard, the ERTA expansion was quite average.

The real impetus to the expansion of the 1980s was investment spending. In recent history, investment spending increased an average of 23 percent during the first year of an expansion, and at a 13 percent annual rate during the first two years. But during the expansion of the 1980s investment skyrocketed 41 percent during the first year and expanded at a 27 percent annual rate during the first two years. The present expansion began with an explosion of investment spending twice as powerful as usual.

The investment incentives of ERTA were quite strong and produced marked results. ERTA's most important pro-investment provision was the Accelerated Cost Recovery System (ACRS). Governing the rate at which new investments could be depreciated for tax purposes, ACRS bolstered the depreciation deduction for business plant and equipment. During the 1970s the erosion of that deduction by inflation and high taxation had substantially penalized business investment.

A key principle of business taxation is that a company should pay taxes only on its profits, and not on its costs of doing business. For that reason businesses have been allowed to deduct, over time, the cost of the plant and equipment used to produce their products or services. The deduction is taken over time rather than at purchase (as with materials or wages) because the expense of using a machine or a factory is considered to occur over the course of its useful life. Depreciation deductions are not based on the actual useful life of a particular piece of equipment, however, but are taken from standardized schedules for depreciating broad categories of plant and equipment.

By the late 1970s inflation and the tax rules had undermined these depreciation schedules and subverted the principle that businesses should pay taxes only on their profits. Imagine a machine that cost $100 the year it was purchased and wears out at the rate of 10 percent a year, so that it must be replaced at the end of ten years. The tax system allows the company to subtract $10 per year from its taxable profits to account for the wear on the machine: a cost of doing business. This $10 subtraction in effect allows the company to sell $10 worth of goods tax free. At the end of ten years, if the $10 in goods which the machine produces has been set aside each year, the company will have accumulated $100 tax free to buy a new machine. In the absence of inflation, this system works well.

But suppose inflation enters the system and all prices rise 10 percent per year. After one year, the $100 machine will cost $110 to replace. After ten years it will cost $259 to replace. But IRS accounting rules, which ignore inflation, allow the company to accumulate only $100 tax free. The additional $159 the new machine costs comes out of after-tax profits, violating the basic principles of fair taxation and harming the economy by discouraging investment.[2]

ACRS was ERTA's[3] solution to this problem. Under the old tax law, it often took as long as eight to ten years to fully deduct the cost of new machinery. ACRS reduced the time period to five years, substantially cutting the after-tax cost of buying new equipment. ACRS did not provide precise compensation for inflation. The way to do that would have been to index the system, adjusting the original purchase prices of plant and equipment for actual inflation and increasing the depreciation allowances accordingly. Nevertheless, ACRS did substantially encourage investment in plant and equipment.

A way to quantify this investment effect is by the "hurdle rate of return"—the rate of return an investment must produce to justify the decision to make it. Hurdle rates vary for different businesses, depending on their particular circumstances and opportunities. As hurdle rates rise, fewer and fewer investments make business sense. In 1979, because of the combination of high tax rates and 10 percent inflation, an investor needed a 16.4 percent nominal rate of return in order to make a 4 percent hurdle. By 1981, with inflation down to 8 percent and the new tax law in effect, an 11.5 percent nominal return would make the same 4 percent hurdle. Of this five point drop in the hurdle rate of return, which made a tremendous number of previously unprofitable projects quite attractive to investors, three points were directly attributable to the tax law change and the remaining two point drop came from the reduction in inflation.[4]

(In some cases the changes may have gone too far. For certain types of investment ACRS actually produced a net tax subsidy, encouraging overinvestment in certain types of equipment. These net subsidies were subsequently eliminated in tax bills passed in 1982 and 1984.)

ACRS helped make the Reagan recovery one of the most investment oriented on record. It is particularly significant that the investment incentives of the bill worked even though other factors in the economic environment, such as high real interest rates, were not conducive to business investment. The ACRS provisions were particularly generous in their treatment of producer durable equipment. Such investment usually expands about 8 percent in the first year and 9 percent over the first two years of an economic expansion. In the ERTA recovery it expanded 21 percent the first year and averaged 18 percent over the first two years. On the other hand, investment in structures such as factories, which was not particularly favored by the bill, behaved normally for an expansion.[5]

In sum, the recovery benefited from both consumption and investment, but it was investment that turned it from an average recovery into a record-setting expansion. The investment boom continued well into the recovery. In 1985, the last year of the ERTA investment incentives, fully 8.4 percent of the nation's real GNP went into real, inflation-adjusted investment in producer durable equipment.[6] During the 1970s this investment figure never exceeded 8.1 percent.

Investment spending is crucial to the long-term health of the American economy. If the nation devoted a greater proportion of its resources to investment spending, our living standard would rise more quickly. But ERTA was clearly part of the solution, not part of the problem. Later in the decade, when most of the incentive provisions of ERTA had been repealed, investment spending slowed somewhat; taken as a whole, however, the investment data from the 1980s hardly indicate a nation headed for economic catastrophe.

Critics of the tax cut also claim it has made us a nation of borrowers instead of savers, and that our profligacy could lead to economic ruin. Once again, it is indisputable that increasing the national savings rate would be a good idea. But most of those who criticize the effect of Reaganomics on saving use a standard of measurement that tends to substantially understate national saving during periods of strong economic growth. Better measurements show that we do not face catastrophe now, nor did ERTA make the existing situation significantly worse.

Before we get into the measurement issue, however, let us consider one way in which ERTA clearly fostered saving. As mentioned in chapter 3, ERTA established the Individual Retirement Account program (IRA) to increase national saving and to make it easier for individuals to save for their own retirement. Under this program taxpayers could deduct from their taxable income up to $2,000 in annual contributions to a retirement account. The contributed funds accumulate interest, dividends, and capital gains tax free; the participant in an IRA plan pays taxes only when the funds are withdrawn, generally after retirement.

The advantages of an IRA to an individual are twofold. First, the taxpayer's tax rate while working and contributing to the IRA will probably be greater than when the funds are withdrawn. The taxpayer thereby receives an immediate saving equal to the difference between the two tax rates. For most taxpayers, however, the biggest advantage is that the funds contributed grow tax free over time. One dollar invested in an IRA program at 8 percent interest grows to $4.66 in twenty years. If the total is then taxed at a 28 percent rate, the taxpayer is left with $3.36. On the other hand, if the dollar is deposited in an ordinary savings account paying 8 percent interest, taxes must be paid both on the initial contribution and on each year's interest as it is earned. At the end of twenty years, the retiree is left with only $2.24, or 34 percent less.

This made IRAs very attractive. Data from the first three years of the program indicate that 12 million taxpayers contributed $28.3 billion in 1982, 13.6 million taxpayers contributed $32.1 billion in 1983, and by 1984, 15.4 million taxpayers contributed $35.8 billion. Most participants contributed in all three years, and much of this money was "new" savings, not just transfers from other accounts. (Because IRA contributions must be "locked up" for many years they can not be readily substituted for other forms of saving that the taxpayer can use at his or her discretion.) Data from the Survey of Consumer Finances indicate that individuals who contributed to an IRA were 50 percent more likely than non-contributors to have increased their overall saving in the year their contribution was made. Careful statistical analysis of the IRA data indicate that about 45 percent of the money contributed to IRAs came from a reduction in household consumption, 35 percent from the tax savings, while 20 percent came from other forms of existing saving.[7] The first category represents new saving to the economy, while the latter two represent a reallocation of saving, either from the government to the IRA or from other savings vehicles to the IRA. Overall, in its first three years, the IRA program increased net national saving in America by some $40 billion, a very respectable figure.

Even aside from the IRA program, however, the effects of ERTA on saving were far more beneficial than is popularly believed.[8] Critics usually cite a statistical series called the personal savings rate, the percentage of after-tax income that is not spent by consumers, to prove the national savings rate has tumbled. This statistic has fallen from roughly 7 percent in the late 1970s to a low of 3.2 percent in 1987. If it accurately reflected the true behavior of households toward savings, we would be in bad shape. Fortunately, it does not.

A look at history makes obvious the shortcomings of the personal savings rate as a measure of national capital formation. The sum of all statistically reported personal savings back to the beginning of recorded U.S. data plus a generous allowance for personal savings from that point back to the time of the Pilgrims would indicate that Americans have saved somewhat less than $4 trillion during our nation's history. Yet the total accumulated wealth of American households was over $14 trillion at the end of 1987. The personal savings rate missed nearly three-fourths of the real savings because it does not count the rising value of personal assets ranging from houses to stock portfolios. A family that took out a $25,000 mortgage in 1950 to buy a house and has since paid off the mortgage now holds an asset that may be worth $200,000 or more. But only the $25,000 spent paying off the mortgage counts as saving. The $175,000 rise in the value of the house is considered a capital gain, which is not counted as income by the National Income and Product Accounts and therefore not included in figures for personal savings.[9]

The personal savings calculation produces another even more

bizarre result. According to official calculations, the house fully depreciated during the four decades the family lived in it, and it is now carried on the nation's balance sheet as being worth zero. Even if the owner sells the house and puts the money in the bank, neither the owner nor the buyer are considered to be saving the $200,000. According to the statistics, they are simply swapping one asset (officially valued at zero) for another and not producing either income or savings. The same peculiar accounting applies to many other assets. The stocks in the family portfolio are valued at the purchase price, not their current market value. Even at the time of purchase there would have been no net saving in the economy if the seller spent the proceeds. Most Americans accumulate far more wealth than the personal savings rate suggests.

In its balance sheets for the U.S. economy, the Federal Reserve[10] compiles a much more accurate measure of household savings: the rise in the net worth of households, or the difference between the increase in their assets and the increase in their liabilities. If after the tax cuts households had gone on a borrowing and spending binge, piling up debt without offsetting increases in assets, household net worth would have declined, and household savings would be negative.

Quite the reverse happened. Between the end of 1981 and the end of 1987, household liabilities rose more than $1.3 trillion, but household assets rose more than $6 trillion. All together, households increased their net worth by $4.7 trillion, or 49 percent, while prices rose only 23 percent. These data indicate a *rise* in the real savings rate of households: In the five years before the rate reduction took effect, using the rise in real net worth as the measure, household savings averaged 7.8 percent of personal income, but in the five years following the passage of ERTA, household savings grew to 13.5 percent of personal income.[11]

The oft-quoted but misleading personal savings rate often falls in a strong economy and rises when times get hard. During a falling stock market and high inflation people see the real value of their existing assets decline. They compensate by saving a greater proportion of their current income. But during good times, with a rising stock market and low inflation preserving or even increasing their store of wealth, people feel less compelled to save out of current income. The rising value of household wealth in the 1980s probably blunted the urge to save.

Some people worry that a stock market crash could wipe out all the gains of the 1980s or that many families have leveraged debt against paper wealth that could disappear tomorrow. But all the figures we have been using come from the end of 1987, when the market had barely begun to recover from its record fall in October of that year. More important, since the end of 1980 the share of household assets in the stock market has only risen from 11.2 percent to 12.2 percent, hardly a significant increase considering that the stock market doubled. Safer holdings such as bank deposits, money market funds, and government bonds have risen from 20.4 percent of household assets to 23.2 percent.

Nor have households run up exceptionally large credit card balances. At the end of 1980 consumer credit amounted to $355 billion or 24 percent of such readily accessible household assets as currency, checking and savings accounts, and money market funds. By the end of 1987 consumer credit had grown to $697 billion, but ready cash had also grown to $2,788 billion. Consumer credit still equaled only 25 percent of ready cash.

On the average, American households in the late 1980s could pay off all their debts, including credit card debt, auto loans, and mortgages on their homes with their ready cash. They would not have had to touch their houses, cars, stock portfolios, pension funds, life insurance, small business holdings, or other assets. Obviously not every household was in this situation, nor has there ever been a time when all were. But taken as a whole, the households of the nation were no more burdened by debt at the end of the decade than they were in 1980. The situation is hardly a recipe for catastrophe or crisis.

The nation's businesses are in a similar position, though they are not quite as comfortable as households. According to the Federal Reserve, from 1 January 1981 to 31 December 1987, American businesses increased their liabilities by nearly $1.2 trillion. But they increased their assets by nearly $2.1 trillion and their net worth rose some $900 billion, or about one-third. At the end of 1980, non-financial business corporations had $196 billion in liquid assets covering nearly 24 percent of their $828 billion in credit market debt. The prime interest rate was over 20 percent. At the end of 1987, these businesses owed $1,697 billion in the credit markets but had $494 billion of liquid assets. Their liquid assets covered 29 percent of their debts while the prime rate was only 8.75 percent, less than half the 1980 rate.

As to the banks, it is obvious that the savings and loan industry is in serious trouble and that commercial banks are overextended in their third-world loans. But the overall picture is not one of profligacy. Private financial institutions saw their net worth rise from $247 billion at the end of 1980 to $490 billion at the end of 1987, an increase of 98 percent. The share of their assets held in very safe U.S. government debt rose from 9.2 percent at the end of 1980 to 15.6 percent at the end of 1987, while corporate and foreign bonds took a roughly constant share of their portfolio. On the whole, banks have increased savings and reserves and reduced the risk in their loans.

All in all, the private sector's net worth rose from $10.5 trillion at the end of 1980 to $15.8 trillion at the end of 1987, an increase of 51 percent. During the same time, the price level rose 34 percent. The real growth of the net worth of the private sector has been 13 percent, or 1.7 percent per year during this seven-year period as shown in figure 8.1. The fight against inflation clearly took its toll. Real net worth increased only 0.5 percent per year from the end of 1979 to the end of 1982. By contrast, growth from the end of 1982 to the end of 1987 averaged nearly $300 billion per year, a 2.2 percent annual rate.

The most comparable period is the 1960s, which combined

FIGURE 8.1

Real Value of Private Sector Net Worth
1979–1987

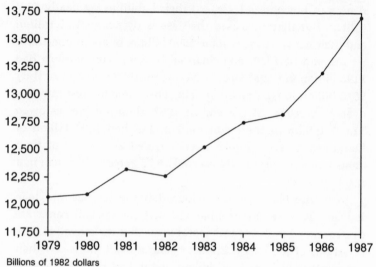

Billions of 1982 dollars

moderate inflation and fairly robust economic growth. During
that decade, the real net worth of the private sector increased
at a 2.6 percent annual rate.

For the private sector, the savings versus borrowing record
has been good but far from outstanding in the 1980s. That is
not true of the public sector, where the financial position deteri-
orated significantly. Net financial liabilities, after adjusting for
inflation, doubled from $825 billion to $1,652 billion between
the end of 1980 and the end of 1987. Fully half of the $1.6
trillion of real growth in the private sector's net worth was
offset by this deterioration in the financial net worth of the
public sector.

Considering the private and public sector together, the overall savings performance of the country has been quite mediocre
during the 1980s. Real national net worth grew only about 1
percent per year from the end of 1980 to the end of 1987.

America clearly must do better. At the same time, the nation's assets are growing faster than its liabilities, and we are far from sinking in a sea of red ink.

The 1980s combined rapid growth in investment with a mediocre performance in savings. This is a bit unusual. Savings and investment usually run in tandem, since the first is a primary source of the second. ERTA changed that normally close relationship by providing very generous incentives for new investment. Despite the popularity of the IRA program and the taming of inflation, incentives to save were less successful, and any extra private savings were consumed by greatly increased public sector borrowing.

ERTA did not flood the country in red ink. But by encouraging investment much more powerfully than it encouraged savings, it created an imbalance in the credit markets. As investors demanded more funds than savers supplied, real interest rates moved sharply higher. This rise did eventually evoke new sources of capital but only partially from American households. The balance was made up in part by American businesses themselves. Gross business savings by American firms jumped 58 percent between 1980 and 1985.[12] In addition, foreign capital flowed into America at an unprecedented rate as the United States became the world's premier investment opportunity.

In the years leading up to 1980, American direct investment abroad in new plant and equipment far exceeded foreign investment here. After the tax cuts the situation reversed dramatically, with foreigners investing in new plants in the United States at three times the rate Americans made similar investments overseas. Direct foreign investment in plant and equipment in the United States rose from $109 billion in 1981 to $220 billion in 1986. Private foreign investment in financial assets rose from $93 billion in 1981 to more than $400 billion in 1986. In short, the United States was internationally recognized as the smart place to invest in the early 1980s. This trend was so powerful that by 1988 critics who had complained about U.S. companies shipping jobs overseas by investing abroad were instead complaining that foreigners were "buying up America."

The lesson of ERTA is twofold: The investment provisions worked quite well. But any tax bill that encourages business investment should also include equivalent encouragement for private savings—one more example of the fundamental need to balance the supply and demand features of any tax cut.

Chapter 9

The World's Tax Cut

"The reason for the world-wide trend toward lower top rates is clear. Excessive rates of income tax destroy enterprise, encourage avoidance, and drive talent to more hospitable shores overseas."[1]

—NIGEL LAWSON, Chancellor of the Exchequer, HMG

In the United States the debate over Reagan's Great Experiment rages on. But abroad the verdict is clear. In a shining example of that sincerest form of flattery, nearly all the industrialized nations as well as most of the newly developing nations have either reduced their tax rates during the 1980s or have scheduled rate reductions for the early 1990s.

The worldwide reduction in taxes is part of a larger worldwide movement toward free markets, again led by the United States. But though the United States, under Reagan, started this trend, Reagan's departure from the scene will not reverse it. Cutting taxes and freeing markets have become essential weapons of worldwide economic competition. The United States would find it difficult if not impossible to return to the high tax rates of the past and still maintain its position in the world. Indeed, international competition coupled with the technological revolutions of the recent past will likely prompt further worldwide progress to even greater economic freedom and even lower tax rates.

The 1980s were an important turning point, not an end but a beginning. And the beginning began not just in the United States, but in the United Kingdom as well. History will likely credit the worldwide resurgence of free markets and lower taxes to Margaret Thatcher as well as Ronald Reagan.

At the start of the decade one could not imagine two nations less likely to lead an economic revival. Through the 1960s and 1970s they had competed for last place in the world growth leagues. While Americans spoke of a national malaise, Europe spoke of the "British disease" afflicting a country that seemed more interested in prolonging economic decline than in reviving past glories.

In the late 1970s Britain levied a top marginal rate of 83 percent on earned income and an utterly confiscatory top rate of 98 percent on capital income. Margaret Thatcher's first budget called for a reduction in the regular top rate from 83 to 60 percent, with smaller percentage reductions in lower rates. The opposition benches cried "rich man's budget" as the chancellor read the proposal, but the Iron Maiden triumphed. In the first year of the tax rate reductions the rich did pay a smaller share of Britain's taxes, but the reduction was quite small compared to the rate cut. Though the top rate was cut by more than 25 percent, the share of taxes paid by the top 2 percent of the British taxpayers fell only from 15.4 percent to 14.7 percent. By the second year of the lower rates, the share of taxes paid by the top 2 percent of taxpayers had regained its pre–tax cut level. And by the fourth year after the tax cut, the top 2 percent were paying a greater share than before the cut: 16.4 percent. In real terms, the taxes paid by the top 5 percent rose 35 percent in the decade, compared to 5 percent for other taxpayers. Rising revenues and the beginning of a revitalization in the British economy soon emboldened the government to eliminate the 15 percent Investment Income Surcharge on all non-salary income. By the second year of this latter cut, the share of taxes paid by the top 2 percent was at an all-time high, and headed higher.[2]

As we have learned, such profound behavioral changes generally indicate that tax rates had been a significant burden on the economy. True to form, after the rate cuts, Britain's long-comatose economy began an astounding recovery. The United

Kingdom has had the fastest rate of growth of the major countries in Europe in every year but one of the last seven. Since
1981 British industrial production has grown more than 20
percent, easily the fastest growth in Europe. The British pound,
long shunned, is regaining its status as a world reserve currency,
and most of Europe envies the capitalist fever that Thatcher
brought to Britain.

In the government's 1988 budget, Thatcher's Chancellor of
the Exchequer Nigel Lawson proposed cutting the top rate of
income tax to 40 percent and the basic rate of tax to 25 percent.
Lawson reasoned that a 40 percent rate in the United Kingdom,
which does not have state and local income taxes, would be
roughly equivalent to the United States's 33 percent top rate
plus the typical state rates of 5 to 10 percent. These dramatic
tax rate cuts, passed in 1988 and in effect since the beginning
of 1989, were derided as excessive by the opposition. At this
writing, Lawson does face a budgetary problem: the British
budget, long in deficit, is headed for a record surplus of some
13 billion British pounds,[3] or nearly 3 percent of British GNP.
He has begun retiring the British national debt, which, coupled
with a booming economy and the tax cuts, has brought a flood
of foreign investment capital to Britain, driving up the pound.
Prime Minister Thatcher has won two landslide reelections and
is now the longest serving prime minister in modern times. Her
critics still heckle, but strictly from the sidelines; the public is
much too busy enjoying the record-breaking prosperity to pay
any attention.

The United Kingdom represents an obvious success story for
tax rate reduction. But some critics of tax cuts point to Sweden[4]
as a model of a nation where prosperity and high tax rates have
long gone hand in hand. Sweden is not technically a socialist
country. Government ownership of industry is rare. Rather
Sweden has high-tax capitalism, and taxes are high enough to
make the head spin. The top marginal income tax rate takes
effect at the equivalent of $35,000 income. Tax cuts during the
1980s reduced that top rate from 87 percent to 75 percent, but

it is still high by almost any standard. Counting social insurance taxes and value-added taxes, a Swedish worker earning average wages faces a 73 percent combined marginal tax rate. Yet Stockholm is filled with Mercedes and Volvos; boat ownership in Sweden is among the highest in the world, and many families own summer homes. Why haven't such staggering tax rates impoverished Sweden?

First, much of the money paid in taxes comes right back in the form of subsidies. The expansive Swedish state consumes about 55 percent of GNP in taxes, overwhelmingly paid by the middle class, and then gives about 45 percent of GNP back in the form of subsidies, largely paid to the middle class. To receive a subsidy you don't have to do anything unusual: just consume food (which is heavily subsidized), or have children (who entitle you to generous child allowances), or live long enough to collect your pension. The staggering level of taxes really doesn't reflect the government's burden on the typical Swede. After paying subsidies, the Swedish government consumes about the same share of GNP as the American government.

Still, rerouting all that money through the government via the tax system does profoundly change economic incentives. For example, the Swedish family's way to the good life is not to save. The interest paid on consumer loans is tax deductible. Given the tax rates, sensible Swedes not only do not save, they pile up debt. Borrowing is the Swedish way to enjoy a great lifestyle while sheltering income from the tax collector. So great are these incentives and so smart are the Swedes, that the government's net tax take from capital income, interest, and dividends is actually negative. Only lower-income, low–tax rate individuals save. Though these spend-and-borrow tactics do help individuals in the short term, the long-term consequences are severe. The government loses tax revenue and the economy loses capital. Sweden's personal savings rate is actually negative.

Another secret to making it in Sweden is to take compensation not in salary but through the company expense account, which can buy your car, your travel, and your meals for you directly and tax free. One economist explained that Sweden has two types of money, pre-tax and post-tax. In a corollary of Gresham's law, pre-tax money drives out post-tax money.

Beating the tax system is a favorite topic at Swedish dinner parties. The dinner itself is often part of the deal. The restaurant is filled, but not with families. No children are present at all, there are three men for every woman, and everyone in the restaurant is in a business suit. As one Swedish economist told me, when you negotiate with your employer, wages don't come up. You talk about lifestyle. Once that is settled, you get together to figure out the best way of paying for that lifestyle. The objective is to have the government pick up as much of the cost as possible.

The result of all this is tremendous wage compression. Virtually no one in Sweden earns more than $50,000. Jobs that pay six figures in the United States pay one-third to one-half as much in Sweden. But the result isn't really equality. Assembly-line workers don't get a business lunch, a company car, or foreign travel. Their compensation comes in very taxable cash. Company executives pay taxes too, but on a smaller portion of their total compensation.

Even better than living off one's employer is to set up a company. The company can be a consultancy, own rental housing, or engage in any activity that can be done after regular business hours. The company need not make money: its purpose is to preserve the income of one's regular job. Tax-deductible company purchases—cars, housing, etc.—can keep that lifestyle in shape, because most of the company's losses are deductible against other income. A hot conversation topic on my last visit to Sweden was the rumor that some clever accountant had found a way to deduct such business losses twice. Two deductions, each worth 80 percent, means that the more you lose, the more you make.

There are other escape routes. Tennis stars, rockers, and other high rollers become expatriates during their high earning years. Others opt for less dramatic departures. One night in Stockholm I was surprised to learn that my waiter was an electrical engineer on leave from Erikson, the huge Swedish telecommunications firm. He was taking his three-month leave to be a waiter in order to "make some money." He made more money after taxes as a waiter than he did as an electrical engineer. The tax man has trouble getting at tips.

Talk of taxes in Sweden makes a guest feel a bit like Alice visiting Wonderland. The Red Queen would understand: the faster you run, the more you fall behind. The secret is not to run so fast. Swedes do not get ahead by working overtime and sharing 80 percent of the proceeds with the state. Instead the Swedish middle class makes it by living off state subsidies, borrowing, taking as much compensation as they can tax free, and working in the untaxed informal economy.

Even in Sweden, however, there is no such thing as a free lunch. Many of Sweden's leading economists and business leaders feel that Sweden peaked in 1970, when it held undisputed title to the world's highest standard of living. With a highly educated work force and world-class expertise in engineering, metallurgy, and telecommunications, Sweden had built for a quarter century on all industrial infrastructure left untouched by World War II. Postwar taxes were high by international standards but far lower than today; Swedish taxes in the 1950s and 1960s were roughly comparable to American taxes after Reagan. In the seventies things turned sour. Taxes rose steadily throughout the decade, hitting record levels by the early 1980s. Sweden is now fourth among Scandinavian countries in per capita income. Its economic growth since 1970 has been well below its historic trend and below average for the OECD. To remain internationally competitive Sweden has reduced the value of the krona by half compared to the German mark. But this drastic devaluation is itself an onerous tax on Swedish citizens, who must pay far more for imported products or raw materials. In recent years the krona has declined faster than any currency save those of Greece, Spain, and Portugal. Even the Italian lira has done better.

This relative decline does not mean poverty. Most Swedes remain oblivious to their nation's eroding economy. As the head of Sweden's largest private economic think tank told me, "It took the English one hundred years to wake up to their decline. Where will Sweden find itself at the start of the twenty-first century?"

It is a good question. The industries that made Sweden strong, particularly steel, are no longer growth industries. Future growth depends on new investment in new industries, particularly the high-risk high-technology start-up companies of today. Whereas the U.S. venture capital market will take a risk on a new venture with prospects for a 25 percent pre-tax rate of return, the Swedish tax system forces this threshold up to the 50 to 60 percent range. Swedish capitalists must often turn their backs on start-up companies with payback periods of as little as three years.

The Swedish tax system, allowing people to consume today, is systematically consuming Sweden's future. Next year, Swedish companies will invest more in other countries than they will at home. High taxes are no longer merely a long-run problem. The day of reckoning comes ever closer. The Swedes themselves seem to realize this. The Swedish opposition parties have called for sharp reductions in tax rates. Now the social democratic government seems willing to go further. The government has proposed lowering the top rate to 60 percent, with further reductions to 50 percent in the 1990s. In the wake of the worldwide tax revolt, Sweden will still have one of the highest personal income tax rates in the world but should see economic incentives substantially improved. Even this bastion of the welfare state demonstrates the basic tenet of supply-side economics: taxes matter, especially since democratic governments will almost always compensate for high taxes with loopholes and benefits that distort economic incentives even more perversely than high taxes alone.

Sweden's social planners have long been committed to equality of income, the elimination of private wealth, and the provision of economic security. The tax system established to achieve these goals has in a sense succeeded: high taxes advanced equality by prompting the very wealthy to leave the country and electrical engineers to become waiters. High taxes plus tax deductions for borrowing certainly discouraged private wealth. The personal savings rate is negative. Basic economic security, plus high taxes on profit, guarantees that few Swedes will undertake high-risk ventures, so the Swedish people and Swedish industry can grow old together. Sweden is not the exception that proves the rule. It is not an exception at all. Sweden proves that the tax system can either encourage work, saving, and risk taking or discourage them. Sweden does not prove that incentives do not matter. Sweden proves that they work both ways.

The social democratic formula is breaking down throughout Scandinavia. Norway slashed its top tax rate from 75 percent to 54 percent over the course of the 1980s. Finland cut its top rate from 71 percent to 51 percent during the 1980s and has scheduled a further reduction in the top rate to 44 percent in the 1990s. The social democrats have not abandoned their goals of greater equality and a higher standard of living for working people, but they seem to recognize that lower tax rates help accomplish these goals. Individuals striving for personal success are the prime engine of social mobility. High taxes discourage that mobility by discouraging new money. Taxes do not break down class distinctions but perpetuate them.

Social democratic governments in Australia and New Zealand have also lowered tax rates. Australia reduced its top rate from 62 percent to 49 percent. New Zealand cut its top rate from 60 percent to 48 percent and plans a further reduction to 33 percent, the top U.S. rate. Israel has cut its top rate from 66 percent to 48 percent, Canada (under a Tory government) from 58 percent to 45 percent, Austria from 62 percent to 50 percent, and

Belgium has scheduled a cut to 55 percent, down from a high of 76 percent in 1979.

After Sweden, Japan is probably the country most often cited in evidence by those who believe tax rates have but little effect on economic performance. Japan, the greatest economic success story of the postwar era, has long maintained very high apparent tax rates, though after a few years of poor economic performance it recently cut its top rate from 75 to 50 percent.

The secret of Japanese tax rates is that few Japanese pay them. Huge tax deductions reduce real Japanese tax rates to levels comparable to or lower than current U.S. rates. Moreover, most Japanese tax deductions, unlike those in Sweden and other high-tax countries, favor long-term economic growth. By far the greatest of these deductions has been for savings. Until 1989 Japanese could deposit money in savings accounts of up to $25,000 in value without paying any tax on the interest. Each member of a family was allowed to have such an account, greatly increasing the maximum amount of tax-free savings available to a household. In addition, few checks were placed on taxpayers who held multiple accounts. By some estimates, as much as 80 percent of total Japanese household savings were completely exempt from tax. The combination of very high tax rates and very large deductions for savings virtually forced the Japanese to maintain one of the world's highest personal savings rates. This was useful during the rapid phase of Japanese economic growth, channeling funds away from consumption into investment in new plants and equipment.

Even in Japan, however, the government's attempt to direct the course of economic life through tax rates has had its downside. As in Sweden, high Japanese tax rates encourage business consumption in place of personal or family consumption. As in Sweden, high tax rates encourage Japanese workers to negotiate lifestyle rather than paycheck, with families the losers. Any visitor to the Ginza in the evening finds its restaurants crowded with groups of males in business suits. No families in sight. A quick look at the price list tells why. The men are having a night on the firm, a tax-free benefit for the worker and tax deductible for the firm, but a luxury few workers could afford to provide for their own families. Such camaraderie has come to be considered an important part of the Japanese corporate ethic, but Japanese families are poorly housed and have what we would consider a low standard of living.

Like the Swedes also, the Japanese seem to be changing their minds. The government has cut tax rates in part because it believes the tax biases that served Japan's postwar needs are no longer as helpful. Japanese leaders now believe that in the 1990s and beyond established industries led by large corporate hierarchies will decline in importance compared to entrepreneurial knowledge-based start-ups. MITI, the Japanese ministry of trade and industry, has been encouraging Japanese businessmen to study the U.S. entrepreneurial style, and the government is studying U.S. entrepreneurial tax rates.

The emerging industrial nations of East Asia have been ahead of Japan in this regard. Hong Kong has always had extremely low income taxes. Singapore recently slashed its top rate from 55 percent to 33 percent. South Korea reduced its top rate from a 1979 high of 89 percent to 70 percent in 1989 and has scheduled a further reduction to 48 percent during the 1990s. Indonesia, Malaysia, and Thailand, who seek to be the Koreas and the Hong Kongs of the early twenty-first century, all slashed their top tax rates during the 1980s.

The growth of a true global market encourages the worldwide tax revolt.[5] As the resources that drive economic growth become more mobile, they gravitate toward places where they can earn the highest after-tax rates of return. The key resource behind economic growth isn't a fixed resource like gold or oil, or even capital equipment, but something far more mobile: the human mind. Nations that wish to compete for that resource must keep the price of government low and the quality of government high.

In the past, governments that controlled centers of financial, cultural, or industrial activities were able to exact high "rents," including high taxes, from those who wanted to live there. As the advantages of geography diminish with the advent of cheap communications and transportation, governments will lose some of this leverage and will be forced to cut taxes. On a recent Sunday night flight from Dublin to London, my wife and I were surrounded by young nurses. They were not traveling as part of a group, but as individuals, each returning to a job in the United Kingdom after visiting family back in Ireland. Irish income taxes, which hit 60 percent at the equivalent of an $18,000 income, have driven the economy downhill and the educated work force across the Irish Sea. The Penal Laws could never make Irishmen into Englishmen. It took Maggie Thatcher's tax cut to do that.

In the world of the future, the advantage will be to those nations that allow their populations to live and work as cheaply as possible. No country is exempt. Robert Walter, an economist at the University of Kiel in West Germany, argues, "We will see a brain drain to the U.S. if nothing happens on taxes here."[6] The smart and prosperous regions of the world will be those which attract the talented and the entrepreneurial with low taxes and few fetters. The economic move to free markets and low taxes has just begun.

Chapter 10

One Step Sideways

"The prospects are pretty high that, in the end, we'll get
something called tax reform, but it won't be real tax reform."

—RICHARD RAHN, Chief Economist, U.S. Chamber of
Commerce[1]

By 1984 the country was learning the lessons of the Great
Experiment. The economy was recovering, inflation had
dropped precipitously and stabilized, unemployment was declining, and, thanks to ERTA, Americans were enjoying bigger
paychecks, in real terms, for the first time in more than half a
decade. In addition, as the first detailed data on the tax cut came
in, the most important supply-side contention was proving
true: The rich were paying more in taxes at lower rates.

In four years, voodoo economics had traveled a good part of
the distance from tabu to totem. In his first run for the Senate
in 1978, Bill Bradley had vigorously and repeatedly denounced
the proposed Kemp-Roth tax cut authored in part by his opponent Jeff Bell. Just five years later in 1983, Senator Bill Bradley
and Representative Richard Gephardt, both Democrats, introduced a tax reform bill that would have cut the top rate of
income tax to 27 percent. Ronald Reagan called, in his 1984
state of the union address, for a further reduction in tax rates
and a doubling of the personal exemption.

ERTA's success also changed the economic agenda. The economic recovery made demand-side stimuli, such as demand-
oriented tax cuts and spending increases less important. And as

the budgetary cost of the transition to low inflation became apparent, and the federal budget deficit made headlines, tax revenues grew more precious.

The nation had also learned an additional, rather subtle, lesson: Just as high tax rates discourage productive activities, overly generous tax incentives can produce too much of the subsidized activity. For example, ERTA's dramatic increase in the depreciation allowances for business equipment reduced the after-tax cost of some such purchases to less than their pre-tax cost. The tax system actually became a subsidy, lowering the net cost of some purchases to below what they would have been if we didn't have any taxes at all, giving a whole new meaning to the adage "you have to spend it to make it."

Because ACRS favored certain industries over others, politicians and economists put a new demand on the tax agenda: the "level playing field," a tax code that would not play favorites.[2] In a way, the concern for a "level playing field" vindicated the central supply-side argument: taxes matter. Members of Congress who never before thought a moment about taxes and incentives were turned into latter-day supply-siders by lobbyists' charts showing that the industries in their home districts were unfairly taxed. Human nature being what it is, it soon turned out that everyone was unfairly taxed and had the charts to prove it.

The success of the tax cut strategy, the new economic and budget environment, and the fair play pressures produced a groundswell of support for a different kind of tax rate reduction: rate reduction coupled with reform, which while it broadened the tax base by eliminating the "unfair" provisions, would also pay for the reduction. In principle, everyone liked the idea. President Reagan and the supply-siders would get even lower tax rates. Critics of the 1981 bill would get to "close loopholes" and make everyone pay their "fair share" of taxes. And everyone could crusade to end everyone else's tax breaks, so that people back home could compete on a level playing field.

The ground rules were laid down by President Reagan in his

mandate to the staff of the Treasury Department: tax reform should promote fairness, simplicity, and growth. (A report to the president by the department in November 1984 was titled just that: *Tax Reform for Fairness, Simplicity, and Economic Growth.*) President Reagan would never concede that the budget deficit should be closed by raising taxes, but he did believe that reform should not make the deficit any larger and required that any tax legislation be revenue neutral. Revenue neutrality was also supposed to limit the tax goodies for favored constituents that had become part of just about every tax bill. With revenue neutrality, one man's goodie would be another man's tax increase.

This great movement for tax reform started as a civics class dream. It had bipartisan support, clear-cut rules of the game, including the bottom-line discipline of revenue neutrality, and was to be written by experts—the permanent Treasury staff—not politicians. By the end of the two-year drafting process, a combination of politics as usual, a preoccupation with that moving target called revenue neutrality, and a greater concern for the appearance than the reality of fairness produced a bill that ignored some of the most important lessons of Reagan's first great experiment.

The Treasury document that opened the process devoted many pages to lofty principles of efficient tax design and scientific reform. By the time the measure cleared the House of Representatives, most of the text was devoted to the lofty principle of constituent interest: The bill provided, for example, that "The treatment of annuity contracts as investment property under section 147(b)(2) of such Code shall not apply to any obligation issued by the South Dakota Building Authority . . ."[3] and that a parking facility met section 142(a) requirements if "Such facility is for a university medical school and the last parcel of land necessary for such facility was purchased on February 4, 1985."[4] Sorry, neither 3 February nor 5 February qualify, though somewhere in the voluminous text there are undoubtedly some juicy benefits for the owners of playing fields leveled on 15 April.

Neither the principle of revenue neutrality nor the spirit of fairness was enough to entirely eliminate the customary goodie-grabbing and constituent-coddling. In fairness to those who shepherded the process, I have to say the Congress did better than usual. But the special favors that were doled out were costly, because the principle of revenue neutrality required full funding for every favor by some corresponding tax increase.

Revenue neutrality in fact is economic nonsense when applied in such detail as it was in 1986. The principle hardened into a rule that any proposal that apparently cost revenue must be coupled with a specific revenue increase. The short-term revenue numbers quickly dominated the process. As we have seen, it is not easy to estimate precisely the revenue effects of any tax change. In this case, the net effect of the procrustean matching of revenue losers and gainers was an enormous error (on the order of $15 billion per year) in the overall estimates of the tax revenue the bill would produce. At first, in 1986, the government collected far more revenue than expected. The data for 1987 suggest, however, that revenue was overestimated, and early evidence for 1988 suggests that people moved some income from 1987 into 1988 to take advantage of the lower 1988 rates. (The data consistently point to underestimation of the responsiveness of taxpayers to tax rates.) Moreover, though the joint committee predicted the tax reform would raise the share of taxes paid by upper-income taxpayers, the early evidence tends to the contrary.

The explanation is simple. Given the enormous complexity of precisely balancing all the revenue-losing and revenue-gaining provisions, the Congress took the easy way out. It ignored the overwhelming evidence for the behavioral effects of tax changes and, for the most part, made its calculations on the basis of direct-effect estimates alone. Frankly, it is hard to see how any committee of 535 governed by the revenue neutrality rule could have agreed on any more sophisticated system.

Consider the process of trading off higher rates for special tax favors to pick up key votes. The direct revenue effect of such special tax exemptions is based on the current level of activity in the favored area. But when a particular economic activity gets a new tax favor, it tends to expand at the cost of other activities. Hence the actual revenue loss will be *bigger* than anticipated by the direct-effect estimates, which ignore such changes.

To pay for the various special exemptions the top rate of the income tax had to be increased from the planned 26 percent to 28 percent, with a special 33 percent[5] bracket for many upper-middle-class taxpayers. These rates are low enough to be on the revenue-increasing side of the revenue-maximizing rate but, as we have learned, an increase in the rate from 26 percent to 28 percent will not produce two twenty-sixths more revenue. Even at relatively low rates, the tax base shrinks as the tax rate is increased. The official direct-effect revenue estimates did not take this into account and predicted higher revenues than the government actually received.

Such errors also derailed the goal of shifting a greater share of the tax burden onto the rich. Both the special exemptions and the increase in the top rate mostly affected upper-income taxpayers. Since in both cases the government overestimated revenues, tax return data for the next few years will probably show the rich paying a smaller share than the reformers intended, and perhaps a smaller share than under the ERTA regime.

Changes in the capital gains tax rate produced the same errors on a larger scale. Despite overwhelming evidence that the 1978 and 1981 reductions in capital gains taxes produced extra revenue the final 1986 bill eliminated the special treatment of capital gains income for the first time in more than a half century. The top capital gains tax rate was increased from 20 percent to the same 33 percent top rate applied to ordinary income. The effective increase was even larger than that because the new law made it much more difficult to write off investment losses against ordinary income. A risk-taking investor whose plans went bad might no longer have even the cold comfort of being able to reduce the taxes on his ordinary salary though he might just have gone through one of the worst years of his life financially.

The prime motive for this increase in capital gains rates had been to increase the share of income tax paid by upper-income taxpayers. Yet the Congressional Budget Office's own research indicated that a 33 percent capital gains rate would take in essentially the same amount of revenue that a 25 percent rate would collect, because of behavioral effects.[6] Congressional direct-effect estimates ignored this evidence and substantially overestimated capital gain tax revenues under the new law. The mistake was most pronounced in the estimates of the new tax burden on the rich.

This undue focus on the estimated direct revenue effects of the tax changes systematically biased the bill against sensible supply-side incentives. Had the reformers included behavioral changes in their estimates, they could have produced a bill with lower overall tax rates. Still, not every provision of the 1986 tax bill was adverse to the supply-side. The very large reduction in the top marginal tax rate was certainly a supply-side move. One might easily argue, as many supply-siders do, that any defects in the bill are insignificant compared to the dramatic accomplishment of cutting the top marginal rate from 50 percent to 28 percent. That dramatic reduction probably increased incentives to work, save, and invest significantly and is likely to produce both unanticipated revenue and additional economic growth for many years to come. On the other hand, the very substantial increase in capital gains taxes almost certainly did significant injury to the economy.

As the 1988 data in table 10.1 shows, the 1986 law may produce a loss of much more revenue than anticipated, most of it to upper-income taxpayers. Lower-income taxpayers also ended up paying slightly less, while middle-income taxpayers paid more. Seeking the illusory goal of strict revenue neutrality throughout such a complex reform was the real culprit in these setbacks.

The second great lesson of the 1986 tax reform is that a little

TABLE 10.1

Potential Revenue Impact of Behavioral Responses

Income Class	Revenue Effect (Billions of Dollars) Due to Response of			
	Wages and Salaries	Business Income	Capital Gains	All Responses
under $10,000	−0.1	−0.0	−0.1	−0.2
10,000–20,000	−1.4	−0.0	−0.2	−1.6
20,000–30,000	+0.1	+0.0	−0.5	−0.4
30,000–40,000	+2.0	+0.1	−0.6	+1.5
40,000–50,000	+0.8	+0.1	−0.8	+0.1
50,000–75,000	+2.7	+0.2	−2.7	+0.2
75,000–100,000	+2.6	+0.2	−2.3	+0.5
100,000–200,000	+3.0	+0.5	−5.3	−1.8
over 200,000	+4.4	+0.5	−18.4	−13.5
Total	+13.8	+1.6	−30.8	−15.5

NOTE: A detailed description of the methodology behind this analysis appears in Lawrence Lindsey "Did ERTA Raise the Share of Taxes Paid by Upper-Income Taxpayers? Will TRA 86 Be a Repeat?" in *Tax Policy and the Economy*, ed. Lawrence H. Summers (Cambridge: MIT Press, 1988).

fairness can be a dangerous thing. In politics, the assignment "level the playing field" turns out to be not a rule of simplicity but a source of endless contention. It is only natural that members of Congress regard a level playing field to be one tilted in favor of their constituents. In the end Congress leveled the investment capital playing field not by smoothing out the rough spots in the 1981 law but by raising the cost of capital for everyone.

The 1986 reform eliminated the Investment Tax Credit, in part to pay for personal tax reductions. The Congress had anyway regarded the tax credit as a villain for promoting investment in short-lived equipment above longer-lived assets, particularly structures. A detailed study by Roger Gordon of the University of Michigan, James Hines of Princeton, and Lawrence Summers of Harvard questions this thesis and argues that the tax code had offered substantial support for investments in structures.[7] Structures are far easier to resell than most movable equipment and they can be depreciated repeatedly. It is easier to finance structure by debt, and the interest is tax deductible.

Gordon, Hines, and Summers concluded that the supposed unevenness of the investment playing field was exaggerated. Thus the 1986 increase in the corporate tax burden brought no added efficiencies to the investment market, just higher taxes, and thus worsened the single most important bias in the American tax treatment of capital. American tax law (primarily through mortgage interest deduction) greatly favors residential housing over business plant and investment, a favoritism that provides little help to homeowners of modest means, because it raises the price of houses and because in their relatively low tax brackets the mortgage interest deduction does not save them much. But the mortgage interest deduction does shift capital away from job-producing industrial plants and toward upscale housing, and the 1986 increase in corporate taxes will make it that much harder for business to compete for capital.

The level playing field argument originated not with the Congress but the economists, and the 1980s made an interesting and useful contribution to the understanding of capital taxation. But the level playing field theme, still in its academic infancy, was seized upon by the political process; and turned into a bulldozer when economists meant it to be a hand hoe. This is another reminder that too–finely tuned theories can come to grief in a political debate. Whether the goal is a full-scale tax revolt or a series of small but essential adjustments in the code, it may be best to keep the agenda simple, or as Reagan critics liked to say of his policies, "simplistic."

The question remains open whether the 1986 tax bill will be good or bad for the economy. We will learn the answer as more tax data becomes available. As to politics of reform, adherents to the Reagan revolution could claim a partial victory: The claim that high tax rates matter to the economy is now widely accepted in Washington, at least in practice. Furthermore, the top tax rate is less than half of what it was when Ronald Reagan took office. But the subtle point that some parts of the tax base are more sensitive than others was lost, with higher capital gains taxes as one unfortunate result.

Because the Congress and even some in the administration

ignored the dynamic effects of tax cuts on tax revenues, the government will end up with less revenue, a bigger deficit, and a distribution of the tax payments borne less by the rich, than it otherwise would have been. Unfortunately, the lesson may still not have been learned. If those who resist the supply-side message run to form, they will call for yet higher tax rates, to try to soak the rich as much as they originally had intended. If they get their way, the behavioral effects will be even more adverse, the rich will pay even less, and the deficit will grow.

One thing is certain: The need for further reform to address the problems the 1986 bill created. We will consider the direction those reforms should take after a look at first principles: the appropriate goals of any tax system.

PART II

Applying the
Lessons

Chapter 11

Of Revenue and Righteousness

> "The art of taxation consists in so plucking the goose as to
> obtain the largest possible amount of feathers with the
> smallest possible amount of hissing."
> —JEAN BAPTISTE COLBERT (1619–83)

Despite the progress of the 1980s the U.S. tax code still needs
reform. The Reagan tax cuts, including the Tax Reform Act of
1986, revitalized the economy but left room for improvements
in our competitive posture. The tax cuts raised the tax contributions of the rich while lowering their rates, yet retained a number of provisions that favor upper-income taxpayers over
lower. The tax cuts increased business investment, a benefit
partly lost in 1986, but did less to encourage savings. The tax
cuts made the nation wealthier but missed opportunities to
encourage the socially responsible use of wealth.

Most important, the tax cuts, having helped rescue the U.S.
(and world) economy from what seemed like protracted decline,
provide an opportunity to ameliorate what may be the nation's
most pressing economic and social problem: the growing economic burdens on middle- and working-class families with
children. Their situation steadily worsened during the seventies
but could not be addressed before the Revolution of '81. From
1973 to 1981 the real after-tax income of a typical American
household declined by 9 percent. And though real wages of

American workers also declined by 8 percent over the same period, the tax share of those wages rose dramatically. Many costs of establishing membership in the middle class, such as buying a house or sending the children to college, rose painfully throughout the seventies and eighties. After ERTA began to take hold in 1982, real after-tax household income rebounded, in large measure because of the success of the Reagan policies. But the fact remains that during the 1970s and early 1980s the American dream became a mirage for too many Americans.

The situation has improved. The country has exchanged economic peril for economic prosperity. Precisely because of the recent improvements, we are now in a position to do a better job of restoring the hopes of American families and extending the promise of prosperity to far more Americans. We can do much of this through tax reform. The Reagan tax cuts and the Reagan recovery got us out from behind the economic eight ball. Every era has its crises, but the late 1970s sometimes seemed like nothing but crises. It was hard to think about fine-tuning success with the news always of failure. It was hard to think about lowering the tax burden on lower- and middle-income families when the nation seemed desperately strapped for cash and the role of tax rates in causing stagflation was the subject of fierce and urgent debate.

Those days of constant crisis are gone, largely because the large tax rate cuts for upper-income and upper-middle-income taxpayers restored the incentives that drive the American economy. As shown in chapter 4, the rate cuts did not significantly reduce short-term revenues. The rich pay more, and the upper-middle class only slightly less than under the old rates. For these fortunate taxpayers, the rate cuts reduced the excess burden—the additional cost, over and above the tax payments themselves, of a high tax rate. The excess burden as explained in chapter 2 is the cost to the individual and the economy of taxpayers being forced into second or third best economic choices by excessive tax rates. By dramatically reducing the excess burden on upper-middle-class and rich taxpayers, the tax cuts increased incentives for them to work, save, and invest, benefiting the economy in both the short and long term. The reforms of the 1980s, by reducing inefficient burdens on the well-to-do, have given us the breathing space to focus on the problems of the less well-off.

In addition to providing an economic base for family tax relief, the Reagan tax cuts offer a base of economic knowledge for directing further reform. We have gained a more precise working knowledge of the relationship between tax rates and tax revenues. We have learned that tax rates above 40 or 50 percent produce no additional revenue, and we also have learned a lot about the trade-offs between rates, revenues, and excess burden at lower brackets. We can predict more confidently the revenue effects of tax increases and reductions at almost any level and how such changes might interact with various tax shelters, subsidies, penalties, and other biases of the code. The several adjustments during the 1980s to taxes on business investment have given us a better understanding of similar issues for those taxes.

This accumulated knowledge can help us design a tax code that will help the United States finance its fiscal responsibilities without sacrificing its families, and keep our social fabric as strong as our economy. The mission for tax reformers of the nineties is to apply the lessons and benefits of supply-side economics to the middle and working class. The job ahead of us is not so much to reduce the total tax bill for average Americans, though we can and should reduce it for families with children; the important job is to eliminate the extra burdens of taxation that do little to raise revenue but discourage thrift and industry and throw up barriers to the pursuit of middle-class prosperity.

The income tax reached its political and economic limits in the 1970s as the nation began to feel the effects of levying rich people's tax rates on citizens of moderate means. The 1981 and 1986 reforms substantially rolled back those rates. Yet middle- and working-class taxpayers still bear burdens far greater than they have through most of the nation's history. If we do nothing in the way of positive reform, we may soon find ourselves again passing the limits of prudence and leaving the path of prosperity. With positive reform we can make the nation stronger and improve the lives of most Americans.

As we have broken down barriers to work, savings, and investment for the well-to-do, to the benefit of all, we must eliminate tax biases that raise the costs of housing and home ownership for average Americans, or discourage savings for college education, a home, or retirement. We must eliminate distortions that curtail investment in plant and equipment, or research, education, and training, forcing workers to work harder rather than smarter. We must stop pushing workers to take their pay in inefficient and often overpriced benefits rather than cash they can control. We must end provisions that punish families in which both parents must work outside the home to make ends meet, or that punish all families that do a responsible job of nurturing our most important resource, the next generation.

If we liberate working- and middle-class Americans from these and other extra and unnecessary burdens of taxation, the United States will be a happier, more industrious, and even better trained and educated nation in the next century, ready to take on all comers in the global competition. Before embarking on these reforms, however, we need a clear understanding of the very purpose of income taxation, and of what we can and cannot accomplish through the tax code.

If economic growth and international competitiveness, or the well-being of America's families were the only objectives of government tax policy, we would probably dispense with the income tax entirely. The income tax invariably discourages maximum economic effort. And it can never be made painless, even for the middle and working class, which no modern state could afford to exempt from taxation.

We levy taxes because the government must have revenue.

Only when we keep that first priority clearly in mind can we design a tax code that also encourages industry and the happiness of the people. It turns out that keeping our eye on the revenue ball positively helps us design an income tax that encourages growth and does not overburden families.

The only reason the income tax is the dominant tax today is that it is a fabulously effective means of collecting revenue for the government. Though the personal income tax contributes but 45 percent of total federal tax revenues, the total for all income taxes, including social insurance taxes and the corporate income tax, is nearly 90 percent. The federal government now takes nearly 20 percent of GNP in total revenue, a figure undreamt of before the days of the income tax when most federal revenue was raised from tariffs and excise taxes. As we explained in chapter 2, these taxes were ineffective revenue producers because substitutes were often easy to come by—and so the tax base quickly narrowed as tax rates rose and people bought less of the taxed commodities be they imported goods or alcoholic beverages. In other words, at high rates excise taxes and tariffs produce large excess burdens relative to the revenue they produce.

The excess burden[1] of a tax is the result of two factors: the tax rate and the elasticity of the demand for the item or activity taxed. Elasticity, though often tricky to measure in practice, is simple in theory. Recall one of our examples from chapter 2. A tax on cars would be much more effective than a tax on Fords because the demand for Fords is much more elastic than the demand for cars. Facing a tax on Fords, people quickly reduce their demand for Fords and buy Chevys. Faced with a tax on cars, people cannot so quickly reduce their demand and buy oxcarts instead. Of course, at some very high tax rate people will start finding substitutes for even so necessary an item as cars, greatly burdening both themselves and the economy in the process.

Thus the second factor in the excess burden story is the tax rate itself. Even if the demand for the item being taxed is very elastic, there will be little excess burden if the rate is low enough. And even if demand for the item is very inelastic, the excess burden can be heavy at very high rates. Economists have long known that at any given elasticity, the excess burden of a tax is proportional to the square of the tax rate. That means that a 20 percent tax will impose four times the excess burden of a 10 percent tax, not just twice the excess burden. A 50 percent tax will impose twenty-five times the excess burden of a 10 percent tax, not just five times as much. Raising tax rates increases excess burdens very quickly.

Note that this formula does not tell us the excess burden of a tax in any absolute sense. Though we know that a 50 percent tax on some item would produce five times the excess burden of a 10 percent tax, we cannot say exactly what that would be without knowing the excess burden of the 10 percent tax. To

FIGURE 11.1

Excess Burden, 20% Tax

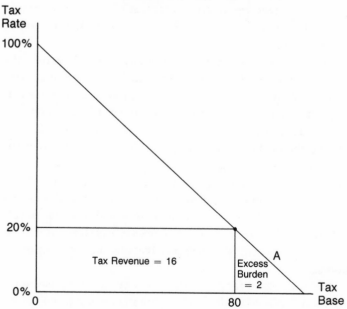

FIGURE 11.2

Excess Burden, 50% Tax

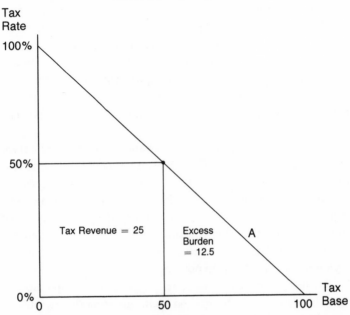

estimate the excess burden we would need a good estimate of elasticity of the demand for the item being taxed. Still, the formula is useful in giving a sense of how dangerous high rates can be. Figures 11.1 and 11.2 show the progress of excess burden at high tax rates. The figures assume that for every percentage point increase in income tax rates the tax base—the amount of reported taxable income—declines by $1.00. (For the purposes of our example the base started at the modest total of $100.) That is our measure of elasticity and is shown in both figures by the "demand curve," line A, a straight 45-degree line. The demand curve governs the relationship between the tax rates and the tax base. On both figures the horizontal axis stands for the tax base and the vertical axis stands for tax rates. The rectangular box, which is a product of the tax rate and the tax base, stands for revenues. The triangle to the right of the box is the excess burden, that additional cost to society and taxpayers of rearrangements made to avoid taxes.

Note the differences between the two figures. For the first figure, the tax rate is 20 percent and the base is $80, or 80 percent of maximum. The excess burden triangle is rather small. In the second figure, the tax rate is 50 percent, 2.5 times higher than the 20 percent rate in the first figure. But the excess burden triangle is 6.25 times larger. And because the base has been cut in half, the revenue box is not 2.5 times but only 56 percent larger.

These results vary greatly if the shape of the demand curve, line A, changes. In reality, line A need not slope at 45 degrees, nor need it be a straight line. The income tax is such a successful tax not only because its base is large—all reported taxable income—but also because in practice its demand curve is fairly forgiving. The demand for income is much less elastic than the demand for Fords, or imported steel. The only way to avoid paying the income tax is to not earn income. The evidence from the Kennedy and Reagan tax cuts suggests that people do exactly that when tax rates get too high. But at moderate rates of tax, which can still produce enormous amounts of revenue, this distorting effect of income taxation is manageable. Whereas a 20 percent tariff might all but eliminate many imported products, a 20 percent income tax rate, in recent practice, has had a much less drastic effect on the income tax base.

There is a direct relationship between a tax's excess burden and its ability to produce revenue. As rates rise, the excess burden mounts up more quickly, the tax base shrinks, and less additional revenue will be raised from a rate increase. For every tax there is a limit at which the most possible revenue is being produced and any additional increase in rates will lose revenue. But this revenue-maximizing tax rate is much higher for taxes with low excess burdens (such as the income tax) than taxes with high burdens (such as tariffs).

This relationship between low excess burdens and high revenue-maximizing rates led to a serious error among some early

FIGURE 11.3

The Laffer Curve

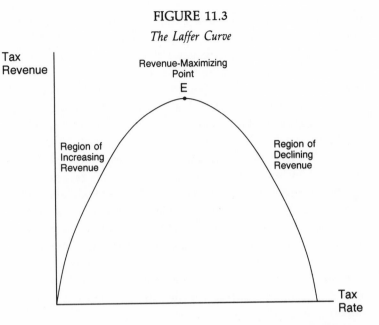

supply-siders. They argued that the revenue-maximizing rate, the famous point E on the Laffer curve (see figure 11.3), was the point at which the government *should* levy taxes. Jude Wanniski wrote in *The Public Interest* of point E:

> It is the point at which the electorate desires to be taxed. At [lower rates] the electorate desires more goods and services and is willing— without reducing its productivity—to pay higher rates consistent with revenues [at the maximum point]. [At lower rates], the elector- ate desires more private goods and services in the money eco- nomy. . . . it is the task of the statesman to determine the location of [the revenue maximizing point] and follow its variations as closely as possible.[2]

Actually the revenue-maximizing point is far from being opti- mal. It is better described as the point at which the taxpayer is being soaked for as much money as possible. Under almost all conceivable circumstances (a war in which the survival of the nation is at stake being one exception), the actual tax rate should be set well below the revenue-maximizing level. To see this, consider further the scenario that produced figures 11.1 and 11.2. Imagine a tax base that involves $100 worth of economic activity. For every 1 percent at which the base is taxed, the tax base shrinks by $1. Table 11.1 shows the resulting tax revenue and excess burden at different tax rates. Note that the total tax revenue collected is simply the product of the tax rate and the tax base. At first this figure rises very steeply, but the rate at which revenue increases slows as the tax rate goes up. At the 50 percent tax rate, revenue reaches its maximum point. At higher rates, revenue declines. The 50 percent tax rate is the revenue-maximizing rate, point E. On this tax base the government can collect no more than $25. Clearly, in this example, the government would never want to raise the tax rate above 50 percent, for it would lose revenue.[3] And none of this is to say that the government *should* set the rate at 50 percent so as to collect that $25.

Remember, tax revenue is no gain to society; it is simply a transfer from one part of society, the taxpayer, to another part of society, the government. The cost of performing this transfer is the excess burden of the tax. At the revenue-maximizing rate in our example, taxpayers not only paid the government $25

TABLE 11.1

Rate, Revenue, and Excess Burden of Hypothetical Tax

Tax Rate	Tax Base	Total Revenue	Total Excess Burden	Additional Revenue	Additional Excess Burden
0%	$100	$0	$ 0		
10	90	9	0.5	$9	$0.5
20	80	16	2.0	7	1.5
30	70	21	4.5	5	2.5
40	60	24	8.0	3	3.5
50	50	25	12.5	1	4.5
60	40	24	18.0	−1	5.5
70	30	21	24.5	−3	6.5

but also changed their behavior to avoid additional payments. The cost to them of this change in behavior—the excess burden of the tax—amounted to $12.50. So the total cost of the tax to the taxpayers was $37.50, the $25 in revenue plus the $12.50 excess burden. Note that the taxpayers would have been even worse off if they had not changed their behavior: if they had not reduced their taxable activities they would have been out $50 in taxes. It makes sense to the taxpayer, to incur a $12.50 change in behavior in order to avoid an extra $25 in taxes.[4]

At a 50 percent tax rate the government gains $25 in revenue at a total cost to the taxpayer of $37.50. On average, the government imposes a cost on society of $1.50 for every $1.00 it collects in revenue. But this average cost is not a useful guide to policy. Rather the government should consider the marginal costs versus the marginal benefits of a change in rates. As table 11.1 shows, the additional, or marginal, revenue collected by increasing the rate from 40 percent to 50 percent was $1. But the additional, or marginal, excess burden imposed by that increase was $4.50. In order to collect the last dollar in revenue, the government imposed a total cost of $5.50 on its taxpayers. That was a very expensive dollar. By contrast, a change in the tax rate from 30 percent to 40 percent produces $3 extra in revenue with an added excess burden of only $3.50. Thus each dollar in revenue cost taxpayers a total of $2.17 ($1.00 in tax plus $1.17 in excess burden). As rates fall off from the revenue-maximizing level, the cost of raising revenue drops dramatically. The excess burden on the first $9 of revenue is only 50 cents, for a total cost to the taxpayer of less than $1.06 for every dollar collected.

Far from being optimal, then, the revenue-maximizing point indicates the point at which increased revenue is most expensive to society. At each step in the rate structure the government should ask itself whether it needs a dollar in revenue enough to impose a cost on the private economy equal to the revenue collected plus the excess burden. By this standard, a 20 percent rate is fairly easily justified and a 30 percent rate is probably acceptable. But a 40 percent rate, which involves an excess burden greater than the revenue collected, is almost certainly imprudent. A 50 percent rate, the revenue-maximizing level, would only be acceptable if the government were so desperate for revenue that its needs completely overwhelmed considerations of the health of the economy or the happiness of citizens.

Nor is there ordinarily any need to impose tax rates highly damaging to the economy or hurtful to individuals. The income tax's broad and relatively inelastic base allows it to collect enormous revenues at relatively harmless rates. The potential base of the personal income tax is the roughly 80 percent of national output that is received by individuals. Today the personal income tax takes in about about 11 percent of all personal income in tax revenue. Because the base is so large, the government could raise this enormous sum, nearly $500 billion, at quite low rates. At present the income tax exempts over half of personal income from taxation, and still obtains its revenue with a maximum tax rate of only 33 percent. Most taxpayers pay only a 15 percent tax rate. From experience with the Kennedy and Reagan tax cuts we also know that the income tax becomes inefficient as rates rise, producing less additional revenue and greater burdens on the economy with every step up the scale.

These considerations suggest that if revenue and economic efficiency (that is, economic growth) were the only considerations in question, the best income tax would be a flat tax on a very broad tax base. For instance, if all deductions, allowances, credits, and exemptions whatsoever were eliminated, we could probably reap the same 11 percent of personal income now produced by the personal income tax with an excess burden of only 1 or 2 percent since such a low rate would do very little to erode the base.

Such a scheme, though on the right track, has drawbacks. Though such a flat rate would reduce rates for most taxpayers, it would raise taxes for some. A considerable number of Americans now pay less than 11 percent of their overall income in taxes. (Though most such people face a 15 percent marginal tax rate, much of their income is exempt from tax, making their average tax rate much lower.) Most of these are low- or moderate-income taxpayers with families. They could not afford the tax increase implied by our truly flat tax, in which marginal and average tax rates are always the same. In other words, efficiency bumps up squarely against fairness. Nearly everyone agrees that in some sense taxes ought to be based on the ability to pay and that the poor should not be more burdened than the rich. Adding fairness to our list of objectives for taxation, we now have a trinity: raise revenue, minimize the damage to the economy, be fair to the less fortunate. There is an old saying that it is not difficult to make a meal that is either cheap and easy, or cheap and good, or easy and good, but impossible to combine all three. The conflicts between raising revenue, encouraging the economy, and being fair are much less pronounced, but at the margin there are real conflicts that must be confronted and resolved.

To resolve those conflicts we first need a better grip on what we mean by fairness. We can certainly agree on some things that seem unfair. The income tax presently generates about $1,500 per person in the United States. But we know that fairness precludes sending everyone a bill for $1,500. No one would seriously propose that we ask a four-person family living on $20,000 to pay 30 percent of its income in taxes while a family earning $100,000 pay but six percent of its earnings. At a minimum, almost everyone would agree that the working-class family should be asked to pay no greater percentage of its income than the rich family. At a minimum, fairness requires proportionality. Most people would probably go even further and say that the low-income family in this example should pay less than their proportional share; that we should have a progressive tax in which the rich will pay somewhat more not only absolutely but as a percentage of income.

Here things get difficult. The economics profession has spent a good deal of effort trying to express this basic notion of fairness, or what in economic jargon is termed "equity," in a more scientific fashion. But attempts to formalize fairness quickly break down. Once progressivity is accepted, the obvious question is: How progressive is fair? No formally acceptable answer has ever been offered.[5]

Generally speaking, when economists, political scientists, or politicians advocate fair taxation they mean one of two things. First, they mean that revenue should be raised in a fair way, and specifically that taxes should be based on ability to pay. Let's call this type of fairness "being fair." They may also mean that taxes should reduce inequalities of wealth, redistributing the goods of society from the rich to the poor. Let us call this goal "creating fairness." Both turn out to be elusive when pursued in a systematic way.

Let's start with "being fair." Though it might seem the simpler of the two goals, through its long history as a goal of political scientists and economists it has failed of attainment.

John Stuart Mill,[6] the nineteenth-century economist and political thinker, argued that taxes should be based on a prescription of equal sacrifice. Taxpayers' ability to pay a tax should be judged by how much of their well-being the tax would cost them. In the example, the family making only $20,000 per year would end up sacrificing more of its well-being than the family making $100,000 per year on almost any practically conceivable tax schedule, however progressive. That is because the last dollar earned by the family making $100,000 is worth less to that family than the last dollar earned by the family earning $20,000. This is the principle of the declining marginal utility of income: additional dollars of income make people happier, but at a decreasing rate. The ten-thousandth dollar is valued more than the twenty-thousandth dollar, which in turn is valued more than the thirty-thousandth dollar. Thus under Mill's prescription of equal sacrifice even if we had taxed the rich family $70,000 and the working-class family nothing, if it happened that the government needed one more dollar in revenue it still would be right to take it from the richer family. With $30,000 remaining they would be less pained by losing a dollar than the $20,000 family. Since the value of each dollar declines with income, the person most able to contribute is always the richest person in society. The richest person will continue to be the right person to tax until he or she ceases to be the richest person. At that point, someone else is richest and places the lowest value on each additional dollar taxed away.[7]

The logic seems flawless. On the other hand, if we tried to apply such a system in the United States today it would be necessary to confiscate all taxable income above $40,000 in order to raise as much money as the income tax now raises. Money, jobs, and talent would flee overseas, the economy would certainly collapse, and the $20,000 family, probably made up of hourly wage workers, certainly would be made worse off by the ensuing depression.

Such obvious difficulties led to an alternative formulation of Mill's basic insight: the principle of equal proportional sacrifice. Under this principle, the total "utility" value of each level of income would be determined, and each taxpayer would be asked to sacrifice the same percentage of his or her utility. In most cases, this will produce a progressive tax schedule. The value of dollars to very high income taxpayers is so low that they must sacrifice a lot of them to make up for the sacrifice of just a few dollars of the lower-income taxpayers. Still, problems emerge.

Consider, for example, two identical twins endowed with the same traits, who received identical upbringing and equal love and attention from their parents. One chooses the life of a college professor, which—if common opinion is true—involves teaching six to eight hours per week with a three-month break in the summer and long vacations at Christmas, Easter, and between semesters. The professor earns the usual rather modest salary which college professors are paid for this grueling regime. The other twin chooses to start his own business, works fourteen hours per day, six or seven days per week, and is amazingly successful, making lots of money.

Under a progressive tax scheme, not only must the businessman twin pay absolutely more taxes than his brother, he must also pay proportionately more. How does this square with the principle of equal proportional sacrifice? We might begin by assuming that since we are dealing with twins, their view of the utility of income is the same. Yet they chose professions with different incomes. Why? The obvious answer is that the college professor is paid not only in money but also in free time. In effect, the extra money the businessman earns compensates him for the extra hours he works.

By our reasoning, the twins are identically happy. Yet under a progressive income tax the businessman would be forced to pay a bigger percentage of his compensation in taxes than the professor. If we truly had a tax system based on the principle of equal sacrifice, these two equally happy twins should pay the same amount of tax. The problem is that money has become synonomous with happiness. The college professor should pay tax on the value of his time off, or the businessman should get a discount for extra hours worked, but the twins should pay the same number of dollars in taxes. Not only should the tax system not be progressive, it should be regressive, taking a bigger share of the money income of the college professor than of the businessman. Of course the twins may not have equal views of the opportunities they face. Perhaps some slight difference in their upbringing caused one to value time off and the other to value earning money. In this case the professor who does not value money should pay more than the businessman twin who values money very highly. By this reasoning, the professor should pay a not only higher percentage of his income in taxes, but a greater absolute amount as well!

Thus any strict notion of being fair fails in practice, because it requires destructive rates on the rich and even the upper-middle class, and in logic, because utility or happiness are so subjective. But what about creating fairness by redistributing wealth? Here we find no problem in logic. Once we have decided that economic equality, or some other standard, is what we mean by fairness, we need not worry that the twins see things differently. That is their problem. But any such scheme founders on the same practical difficulties as attempts to be fair. To create fairness and also fund the government at adequate levels we would have establish even more draconian standards than confiscating all income above $40,000. The Trumps and the Rockefellers would still be vastly wealthy even if we allowed them additional income of only $40,000 per year, so we would have to start taxing wealth as well as income. The excess burden effect would be even more pronounced. Capital and jobs would flee the country even more quickly. The government would become desperate for money and would soon either give up the taxes on the rich or raise taxes on the middle class or surrender the scheme altogether. By that time wealth would have been considerably rearranged, but equality would be nowhere in sight. The country and the people would be much poorer and quite miserable.

By now, some readers who want to create fairness should be shouting "that isn't what we meant at all." No, of course not. We like to imagine that we can come up with a strict notion of fairness and then apply it moderately. Try it. Pick any tax rate for the rich low enough not to destroy the economy. (Or if you pick a high number like 91 percent, apply it high enough up the income scale, and with enough deductions and loopholes so that the damage is limited.) Now pick any tax rate for the middle class high enough to support the government. (We'll even eliminate the working poor from the tax rolls altogether, to make it easier for you.) No matter what reasonable numbers you chose, it is still going to be very much easier and less painful for the rich to pay their high taxes than for ordinary folks to pay their moderate taxes. The tax system is not going to "be fair." The same calculations apply if you try to "create fairness" without destroying the economy or bankrupting the government. As the lady said, "I've been rich and I've been poor, and rich is better."

These conundrums of fairness are almost enough to make one give up on progressivity altogether. As James McCullough wrote in the last century, the introduction of progressivity seems to leave the tax system "at sea without rudder or compass."[8] Proportional taxes at least unite the interests of the nation behind a specific standard, while progressive taxation, McCullough argued, invites political mischief.

Such has proved the case. In the seventy-five years of progressive income taxation in the United States, the top marginal tax rate has been 50 percent or greater for sixty-one years. The top rate has exceeded 60 percent for fifty-four years. It has been 70 percent or greater for forty-nine years, 80 percent or greater for thirty-one years, and 90 percent or more twenty-three years. And in nearly every case a rise in the top rates has been used to cover or excuse a rise in the tax rates and tax payments of poorer taxpayers. Perhaps it really would be better to draw a single line in the dirt and unite all citizens on one side of it.

What then becomes of fairness? We need not abandon it. But we do need to discover what we really mean by it. Our common concern that the working or middle class not be forced to pay what they cannot afford was not merely a rough-and-ready version of the more formal ideas of fairness suggested earlier. It was a different and better idea: Low- and moderate-income taxpayers must be allowed to obtain the necessities of life, by modern American standards, before we treat any significant portion of their income as discretionary and tax it away.

Lower-income taxpayers are less able to avoid income taxes than those with more income. In the first place, most of their income is from wages and is hard to hide. More important, their demand for income is less elastic than that of the well-to-do. They need every additional dollar they can get even if those dollars come at a high cost in taxes. More comfortable taxpayers pay taxes out of what is in some sense discretionary income: They can lower their tax bill by giving up some income (and taking more leisure) or by rearranging their finances (in a suboptimal way) to avoid taxation. These rearrangements will carry a price and burden the economy. Nevertheless, for people who have the option of making such rearrangements taxes are, if in an attenuated sense, voluntary. For low- and moderate-income taxpayers, who lack such choice, taxes are hardly ever voluntary. Where there is no escape from the law, the law can quickly become oppressive. As we have seen, it often has. The government early discovered that moderate- and lower-income taxpayers produce lots of revenue. In large part this is because there are so many of them. But in part low- and moderate-income taxpayers have been good revenue producers because they have no escape.

Deciding what level of income enables people to obtain the necessities of American life is a judgment call. But democracy can make this judgment pretty well if it follows several important rules of designing a tax system. If we start with the number one rule that the purpose of a tax system is to raise revenue, and adhere also to the corollary that revenue should be raised in a way that produces the least possible additional burden on the economy, we can be sure the top rates will not be too high. Sticking rigorously to the first two principles and avoiding political posturing over defining the third, fairness, will make that last easier to achieve. Top rates have historically set the parameters for lower rates, so keeping top rates moderate should ensure that lower rates do not become oppressive.

The probable result of keeping our eye on the revenue ball would be a relatively flat, pro-growth tax rate that is nevertheless gentle to moderate- and lower-income taxpayers, especially those with families. In the final chapter I outline just such a tax code. It has only one rate. But it is progressive in the sense that it provides generous exemptions to remove many working-class families with children from the federal income tax rolls and greatly reduces the tax burden on middle-class families in the same situation.

Recall that a perfectly flat tax of 11 percent with no exemptions, deductions, etc. would produce enough revenue to fund today's federal government. Form 2000, presented in chapter 17, taxes all income at a single rate of 19 percent. But it raises the current individual exemption to $6,000, or $12,000 for a married couple, raises the exemption for children to $3,000 each, and adds an extra $2,000 for each child under four years of age. A family of four with two young children would pay no taxes on its first $22,000 of income. These and several other adjustments push the rate up to 19 percent from the 11 percent of a pure flat tax, but these adjustments would do much to accomplish that goal we have been calling fairness.

Achieving fairness through exemptions rather than staggered rates has great advantages. It helps get us off the slippery slope of a steep tax rate structure. Politically and psychologically, if not logically, it should be easier to hold down tax rates if we establish the principle that all Americans pay the same rate. When the politicians play divide-and-conquer we all stand to lose. Most important, a flat rate would never be allowed to rise to levels where it causes significant excess burdens to the economy.

There is one final advantage to a flat rate. Taxes are used not only to raise revenue but to control behavior. Our system has frequently imposed very high tax rates on top earners, but it has also allowed them to avoid taxes through meritorious expenditures such as contributing money to charitable organizations, purchasing city or state bonds, or spending money on a home rather than a vacation. These loopholes are sometimes useful and, as we shall see in several chapters, can be superior to direct government spending as a way to achieve certain goals. Tax subsidies can sometimes target individuals more precisely than government programs, and taxes are administratively less costly than new government programs because the IRS bureaucracy is already in place. Tax programs can avoid both duplication of services and the problem of people "falling through the cracks." In practice, however, tax loopholes are rarely as well designed or as cost effective as their proponents believe. It is good policy to be cautious in their use. A flat, low-rate tax blunts the government's ability to direct our behavior through the tax code, making politicians a little less quick on the draw with new behavior modification strategies. Moreover, a flat tax ensures that whenever the government does enact a new loophole, every taxpayer will be eligible for the same benefit. Since every taxpayer will be taxed at the same marginal rate, deductions for tax-favored activities will affect each the same. This was not the case under the sharply progressive codes of the past, which caused some conspicuous injustices.

Before the Reagan tax cuts, for example, rich homeowners in the 70 percent brackets received huge tax rewards from the home mortgage interest deduction and the deduction for state and local taxes. Though most taxpayers did not benefit at all from the interest deduction, every dollar the rich paid out in mortgage interest on lavish homes cost them only 30 cents after taxes. And while a dollar in local or state taxes cost most tax-payers a dollar in after-tax income, the after-tax cost to the rich was but 30 cents. In effect, the residents of poor towns with modest public services paid for the lavish public services the rich voted themselves in wealthier areas. The flat tax ends such anomalies. With a flat tax there would be no such thing as a loophole for the rich. Loopholes, for better or for ill, would be for everyone. All would have the same choices to spend their money on themselves or on tax-favored government-approved objects like charity and housing.

Some may argue that the old combination of high rates for the rich plus a generous schedule of loopholes for socially beneficial activities did channel the wealth of the rich away from conspicuous consumption and into more useful directions. But it was an enormously inefficient system, for it discouraged not only conspicuous consumption but work, savings, and investment as well. If we wish to limit conspicuous consumption we can do so directly through sumptuary taxes on luxury cars, boats, household servants, second homes, and the like instead of discouraging people from earning income in the first place.

The proper purpose of the income tax is to raise revenue in the way most painless to the people, the economy, and the nation. The most effective way of raising revenue would be by a flat-rate tax on as broad a tax base as possible. The rigorous pursuit of fairness through steeply progressive tax rates is too costly for all concerned; in designing a tax system to meet the needs of the next century we cannot afford wasteful digressions. But we can afford generous treatment of hard-pressed families and, the daily headlines to the contrary, another tax cut. But that is our next story.

Chapter 12

The Great Surplus of '99

> "The Reagan Administration's economic policies are neither careful nor protective of the nation's future. . . . They have touched off a national borrowing and buying binge that will have to be paid for in the morning."
> —Editors, *The New Republic*[1]

Now for a short civics test. Answer "true" or "false." To balance the budget in the 1990s the Congress must either increase taxes or cut spending from current levels.

The right answer is "false." If you responded "true," however, I won't take off too many points. There is probably no more widespread myth about the U.S. budget system than the supposed need to raise taxes or cut spending.

Let's consider how the myth got started. We do have a budget deficit of some $160 billion.[2] For the Congress to balance the budget in a single year, it would have to enact some $160 billion in combined tax increases or spending cuts. Since most of our budget is "uncontrollable," in that it is comprised of defense, Social Security, Medicare, and interest on the debt, cutting $160 billion is impossible. So the pundits say we need a major tax increase as well.

The fallacy in this analysis is that no responsible economist would suggest that the United States try to reduce its budget deficit by $160 billion in a single year. The result would almost inevitably be a very sharp recession, or even a depression, as the government desperately sucked spending power out of the economy. Most sensible people favor narrowing the gap by $30 to $40 billion per year, ridding ourselves of the deficit over four or five years. That requires neither raising taxes nor reducing spending below current real levels, for the current tax code will *automatically* provide $75 billion to $80 billion more in income tax revenue each year for as long as economic growth continues at its current rate. With an automatic $300 billion revenue increase already scheduled for the next four years, we could increase spending by $140 billion (roughly enough to keep up with inflation) and still bring the deficit down to zero in just four years.

This chapter began with a trick question. The Congress does not need to raise taxes because taxes are going up anyway. There is no voodoo involved. Both the real growth in the economy and continued inflation effectively increase average tax rates and tax revenues over time. In the 1960s Keynesians called this effect a "fiscal drag," or a "fiscal dividend,"[3] depending on whether they were advocating more stimulus or arguing that such stimulus was largely self-financing. Table 12.1 summarizes this relationship for each of the major types of taxes the government collects, in each case showing the effect on tax revenue of a 1 percent increase in the economy's real output as well as a 1 percent inflation.

Start with the personal income tax. We are all aware of the phenomenon known as bracket creep by which inflation pushes us into higher tax brackets without our real income increasing.

TABLE 12.1

Tax Revenue and the Economy

Type of Tax	FY89 Revenue* Collections (in billions)	Percent Change in Revenue with	
		1% Real Growth	1% Inflation
Personal Income	$425	1.3–1.4%	1.0–1.1%
Corporate Income	107	1.4	1.4
Social Insurance	364	1.0	1.0
Other	80	0.4	0.0

*Estimates from the *Budget of the United States Government FY1990* for FY89.

As discussed in chapter 4, ERTA's indexing provisions curbed this highly destructive practice. With indexing, if both your income and prices rise 1 percent, your tax payments—not your tax rate—will also rise 1 percent, and taxes will take the same percentage of your income as before. As a general rule, therefore, 1 percent inflation will cause personal income tax revenue to rise only 1 percent. But because not all parts of the income tax are fully indexed, tax revenues do rise slightly faster than inflation, or a bit more than 1 percent for every 1 percent rise in prices.

Of more importance is what happens when you get a real raise, not just an inflationary increase. Since indexing does not apply to changes in real income, you may be pushed into a higher tax bracket when your income rises. Even if your tax bracket does not change, your tax payments will go up because you will be paying on a bigger income. Moreover, your *average* tax rate will rise because a smaller percentage of your income will be protected by basic exemptions and deductions.

Consider the case of a four-person family earning $30,000 in 1989. In 1989 the family is allowed a deduction of $2,000 for each person plus a standard deduction of $5,000, for a total of $13,000. The family's taxable income is then $17,000. The tax rate on *taxable* income up to $31,000 is 15 percent, so this family pays a tax of $2,550, which is 8.5 percent of its *total* income, or an average tax rate of 8.5 percent. Now assume the family's real income increases by 10 percent to $33,000. Its deductions are unchanged, so its taxable income rises to $20,000. The tax on $20,000, at the standard 15 percent rate, is $3,000. The family's tax payments rise 17.6 percent ($450 on top of $2,550) though the family's income went up only 10 percent. On average, every 1 percent rise in the family's income caused a 1.76 percent rise in its tax payments. The family's average tax rate rose from 8.5 percent to slightly more than 9 percent. This increase occurred even though the family remained in the same 15 percent tax bracket. A greater fraction of the family's income was taxed at the 15 percent rate while a smaller percentage was in the "zero" rate. Note that unlike bracket creep, in which inflation increases the rate applied to the same real income, this family is paying a higher average rate because it really is making more money. This is fundamental to any progressive tax code. The family is still better off.

On average, if everyone in the United States got a 10 percent raise, tax revenues would rise about 15 percent. Ordinarily this would imply that every 1 percent of real growth would produce about 1.5 percent extra revenue. But not all real economic growth can be attributed to salary increases for those currently working; about one-third is due to new workers joining the labor force. New workers add to tax revenues, but they do not produce the same average increase per point of economic growth that occurs when existing workers get higher wages. The actual average effect is thus about 1.3 to 1.4 percent extra tax revenue per point of economic growth.

Corporate income tax revenues also rise much faster than the economy, as long as the economy is expanding.[4] Corporations pay a flat tax rate, and so are not subject to bracket creep. But corporate taxes are increased both by inflation and real growth because of the way that the tax system defines corporate profits.

Imagine the production process as a giant pipeline: Raw materials, labor, and capital enter one end and finished products come out the other. Corporate profits are the difference in value between what goes into the pipeline and what comes out, or the difference between costs and final sales. When the economy slows down, fewer finished products are purchased and items build up in the pipeline, a process known as inventory accumulation. Corporations thus incur the costs of producing the inventory without having any final sales, and corporate profits fall.

When, on the other hand, the economy speeds up, existing items in the pipeline, already largely paid for, are ready to move. Final sales increase faster than input costs, and corporate profits rise quickly.

This "pipeline effect" is most dramatic at turning points in the economy. When the economy turns up or down, corporate profits can easily change as much as 3 to 5 percent for every 1 percent change in the economy. As business expansion continues, the ratio drops to about 1.4 points of corporate profit for every 1 point of economic growth. As business expansion persists, rising demand for products can only be met by new investment: The pipeline itself must be expanded in order to accommodate the greater flow of products. This is where the tax system plays a part. Suppose a business invests in expanding the capacity of its pipeline by 10 percent. We might expect sales, profits, and costs, including capital costs, to rise together in proportion and the capital costs of a 10 percent bigger pipeline to be also 10 percent higher. But the tax system does not allow corporations to deduct the capital costs of the bigger pipeline right away; these added costs must be depreciated over many years. Because the costs of the expansion cannot be fully counted, profits appear to rise much more quickly than economic activity expands. Thus corporate profits, and therefore corporate taxes, increase more than point for point with economic activity during periods of real economic growth.

Inflation has a similar effect. Again, consider the goods moving through the pipeline. During periods of inflation, the value of the inventory in the pipeline rises with the general price level. The corporation does not really gain, because the cost of replacing the materials at the beginning of the pipeline also rises. But the tax system views the rising value of inventory as a source of corporate profit. This is particularly true for corporations which use the first in–first out (FIFO) method of accounting, under which the cost of products is based on the original cost of the materials that went into them, not their replacement or current costs. The last in–first out method (LIFO) uses replacement or current costs. A surprising number of firms use FIFO rather than LIFO, even though it overstates their corporate profits and therefore their corporate taxes.

The tax system also fails to take into account the effect of inflation on the capital costs of the pipeline itself. When inflation is high, the depreciation allowances for the cost of the pipeline are far less than the cost of actually replacing the pipeline at inflated prices. The result, since corporations cannot fully deduct the true capital costs of production from their profits, is an artifical rise in both profits and taxes. All these factors combine to increase corporate tax payments about 1.4 percent for every 1 percent increase in the price level.

Social Security tax payments tend to rise point for point with both real economic activity and inflation because they are indexed to the price level and have a proportional rather than progressive rate structure. Unless social insurance tax rates change, these revenues will continue to grow almost exactly as fast as the economy.

Excise taxes, such as those on gasoline, alcohol, and cigarettes, included as "Other" in table 12.1, are generally levied on a "cents per unit" basis, and so are totally unresponsive to inflation. Sales of goods taxed in this way tend to increase more slowly than the expansion rate of the economy. As a result revenue from these sources does not rise as fast as overall economic activity. All together, however, tax revenues will grow significantly faster than the economy, and this rapid expansion will balance the federal budget if we are at all sensible about spending. The only question is how fast we can expect the economy to grow.

Long-term economic projections are chancy, but let us consider two possibilities. The long-term growth of the U.S. economy since the end of World War II, averaging out recessions and expansions, has been 3.2 percent per year. Though there is no reason to expect that we will do better in the future, there is also no reason to expect worse. We might reasonably project an average growth of 3.2 percent over the next twenty years. If we limit our base to more recent years, say from 1981, the peak of the last business cycle, through 1986, which includes the deepest recession we have experienced since the Great Depression, we get an average growth in the economy of only 2.7 percent per year. Projecting that figure forward would produce

TABLE 12.2

Year	Revenue		Spending*	Difference	
	3.2%	2.7%		3.2%	2.7%
1989	$976	$976	1137	−$161	−$161
1994	1425	1386	1382	+43	+4
1999	2100	1982	1752	+347	+230
2004	3115	2853	2142	+973	+711
2009	4649	4127	2880	+1769	+1246

*Data for 1989 from the FY1990 Budget. It shows $971 billion in program spending and $167 billion in interest. Under this scenario the program spending grows with inflation until 1994 and at inflation plus 2 percent thereafter. Interest payments are calculated as 7.6 percent of the outstanding debt and are then added to program spending to get total spending.

what we might call the bearish long-term forecast. Table 12.2 shows what would happen to revenues with these rates of growth over the next twenty years, assuming inflation continues at the average rate of the past several years, or about 4 percent. In both cases, revenues grow quickly over time, though an increase of just 0.5 percent in average real growth adds $530 billion per year by the twentieth year. This is an important indication of just how sensitive the U.S. budget is to continued economic growth.

To reduce the deficit we do not need to cut spending. But we must show some self-control. After all, the Congress could spend every penny collected in revenue and then some. To illustrate the long-term budget needs of the country, the "spending" column in figure 12.2 employs a five-year "flexible freeze" such as President Bush championed during his campaign. The flexible freeze limits spending growth to the level of inflation for five years, then allows real program growth of 2 percent per year. Thus program spending rises at a 4.0 percent annual rate through 1994 and at a 6.1 percent annual rate thereafter. We assume the interest rate on the national debt, which cannot be frozen, will be about 7.6 percent[5] annually.

Table 12.2 shows that a tax increase is completely unnecessary. If spending is limited to the growth of inflation until 1994, we will have either a balanced budget (with slow growth) or a $40 billion surplus (with average growth). After 1994, a large surplus arises and begins to grow even though spending is allowed to grow faster than inflation. By 2004 we will be showing annual surpluses of roughly $800 billion and will have paid off the existing national debt.

Of course, this will not happen. Given such enormous revenues, the Congress will try to increase spending. Assuming the freeze holds until 1994, both spending and taxes will be 19.5 percent of GNP in that year. Over the next fifteen years, taxes would automatically grow to between 22.3 and 22.9 percent of GNP. The Congress could drastically increase the size of government and the government's share of the economy if it appropriated all of the extra tax revenue for that purpose.

Instead, the country should insist on a series of tax cuts in the latter part of the 1990s. The $300 billion surpluses forecast for 1999 would easily finance a 15 percent reduction in tax rates across the board. If the entire surplus were applied to reducing the income tax rates in the current code, the bottom rate could be reduced from 15 percent to 10 percent and the top rate lowered from 28 percent to 20 percent. Form 2000, the personal income tax code proposed in chapter 17, is designed to produce roughly the same amount of revenue as the current code. So even if in the early 1990s we adopt Form 2000 with its single rate of 19 percent, we would be able to reduce that rate even further in the late 1990s. Assuming we control spending for the next five years, the country will be able to afford substantial tax relief by the end of the century.

All of this may seem magical given the headlines about the government's current fiscal crisis. Yet these calculations do not assume any behavioral changes on the part of the public, or any sharp drop in interest rates, or any unusual rate of economic growth. The only magic involved is the magic of normal economic growth compounded year after year, coupled with permanent restraint on the growth of government spending.

The current tax burden on American families remains too

high. As with the Reagan tax cuts, Form 2000 rearranges the national tax burden to shift it further from lower- and moderate-income families. By exchanging lower rates for fewer loopholes, it reduces excess burdens, making the entire tax system more efficient and less disruptive to the economy. As time passes we can do even better: we can have not only more tax reform, such as Form 2000 proposes, but another round of tax cuts, particularly for the Americans who need them most.

Present-day pundits, stuck in their static analysis of a single year's budget, never calculate the effect of revenue growth on the prospects for the U.S. budget. Hence the persistent calls for tax increases. But tax increases would tend to slow the rate of economic growth and reduce future revenue growth. Much better to keep taxes at current rates—or lower them—and assure continued economic growth not only for the treasury but for all Americans. It is to this task that the next chapter turns its attention.

Chapter 13

Taxes for a Growing Economy

"There is no alternative."

—Margaret Thatcher

Stated simply, there are two paths to economic growth: working harder or working smarter. Working harder has its limits but may be the best way to fund investments toward working smarter in the future, as the Japanese "economic miracle" exemplifies. With its industrial base in ruins and its economy reduced to subsistence level at the end of World War II, Japan recovered because the Japanese worked excruciating hours in sweatshop conditions. That hard work created the surplus capital that became Japan's industrial base.

The United States faces no such dire necessity. But we have been working harder lately, mostly because of changes in demography. The biggest surge in work effort has come from increased female labor-force participation. Though women still do the bulk of work at home, they are also taking more paid work in the labor market, creating extra output. The aging of the baby boomers is also having an effect, since people in their thirties and forties work harder and more seriously than people in their teens and twenties. As in postwar Japan, extra work has generated surplus production that society can either consume or invest in learning how to work smarter.

The choice is an important one. Working harder fosters economic growth for only a short period and soon loses its attractiveness. Most people prefer more leisure to a long work week. The demographic transition of women to the labor force may prove temporary. The gains from the baby boomers maturing will necessarily reverse themselves as that cohort enters their sixties and seventies. There are already signs in the popular culture that some Americans feel they work too hard and want to slow down. The strains of professional life and two–wage earner families are becoming regular themes of TV and movies and a constant subject at dinner parties. On the other hand, as the intellectual demands of certain jobs, including traditional industrial jobs, increase, many younger Americans are discovering they do not have the training to work at all, at least not at a good job for good pay. For the sake of our families and our social fabric as well as our competitive position in the world market, the United States must put more emphasis on working smarter. We should consider the current temporary increase in work effort a bridge to that goal.

There are many routes to working smarter. One way is to give each worker more and better tools to work with, a process economists call capital formation. These new tools may require a more educated work force and new training—human capital formation. Another route to working smarter is to get more output from our old tools, a technique known as process innovation, generally involving the reorganization of work. The assembly line is a prime example. Technological progress may also breed whole new industries and outputs, a process we call product innovation.

All these forms of working smarter require investment, the sacrifice of current production and consumption for the sake of future output. Often we limit the term "investment" to the purchase of new plant and equipment and the postponing of current consumption to foot the bill; the same sacrifice is required for all the other forms of working smarter. Building human capital takes time. Workers must be withdrawn from their present tasks or must train after hours to acquire new skills. This time spent learning is stolen from current production. The research workers who drive technological progress are part of the investment process as well. Neither their talents nor their often expensive tools produce anything for current consumption.

An increasing number of employees are in "systems analysis" or "operations research." Most of their efforts seem modest: a slight tinkering with one part of the assembly line, a rearrangement of machines or factories to reduce transport costs, a more efficient package design. Each such worker is really an investment worker, not a production worker. Or as their critics might say, "They don't produce a damn thing." The critics are right. No systems analyst can point to something and say, "I made that." But heaven help the economy that does not devote some of its most talented workers to "not producing a damn thing."

The ultimate investment worker, the individual most committed to working smarter, is usually overlooked by traditional economists and the public alike. That worker is the entrepreneur. Joseph Schumpeter, one of the leading free market economists of the twentieth century, called the entrepreneur "a gap filler and input completer." It sounds unromantic, but without entrepreneurs the economy would be nothing but gaps and inputs in need of completing. The factories would keep running for a while but, like a marching band without a leader, the organization would quickly deteriorate as the landscape changed. The entrepreneur does not produce a damn thing, but without entrepreneurs nothing gets produced. As a class, they spend their time looking for a shortfall in the current production process: a way to do something more cheaply, or do something with greater quality at the same cost, or come up with a whole new product. Entrepreneurs are responsible for every gadget, system, service, or transaction that takes place in an economy. Everything that humanity values, materially or esthetically, came from the mind of an individual who took some time off from the process of current production to fill a gap or complete an input.

By "entrepreneur" we usually mean someone who starts up a new company. But the essential work of an entrepreneur can be done inside existing organizations, even large ones. The essence of entrepreneurship is redirecting old capital and creating new capital in pursuit of useful innovation and at some personal risk to the entrepreneur. Like a ganglion in the nervous system or the hub city in an airline network, the entrepreneur is a point of concentrated intelligence in the system at which decisions are taken that provide leadership for the whole. A principle consideration in designing a pro-investment tax policy is that entrepreneurs do this job of directing capital much better when the tax system does not overly influence their decisions.

I recently spoke at a meeting where a politician with a national reputation (who shall remain nameless) was also present. The politician defended his pro-growth credentials by pointing to the countless commissions, working groups, and task forces he had formed to improve the business climate in his state. He cited the number of new businesses that had been created with the financial backing of these various economic development authorities. During his campaigns the public was treated to testimonials to his economic stewardship by members of the business community the state had sponsored.

This gentleman's efforts, no matter how well intentioned, were at best irrelevant to economic growth. Politicians who assert their role in directing funds to the "industries of the future" want to play entrepreneur with someone else's money. They are ill suited to the role. The politician who takes over the direction of capital is quickly revealed as this year's amateur following the advice of last year's experts.

The best and brightest politicians, including this gentleman, dutifully keep abreast of economic trends. But to break a trend requires the concentration of a specialist. A good political leader practices conciliation and consensus and is sensitive to the current power structure. The really important entrepreneurs annoy their peers and threaten power structures. The politicians have custody of the rule book. At their best entrepreneurs change the game.

As it happens the state represented by this politician ranks near the top of all states not only in the volume of business commissions, "development authorities," and special tax subsidies for favored businesses but in its general personal and corporate tax burdens. It has had a continuous net out-migration of people, and particularly of entrepreneurs, and as a result faces a severe fiscal crisis.

The first principle of tax policy with regard to investment in economic growth should not be to ameliorate high rates with selective breaks for favored activities, but to keeping general taxes on investment activity to a minimum. Nothing better concentrates the mind than risking one's own money, while few things are more distracting than getting a government subsidy to play with. Whether the investment is in physical capital, human capital, or a new firm, tax policy should be as averse to subsidizing it as to taxing it.

The second principle is symmetry. By taxing the profits of an investment, the government becomes a partner in the investor's success. The government then should also be a partner if the investor loses money. By sharing equally in the risks and the rewards, the government remains neutral in the decision to take a risk. Ideally the tax system should be irrelevant to each investment decision; second best is for it to be irrelevant on average, with full offsets for losers against the profits of winners. When the government abandons symmetry and shares only in the profits but not the reverses, it discourages investment and risk taking.

The first step toward improved tax treatment for investment is to establish a *cash flow corporate income tax*. [1] The present corporate income tax is a hash of provisions assembled over the years and often designed to offset each other. The current system is also biased against equity capital (stocks) in favor of debt capital (bonds and bank loans), a bias that raises interest rates, depresses stock prices, and makes the financial system less sta-

ble in hard times. Under the cash flow tax the base would be
the revenue the firm takes in from sales, less the cost of producing the goods sold, and less any net investment expenditure the
firm makes. No deduction would be allowed for interest or
dividend expense. All existing depreciation schedules and investment credits would be abolished. In effect, the corporation
would be taxed on the difference between the money it takes
in during a year and the money it pays out during that same
year to purchase capital, labor, and raw materials.

The cash flow corporate income tax makes two major changes
in the way corporations are currently treated. First, firms would
no longer depreciate their investments over a number of years,
but instead deduct the cost of those investments in the year
they are made. The deduction for depreciation derives from the
principle that a business should be taxed only on its profits, not
on costs of doing business, such as the purchase of machinery.
Traditionally the deduction has been spread over time on the
theory that the cost of a machine is incurred *as the machine wears
out;* before it wears out, it is not an expense but an asset. (It
could, for instance, be resold.)

One problem with this system, as discussed in chapters 3 and
8, is that the accuracy of depreciation schedules is very sensitive
to economic conditions, most notably the underlying rate of
inflation. During periods of high inflation, firms can generally
deduct only a small percentage of the real cost of replacing their
equipment, because the deduction is based on the original purchase price, not the inflated replacement cost. The result is an
underestimation of business expenses and overestimation and
overtaxing of profits, particularly for businesses with heavy
investments in machinery. Indexing for inflation would solve
that particular problem, but even so, standardized schedules
can not be very accurate. Just about any depreciation system is
based on guesswork about how quickly tools wear out (or
become obsolete). The ACRS system adopted in the 1981 tax
bill fits all investments into only four classifications. Most industrial equipment was given a five-year estimated life, despite

tremendous real variations in the longevity of such equipment. Assets that lasted longer than the five years were greatly favored by the tax code, while assets that wore out more quickly were penalized. As our society becomes more complex, and machines more often become obsolete before wearing out, it will be increasingly important to curb such distorting influences on our investment decisions.

The cash flow corporate income tax eliminates these problems by allowing the firm to deduct the cost of the machine in the year it is purchased. There is no need to worry about what future inflation will do to the cost of buying replacement equipment or how to design a tax depreciation schedule that accurately estimates a machine's useful life.

The cash flow system also enhances the principle of symmetry. The government becomes a partner with the corporation, for richer or for poorer, in the purchase of the machine. At the time of purchase, the government incurs a cost equal to the corporate tax rate times the value of the machine, because the firm deducts the cost of the machine from its taxable income. Then the government receives a flow of tax revenue as the machine starts to produce. Its share of the revenue produced by the machine, the corporate tax rate, is the same as its share of the cost when the machine was purchased. If the machine turns out to be profitable, the government comes out ahead. If the machine turns out to be unprofitable, the government loses, but so does the corporation. Since on average and over time a strong steady stream of investment helps the economy grow, overall the government will come out ahead.

The second major improvement of the cash flow tax is to eliminate the present subsidies for corporate indebtedness. Under current law a firm is allowed to deduct the interest cost of borrowing to finance operations. However, if it issues new stock or rewards existing shareholders with a dividend payment, it is not allowed a deduction. Consequently, the after-tax cost of debt capital is much lower than the after-tax cost of equity capital. The cash flow tax eliminates the deduction for interest payments. Some might argue that interest should be deductible because it is a cost of doing business. Actually, interest is the cost of delaying payment for an investment. Under a depreciation system the tax benefits of the investment are also delayed, which might justify deducting interest. But under the cash flow tax all investments are deducted immediately. An additional deduction for interest would be an asymmetrical subsidy for delaying payment.

Eliminating the corporate interest deduction probably would slow the recent wave of leveraged buy-outs (LBOs), which take public companies private by turning equity (public shares) into debt. When LBOs are motivated by a real need for new management or corporate restructuring they are a fine idea. But many such deals result from the tax subsidy for debt making companies more valuable in the debt market than in the stock market. In such cases, when no substantive improvements are made by the LBO, the leveraged company may end up in perilous financial condition, putting both workers and the financial health of the corporate sector at greater risk. Take away this tax subsidy and LBOs will more often be limited to deals that make good sense for all involved.

The transition from our current corporate tax to a cash flow tax would require some difficult decisions, most notably how to treat depreciation deductions and interest expenses incurred before the transition. There is no reason why a reasonable compromise on these issues can't be reached. After the transition the cash flow corporate tax would lower the cost and the riskiness of undertaking new investment.

The second step towards building a tax system for a growing economy is a *thorough reform of capital gains taxation.* The taxation of capital gains is probably the most controversial issue in tax policy: Though the capital gains tax is destructive to the economy, it is mostly paid by relatively well-to-do taxpayers, which makes it politically attractive.

Stated simply, capital gains are profits made by buying an asset at a low price and selling it at a higher price. Why treat income from capital gains any differently than other income? The matter is not in practice simple. Investments that yield capital gains income are generally riskier and more subject to inflation and other forms of taxation than other investments. Taxing capital gains at the same rate as other income often results in an *over*taxation of the true profit of the investment, a distinction historically recognized by the tax code in partial exemption or reduction of rates for capital gains income.

Prior to the 1986 tax reform, long-term capital gains were taxed at only 40 percent of the tax rate applied to ordinary income. A taxpayer in the top 50 percent tax bracket paid 20 percent on capital gains. A taxpayer in the 30 percent tax bracket paid only 12 percent. This provision, known as the capital gains exclusion, seemed to primarily benefit upper-income taxpayers. For example, in 1985 (holding taxpayer behavior and economic conditions unchanged) the capital gains exclusion lowered personal income taxes by $34 billion. Of this, a total of $19 billion, or 56 percent, went to the top 2 percent of American taxpayers. Only 6 percent of the value of the capital gains exclusion accrued to taxpayers in the bottom half of the taxpayer population. On its face the capital gains exclusion appeared to be overwhelmingly a privilege of the rich.

There are a number of problems with this conclusion. It is unlikely that the treasury really would have collected the extra $34 billion had the capital gains exclusion been eliminated. The exclusion lowered the tax due on the sale of the capital asset, and without the exclusion, fewer taxpayers would have found it profitable to sell their capital assets. Moreover many recipients of capital gains are "rich" solely because of their capital gain, and only for one year. A small businessman who retires and sells his business for a $500,000 gain will be counted as rich that year even though his usual income was relatively modest. A detailed analysis of 1984 capital gains recipients finds that 43 percent of taxpayers with gains over $100,000 had ordinary, recurring income of $50,000 or less.

Almost any middle-class American could find himself among

the ranks of the "rich" for one year. If you own some rental property or a vacation home, you will likely find that the year you sell it your income doubles or triples. The same will happen, though to a lesser extent, the year you sell some of your accumulated stock to pay for your child's college tuition or a wedding. The capital gains tax falls particularly heavily on the elderly who, even if they are of modest means, have had time to accumulate capital gains on their assets. Under the Tax Reform of 1986, which increased the effective tax rate on capital gains by eliminating the exclusion, taxpayers over sixty-five will pay about 11 percent of the total income tax but more than 26 percent of the capital gains tax.

The exclusion thus had been a way of making capital gains taxes more, not less fair. When capital gains income is lumped together with other types of income, the tax code cannot distinguish between those who are "king for a day" and those who live like royalty their whole lives. The United States is now almost unique among the major industrial nations of the world in taxing capital gains at the same rate as ordinary income. Most nations tax capital gains at only a fraction of ordinary tax rates, and they are right to do so. Some taxes are better than others, and the capital gains tax ranks near the bottom of the list. It is a tax on transactions, not on income, and thus can be avoided simply by postponing the sale of an asset. Such artificial postponements can blunt the efficiency of financial markets, discourage new investment, and prolong investments that have outlived their usefulness. Most of the capital gains tax base is composed of items that should be taxed either lightly or not at all: inflationary gains, the return for taking risks, and the shareholder's portion of the retained earnings of corporations.

Consider the effects of inflation. Suppose I bought one unit of the Dow Jones Industrials in 1967 at $879 and had the foresight to sell at a record $2,700 before the October 1987 crash, for a gain of $1,821. Under the current 28 percent capital gains tax rate (33 percent for some taxpayers), I pay capital gains tax of $510. After tax, my $879 has grown to $2,190. But to retain the same purchasing power my $879 had in 1967, I would need more than $3,000. After inflation, my capital has declined in value. I was forced to pay a whopping capital gains tax even though I suffered a real capital loss.

Or consider a farmer who retires and sells the farm he bought forty years ago for $50,000. Assuming that the price of the farm kept pace with inflation, he gets $275,000. He takes no *real* capital gain on the farm because that $275,000 has exactly the same purchasing power as the money paid for the farm forty years previously. Nonetheless, the capital gains tax law says he must pay $63,000 in capital gains tax.

One solution to this problem is to allow taxpayers to adjust the purchase price of their asset for the inflation up to the time of sale. This is known as indexing the basis of the asset. For the purpose of calculating the taxes due, each taxpayer would increase the purchase price of the asset by the amount of inflation since the time of purchase. The taxpayer's capital gain (or capital loss) would be the difference between this inflation-adjusted price and the price for which he actually sold the asset. For example, in my stock market investments the initial $879 would be adjusted to $3,002 to reflect the inflation between 1967 and 1987. Comparing the adjusted basis to the sale price of $2,700, I would have a capital loss of $302, rather than a capital gain of $1,821. Instead of paying capital gains tax of $510, my capital loss reduces my tax liability by $84 or 28 percent of my $302 loss. Investors who did make real capital gains would pay taxes on their profits, but only their real profits.

The major problem with allowing taxpayers to index capital gains is that it is extremely costly for the treasury. The very fact that our hypothetical taxpayer with excellent investment timing had no *real* capital gains also means that, under indexing, no capital gains tax revenue would be collected from that taxpayer. Indexing sharply increases the possibilities for taxpayers to reduce or eliminate their capital gains tax liability. A partial rate reduction for capital gains is a much more cost-effective way of recognizing the inflation problem given current constraints on the treasury.

After inflation, the most significant component of the capital gains tax base is the return on risk. For large institutional investors, many of which are tax exempt, capital gains taxes hardly affect the return on risk. Other large investors that are not tax exempt nevertheless often are diverse enough to fend off a good deal of their supposed tax burden by trading off losses and gains in any given year. It is worth noting, however, that most of the nation's independent venture capital funds, which have been leaders in funding leading-edge hi-tech firms, did not exist before the Congress sharply cut capital gains tax rates in 1978.

Still, most of the money for start-up businesses in the United States comes not from venture capital industry or from pension funds and other tax-exempt entities but from mom and pop, aunts and uncles, friends, and the entrepreneur's own savings. With little collateral, the entrepreneur can only offer these investors a share in the profits. Most of these entrepreneurs and investors don't make it: they lose their money. Those who do make it tend to make it big. How should the tax system treat the ones who win or the ones who lose?

The principle of symmetric taxation offers a key. Before the 1986 tax reform, profits and losses were treated roughly symmetrically. Taxpayers who were full partners in an enterprise paid taxes on their share of the profits and were allowed to deduct any losses against other taxable income. This was purely symmetric taxation and it occurred at ordinary tax rates. Alternatively, some forms of investment entitled the taxpayer to receive capital gains tax treatment on profits or losses, so that investors who sold their stakes at a profit paid tax at the capital gains tax rate. However, the right to deduct capital losses against other taxable income was limited to $3,000 in excess of any capital gains for the year. As a result major losses were often not fully offset for tax purposes. This result was not quite symmetry, but offsetting asymmetries.

The Tax Reform Act of 1986 changed this. First, passive

investors in partnerships became subject to full taxation of their profits but were not allowed to deduct their losses. The tax collector became a full partner with the winners but not with the losers. Second, those who invested in other ways lost the favorable treatment of capital gains but were still stuck with the limit on the deductibility of losses. Symmetry was violated both ways, with the government always the winner.

The big investors in the venture capital industry were unaffected by these changes. Since a large portion of their investments produce capital gains, against which capital losses can be deducted, their losses are never "wasted." But the entrepreneurs and their small-time investors are not diversified. Almost all of their income is ordinary income. If the family venture goes bust they no longer have even the cold comfort of a healthy tax deduction. Under the new system the government still shares in the profits but does not share in the losses if the venture fails. Most important from the perspective of economic policy, by violating the principle of symmetric taxation, the government effectively taxes the returns on risk *more* heavily than it taxes other types of income. This is hardly a recipe for a dynamic economy.

Thus the second reason for a change in the capital gains tax is an allowance for risk taking. Unfortunately, allowing a full deduction for losses does encourage tax shelter abuses. But if the government cannot afford to be a full partner with the losers because of the tax shelter problem, it should not be a full partner with the winners. Direct investors in businesses should receive special capital gains tax treatment, a partial exclusion of capital gains from taxation sufficient to lower the effective top tax rate on their capital gains to between 15 and 20 percent.

This treatment should also apply to investors in common stock, but for different reasons. Corporate retained earnings comprise the third major source of capital gains. A corporation has a choice between paying its profits out in the form of dividends, which are taxed immediately to the shareholder, or reinvesting them in the corporation. When reinvested, retained earnings increase the amount of corporate assets behind each share of stock and over the long term increase the stock price. When the taxpayer sells the stock, he should reap a profit roughly equal to the value of the retained earnings.[2]

Because we do not wish to discourage the valuable practice of reinvesting earnings in the business, the taxpayer should pay the same tax whether profits come yearly as dividends or in one lump sum as a capital gain from the reinvestment of earnings. If there were no corporate income tax (or we had a cash flow income tax allowing immediate deductions of all net investment, including reinvestment of retained earnings), we could accomplish our end by taxing capital gains and ordinary (that is, dividend) income at the same rate. But under our current corporate tax, the retained earnings do not build up tax free but are subject to the corporate tax rate, which under current law is higher than all of the personal tax rates. The accumulating earnings are taxed at a higher tax rate than if the taxpayer had invested in some other asset.

Corporate retained earnings are a major part of our national savings. So as not to discourage investment in growth corporations—those that tend to reinvest rather than pay dividends—the capital gains tax on shares of stock in business corporations should get the same special exclusion as profits from investments in new ventures, lowering the effective capital gains rate on the sale of stock to 15 to 20 percent range.

Reducing the capital gains tax rate on business investment would expand the capital gains tax base, perhaps enough to actually increase revenue. Because capital gains taxes are not levied when the capital gains "happen," or accrue, but when the taxpayer chooses to sell an asset, taxpayers have great discretion over whether and when to pay capital gains taxes. Because capital gains income is so discretionary, the revenue-maximizing rate for capital gains taxes is much lower than for regular income taxes, and the rate at which the excess burden of the tax becomes unacceptable is lower still.

Consider an investor who bought some stock for $50 which

is now worth $200, for a net capital gain of $150. He expects to make $20 in profit each year from the $200 stock, a 10 percent annual return. But there is another security that the investor thinks will yield a 12 percent return. In the absence of capital gains taxes, the investor would sell the 10 percent investment and buy the 12 percent investment. Under the current tax law, however, the taxpayer would owe $42 in capital gains taxes (28 percent of the $150 profit) after selling the $200 stock, and retain only $158 to invest in the new asset. At the expected 12 percent rate of return, this would yield only $18.96, or less than the $20 the investor would make by keeping the original stock. Most people would choose not to sell, and the government would collect no revenue. Under the ERTA maximum capital gains rate of 20 percent, however, it would have been profitable to sell one stock and buy the other, and the government would also have made some money.

The current tax rates on capital gains, at record high average rates, are indefensible. We know that relatively high capital gains taxes discourage investment. We can also be pretty sure that a reduction in the current rates would either increase revenues or at least produce no more than trivial losses.[3]

The revenue consequences of rate reduction can be made even more favorable. The tax code currently complicates the taxation of capital gains by exempting from capital gains tax the assets in a taxpayer's estate at death. This exemption, reasonable in itself, is coupled with a provision that allows the heirs to "write up" the initial purchase price of the asset to its value at the date of death. They do this without paying any capital gains tax. In effect, the appreciation of assets during the decedent's life escapes capital gains tax entirely. This exemption causes taxpayers, particularly elderly persons concerned about leaving a large estate, to hold onto assets longer than they otherwise would, thus locking money into low-yielding assets, wasting national capital resources, and reducing capital gains tax revenue. Properly altering the exemption would both increase capital gains tax revenue and reduce the distorting effect on the economy of the capital gains tax.

There are two ways of reforming the capital gains tax treatment of assets left in an estate. The first, known as the "carryover basis" rule, would prevent heirs from adjusting the value of the property they inherit unless they paid capital gains tax. If an heir chose not to adjust, but sold the asset at a later date, the tax then due would be figured on the original purchase price, exposing to taxation the entire gain over the decedent's and the heir's lifetimes. The second alternative is a "realization at death" rule. This rule would assume for tax purposes that all property in the estate was sold at the time of death. The capital gains taxes on this assumed act would be due with the income taxes owed for the last year of the decedent's life. Either of these rules would reduce the incentives to hold existing assets, and thereby increase capital gains tax revenues. They would also mollify those who regard reduced capital gains taxes as a "loophole for the rich." And they would fall harder on large accumulations of inherited wealth than on the proceeds of new entrepreneurial enterprises.

The staff of the congressional Joint Committee on Taxation estimated that the annual revenue gain from taxing capital gains at death would be $4.9 billion in fiscal 1989. By combining taxation of capital gains at death with a sharp reduction in capital gains tax rates, we can encourage entrepreneurship, risk taking, and corporate investment while eliminating perverse incentives for investors to hold assets no longer profitable.

None of the changes discussed in this chapter positively encourage or subsidize business investment: They only remove existing roadblocks. In order to take full advantage of our hard work today and build the capital to work harder tomorrow, we must do more. Investment requires saving and the nation's savings rate is still among the lowest in the industrialized world. The American tax system, though vastly improved since the late 1970s, is still biased against savings. In order to take advantage of our current hard work, we must not only correct the remaining biases against saving but positively encourage it. The next thirty years will be a window of opportunity for the United States. We must make sure that opportunity is not wasted but saved.

Chapter 14

Saving the Future

> "What reason is there that he which laboreth much, and, sparing the fruits of his labor, consumeth little, should be charged more than he that living idly, getteth little and spendeth all he gets, seeing the one hath no more protection from the commonwealth than the other?"
>
> —THOMAS HOBBES, *Leviathan II*, 1651

Setting aside resources from current consumption so that an economy can work smarter in the future is the key to rising standards of living. But setting aside resources is not free. It requires a sacrifice of current living standards, the process known as saving.

One of the iron laws of economy is that a society cannot, in the long run, invest more than it saves. At present we are investing more in the United States than we are saving only by borrowing from abroad. This extra investment is beneficial, but it is unlikely that foreigners will continue to lend to us indefinitely. Ultimately we must raise our national savings rate or reduce our rate of investment.

The economics profession is quite clear that the national savings rate for the country must be raised. It is far less clear about how to do that. Most theories about why people save are based on the assumption that individuals save during what they regard as good times in order to prepare for hard times. People in their forties and fifties realize they are at their earnings peak and set money aside for retirement. Families also save for unusual expenses such as college education or illness. As a rule, however, the traditional motives for savings have been blunted by government programs to care for the aged and disabled, to finance college, and to cushion unemployment. People may be saving less in part because they have less fear of hard times.

This does not explain why Americans save less than, for instance, Germans, who have a welfare state at least as elaborate as ours. One possible explanation is that the German people define "good times" and "bad times" differently than Americans. As a rule, Germans have known harder times than Americans, who have never seen their nation and their economy completely destroyed by war. Bad times may seem more likely to the German people than to the American people, and they may be more impressed with current "good times" than Americans, who tend to expect good and ever better economic conditions. Germans may save more today in what they regard as "very good times" to compensate for the "very bad times" they fear.

One should not make too much of these ventures in mass psychology. They are plausible but not testable, nor do they provide any policy prescriptions. The United States could hardly arrange for a period of hard times in order to increase the national savings rate a few percent. An alternate—and more useful—explanation for low American savings rates is that our tax system punishes saving and rewards borrowing. With a tax system that virtually assures that money put into savings will have little more or even less purchasing power when it is withdrawn, it is not hard to see why Americans would rather consume than save.

In chapter 3 we noted that during the late 1970s inflation and taxes reduced the real return on interest income from most conventional sources to well below zero. Even today, with substantially lower inflation and taxes, many savings vehicles produce a negative return. A family in the 28 percent tax bracket earning 5.5 percent on a savings account keeps about 4 percent after tax. With inflation ranging from 3 to 6 percent, their real return ranges from 1 percent to minus 2 percent. More risky savings vehicles, such as corporate bonds, which often failed to pay positive real returns in the late 1970s, do pay a positive return today, but they do not pay nearly as much after taxes as they would if bondholders were fully protected from inflation.

The tax cuts of the 1980s went some way toward correcting the bias against savings. We could nearly eliminate that bias with another change in the tax code: The government should tax only that portion of interest income that exceeds the rate of inflation (the real interest rate). If savers were taxed only on the interest they earned above the inflation rate, they would at least be guaranteed a positive return and, all else being equal, a significantly higher return than they get today.

The tax system currently discourages savings. It also encourages people to borrow (dis-save) to finance current consumption. Again things are not quite as bad as they used to be. Back in 1980 most credit cards charged about 18 percent interest. Interest payments were deductible, cutting the after-tax cost of borrowing to just 9.2 percent for a family earning $50,000. With inflation running at 13.5 percent, the cost of waiting until next year to make a purchase in cash was actually 4.3 percent higher than buying now on a credit card. Spending was rewarded, thrift discouraged. The new tax law enacted in 1986 eliminated the deduction of interest payments except for home financing. The reformers intended this change as an incentive to thrift. But it appears to have had little practical effect beyond encouraging people to use home equity loans to finance consumer purchases. The reform thus did little to limit consumer debt and exacerbated another problem: America overborrows to finance housing.

Subsidized borrowing severely distorts the housing market.[1] People spend too much of their income on housing because it is tax favored. In most areas this tax favoritism bids up the prices of existing houses, though it may also encourage developers to build bigger, more expensive homes. Such tax distortions cause the housing market to favor high-income taxpayers for whom the home mortgage deduction is valuable enough to justify buying a home with a higher price tag. As a result, many would-be homeowners of more modest means may find themselves priced out of homes they could otherwise afford.

The solution is to make the tax system as neutral as possible with regard to borrowing and lending. Since under our suggested reform only the real interest rate received by lenders would be subject to tax, only the real interest rate paid on home mortgages or home equity loans should be deductible. In addition, limiting the maximum deduction for real mortgage interest to $10,000 would blunt the urge to finance consumer spending with mortgage debt as well as substantially solve the problem of tax subsidies raising housing prices. If lavish homes—or lavish prices for quite modest homes—were no longer deductible, moderate-income families would do better in the real estate bidding wars.

Such reforms would help eliminate the bias against savings. But we can do more. With a very modest loss of tax revenue we can build a tax program to substantially encourage the savings we need to sustain our investments in working smarter.

Under almost any circumstances a tax reform to encourage a national savings rate higher than today's would probably be a good idea. Such a reform is both particularly urgent and opportune right now because of the changing demographic characteristics of the American population and the long-term effect of such changes on the Social Security system and the federal budget. Right now we have enough prime age workers to both work harder and save more, so that we can work smarter in the future. In another thirty years we will be forced to work less hard as the proportion of people of prime productive ages declines and the number of older Americans increases. If we have not by then invested enough in a larger, smarter economy, we will be unable to adequately support today's workers in their retirement, and our global competitive position may erode.

Under the current set of economic and budgetary assumptions used by policy makers, the present annual surpluses in the Social Security system are forecast to increase substantially during the 1990s and continue through the first quarter of the twenty-first century. But the system will start running substantial deficits in the 2030s. These deficits are expected to grow markedly, consuming all of the accumulated surplus by mid-century.[2] The reason for this great shift in the cash flow position of the Social Security system is demographic. In the short run, the rapid rise in the size of the birth cohorts of the 1950s will increase the number of working-aged people relative to the number of retirees. For example, in the late 1990s the number of people aged twenty-five to sixty-four will increase at the annual rate of 9.0 per thousand, but the number aged sixty-five and over will increase at a rate of only 7.7 per thousand: The number of workers will rise 17 percent faster than the number of people of retirement age. When the children of the 1950s retire, however, the worker base per retiree will shrink.[3]

This demographic bulge suggests three problems for national savings. First, since the surpluses that the Social Security system will amass during the 1990s are not now committed to savings, this temporary windfall could be used by the federal government to permanently increase federal spending. Second, the nation must increase its rate of saving to provide baby boomers a comfortable retirement. Unless saving is increased now, so that we have a substantially larger economy by the second quarter of the next century, the burden of these retirees will substantially reduce living standards throughout the country. Finally, even if these problems can be worked out, the Social Security system will still face major deficits and an exhausted trust fund by the middle of the next century. As a result mid-century retirees probably will not be able to rely on Social Security for as large a portion of their retirement income as today's retirees. Many will retire into relative poverty unless they have built nest eggs of their own. America needs a long-term program to encourage retirement savings.

The idea of a tax-favored savings program is not new. Tax-exempt pension programs and savings programs for the self-employed have existed for many years. ERTA extended eligibility for Individual Retirement Accounts (IRAs) to all working

Americans. Under this program, taxpayers can contribute tax-free funds to an account that can accumulate interest, dividends, and capital gains, also tax free; tax is levied only when the funds are withdrawn from the account. The primary advantage to the saver in such a program is the tax-free growth of the funds. One dollar invested in an IRA at 8 percent interest grows to $4.66 in twenty years. If then taxed at a 28 percent rate, the current standard rate of income tax for most savers, the taxpayer retains $3.36. On the other hand, a taxpayer saving outside the IRA program, pays taxes on the initial dollar when it is earned and each year on the interest. Even though the taxpayer receives the same pre-tax return of 8 percent, the compounded tax on the earnings leaves him or her with only $2.21, or 34 percent less at the end of twenty years.

The major difficulty with promoting savings through the existing IRA program is that contributors may not withdraw their funds until age fifty-nine and a half without substantial penalty. Retirement is an important motivation for savings, but hardly the only one. Young families save for the down payment on a home, and later for college tuition. Only after the kids are out of college do most families focus on retirement savings. Government data confirm that the existing IRA program primarily attracts taxpayers in their fifties and sixties.

The government should turn the IRA program into an Individual Savings Account program, to encourage contributors to save for a home, for education, or for retirement, for medical expenses, or temporary disability. In practice, it would probably be impracticable to monitor the use of the funds after withdrawal. But the government should do what it could to ensure that ISAs were used to save for worthwhile longer-term goals. For example, it could require that funds be kept in the ISA account for at least three to five years before they could be withdrawn without penalty. This more liberal policy regarding withdrawals would greatly enhance the attractiveness of saving for younger families.

A second defect of the current IRA system was added in the

Tax Reform Act of 1986. The maximum $2,000 contribution to IRAs was limited to married taxpayers earning under $40,000 and single taxpayers earning under $25,000. Married taxpayers earning between $40,000 and $50,000 were allowed partial deductions, as were single taxpayers earning between $25,000 and $35,000. These income limits barred roughly half of all taxpayers who had previously contributed to IRAs from making additional deductible contributions. The new ISA system should be open to all taxpayers.

The 1986 reformers limited the IRA deduction in part out of fear that well-to-do Americans would simply roll existing assets into the program and not increase their savings. Economic studies suggest that this had been happening to a limited extent, but that the program attracted a significant amount of net savings. Moreover, restricting contributions on the basis of total income is an inefficient means of excluding rollover savings. Young people with high incomes but little wealth might be highly motivated by an IRA or ISA program. It is older savers with low incomes but lots of existing assets who are more likely to be "rollovers."

Rules to discourage rollovers should focus not on total income but on the capital income, which is a more accurate indication of whether the taxpayer is capable of rolling over into the ISA or will increase net savings in contributing. The most effective way to protect against rollovers is to place a floor on the deductibility of contributions, based on the taxpayer's capital income, and then raise the current ceiling on deductible contributions to $5,000 per worker. Most of the additional contributions under the higher ceiling would necessarily be net savings: Few households save more than $2,000 in a year. The floor on deductibility should be equal to half the capital income of the taxpayer.

Under this plan, a two-earner married couple with $3,000 in interest and dividend income could contribute up to $10,000 to their ISA, but only the contribution in excess of $1,500 would be deductible. This floor helps ensure that our couple only gets a deduction on "money it would not have saved anyway." We measure the floor by capital income because that roughly indicates the possession of assets that could be rolled over. People without much capital income by definition do not have much in the way of financial assets to roll over. Young couples starting out in life with no assets would find this program a very attractive way to build a nest egg.

The usual objection to such a dramatic tax favor for a savings plan is that it would cost too much in tax revenue. That argument lacks merit, particularly today. The ISA program would cost the government revenue as contributions are made. Most of that revenue would be recouped in the future when the funds were withdrawn by the taxpayer. An ISA program would shift the timing of tax revenue, but the present value of the tax revenue year would not greatly change. Consider a taxpayer in the 28 percent bracket who contributes a dollar to an ISA. For twenty years the contribution grows at 8 percent per year. The ISA program reduces the government's revenue by 28 cents the year the dollar is deposited into the account, and by a few cents each year the interest is compounded tax free. The government's revenue then increases by $1.30 when the funds are withdrawn. By definition,* the present value of the taxes received when the funds are withdrawn is 28 cents, exactly equal to the taxes forgone when the funds were deposited in the account. The only cost to the government of shifting tax receipts through time via an ISA is the forgone taxes on the accruing interest, an amount far less than usually claimed as the revenue cost of an ISA program.

As a rule, individuals would be able to earn a higher return on the ISA than the rate at which the government must borrow, which would mean that the present value of tax revenues may actually be increased by an ISA program. For example, if the

---

*The present discounted value of an initial investment plus accumulated interest at some point in the future is equal to the initial investment if one assumes that the discount rate is equal to the rate of interest, a reasonable assumption since the government can act as both borrower and lender in capital markets.

government must borrow at 8 percent to fund the forgone taxes on the ISA, but the individual earns 10 percent in the ISA account, then both the government and the individual will be better off in the end.

Because of the demographic trends mentioned earlier, shifting current government revenue into the future is a good idea. In fact, the upcoming fiscal imbalances in the Social Security system make it imperative to shift tax revenue from the 1990s to the 2040s. The ISA would be a perfect tool for the job. During the 1990s and early in the twenty-first century, the baby boomers will be at their peak earning and saving years. They will be willing and able to save and would be highly motivated by a tax-free savings plan. During the same time, for the same demographic reasons, Social Security tax revenues will be temporarily inflated, producing a large Social Security surplus. Later in the twenty-first century, as the baby boom generation retires it will withdraw funds from ISAs (and pay the taxes due) at the very time the Social Security system will encounter difficulty meeting its obligations to the new retirees.

The revenue effect of an ISA program meets both the surplus problem of the 1990s and early twenty-first century and the prospective deficits mid-century. The ISAs reduce government revenue only in the 1990s and early 2000s, coincident with large government surpluses in the Social Security accounts, and to the extent that ISAs reduce government revenues at that time, they will discourage the government from using the Social Security surpluses to justify a spending binge or the undertaking of new obligations that would bankrupt the treasury twenty years hence.*

---

*In theory Social Security revenues and general revenues are quite distinct and a Social Security surplus should not effect general spending. In practice the distinction breaks down. For instance, a Social Security surplus makes it easier to finance the general deficit: Social Security funds can be used to buy government bonds, reducing the government's interest charges. Alternatively, since the revenue capacity of the personal income tax is limited by FICA taxes and vice versa, Social Security funds could be switched to general revenues by the camouflage of matching Social Security tax cuts and personal income tax increases. More boldly, the politicians could simply take the Social Security funds

The ISAs would increase government revenue when the contributions are withdrawn at mid-century, exactly the time the government would need extra funds to help finance Social Security payments. Assuming current saving rates, the extra taxes collected on withdrawals from the program would exceed the taxes forgone on new contributions by $90 billion real dollars in 2040. That is roughly equal to the real Social Security deficit now estimated for that year. In the near term the revenue effect of the ISA program would consume roughly two-thirds of the projected Social Security surplus in the year 2000 and between 40 and 50 percent in the first two decades of the twenty-first century. In effect the government would be banking the tax reductions of the early twenty-first century for use when taxpayers withdraw their money mid-century.

The main reasons to implement an ISA program are to encourage Americans to save for their own needs, to wean the United States from its addiction to credit, and to build capital for investment. The time to begin this process is in the 1990s, when we will have an unusual demographic opportunity in the baby-boom generation reaching middle age and working harder than ever. But unless we encourage savings now, their hard work may go for nought as they become the first generation in American history to retire less comfortably than the previous generation.

The government should be frank with the baby boomers about the prospect they face. Only a higher national savings rate will build a capital intensive, "working smarter" economy capable of supporting them in their old age. Only increased personal savings will make up for inevitable contraction in Social Security benefits. A little frankness about the future, and a program to encourage savings now, could change that future before it is too late.

---

and spend them, either on temporary benefit increases or general spending. It really is best, therefore, to think of Social Security and general revenue funds as substantially fungible, an assumption we make throughout the argument presented here.

Chapter 15

Helping Hands

> "Thus is the problem of Rich and Poor to be solved. The law of accumulation will be left free; the laws of distribution free. Individualism will continue, but the millionaire will be but a trustee of the poor; entrusted for a season with a great part of the increased wealth of the community, but administering it for the community far better than it could or would have done for itself."
>
> —ANDREW CARNEGIE[1]

The saying goes, "A rising tide raises all boats." That is true only if the boats are seaworthy. Economic growth is necessary for us to meet the needs of the poor, the sick, and the disadvantaged, but it is not sufficient. Some people will always need the special help of others no matter how rich the nation may become.

Our tax system should do more than foster growth. It should help us provide for those who cannot provide for themselves. A growing economy and an efficient tax system do help this process by making it easier to fund government social programs. But a quarter century of churning ever more dollars through government has not solved our social problems.

The 1980s close with roughly the same percentage of the population in poverty as in 1965. Those who blame this on "cuts" in social programs are playing fast and loose with the facts. Today government transfer payments comprise one of every seven dollars of personal income, compared to one of thirteen dollars in 1965. Federal and state transfer payments, including roughly $300 billion for Social Security and Medicare

(without which many of our elderly would be poor), are nearly
$600 billion. That is more than $16,000 for every man, woman,
and child in poverty. Of course, most of this money never
reaches the poor. Most is paid to people who are not poor to
begin with as part of what have come to be known as "middle-
class transfers." And a great deal of money goes to administrative costs.

While inflation from 1978 through 1987 amounted to 74 percent, federal spending grew 179 percent on medical care, 112
percent on nutrition programs, and 244 percent on housing
programs for the poor.[2] For all the money we have spent, poverty seems as great a problem as ever. We still see daily evidence
of people without adequate food, housing, health care, or hope.

Government is good at moving money but it is a terribly
inefficient provider of services in complex situations. The government will send more than $300 billion to the elderly this year
at a cost of pennies on the dollar thereby greatly reducing
poverty among the elderly. In fact, Social Security and Medicare have been our most successful anti-poverty programs. In
the United States today few old people who worked during
their lives are poor, though in the past it was quite common to
"die in the harness" or retire into poverty. Simple government
transfers work for these people because their problems are relatively simple. Unlike the underclass, they did not live lives of
disorganization and despair in the inner city or the hills of
Appalachia, or face a lifetime of discrimination. They had all
the personal resources for living ordered and frugal lives. Their
single problem is that, but for Social Security and Medicare,
they would be short of money.

When cash is the only problem, government can define a
category of apparently needy people, send them checks, and
solve the problem reasonably efficiently. But the government
cannot help an individual whose life has fallen apart by desig-
nating him as part of that great mass, the poor, and sending a
check. Real poverty is an affliction of individuals who need not
just cash but help from other people.

Our most pressing social problems are the problems of people who lack not just financial but personal resources. There are an estimated 300,000 homeless people on the streets in the United States. A government program that gave each one of those people a check for $10,000 would cost a total of $3 billion. (If you don't think that you personally could get your life in order for $10,000, name the amount.) One year after the implementation of such a program, how many homeless individuals would still be living in the streets? I think we would all be delighted if the number fell by as much as a third.

The problem is not money. These individuals lack the supportive relationships of family and friends that allow the rest of us to cope with day-to-day living. Many are mentally and emotionally ill, or simply ill-trained for life. A check from the government, by itself, will not solve such problems. Government will never solve their problems because it will never know these people except as members of a vast group of those who are statistically qualified for government aid. Really caring about people requires knowing them. The problems of people are best faced by other people on a person-by-person basis. Invariably, the closer the provider of social services is to the individual in need, the more effective is the help. Personal helping may be as informal as individuals helping friends and neighbors who are down on their luck. Often, more formal and organized programs are needed, such as small community-based charitable groups who run shelters or soup kitchens or care for preschool youngsters while their parents work. Local church or secular groups may operate these charitable activities; almost all such groups are closer to their clients than government agencies can ever be.

These groups are more effective at providing social services because they have to be. The volunteers who staff these charities are there because they want to make a difference, not draw a paycheck. Unless some obvious good is done, the volunteers quit and the charity goes out of business. Similarly, the financial support for these local groups is provided by local donors who see the good being done and want to lend their financial support. If the donors do not see results, the money stops flowing. Unlike the government, voluntary providers of social services are subject to the test of the market, which in charity work is also the test of the heart. The country's charities must do good or they will not do well. A government agency obtains funding by demonstrating that the problem is still there and growing. A charity continues its funding by solving the problem.

Charities do more than care for the needy. Nearly every social service we now take for granted—hospitals, schools, libraries, scientific research, and the arts—have been traditionally supported by charitable activity, not state funding. Government encroachment is relatively recent, and the government's performance has rarely been as successful or as efficient as the charities it sought to supplement or replace.

Sometimes the difference in efficiency between the charitable and government sectors is so extreme as to be absurd. John Chubb of the Brookings Institution is the author of an important new study on American education, *What Price Democracy?* (Washington, D.C.: Brookings, 1989). Chubb tells of calling the New York City Board of Education to find out how many employees worked in the central administration. Not the number of principals and the like in the various schools, mind you, but the number of bureaucrats in the central office. Chubb placed more than a half dozen calls before finding someone who knew the answer. But that person was not authorized to disclose the number. It took more than a half dozen more calls to find someone who both knew the number and was authorized to tell a member of the public what the number was. It turned out there were six thousand bureaucrats sitting in the school system's central office.

Then Chubb called the Archdiocese of New York to find out how many people worked in the central office of the archdiocesan school system, which serves about one-fifth as many pupils as the New York public schools. The first person he reached said she didn't know, and Chubb thought he was in for another runaround. Then she added, "Wait a minute, let me count." The answer was twenty-six.

Because charitable organizations are so efficient, many observers have suggested the government funnel money to these organizations. In fact, between one-third and one-half of all the funds received by charitable organizations are either government grants or government fees for services such as running hospitals, orphanages, and other caring facilities.[3] Programs such as vouchers for education would carry this a step further. Though this approach may make public spending more efficient, it doesn't go as far as it might. Direct government funding of private charities still costs society both the dollar raised in taxes, plus the excess burden of raising the dollar in taxes, in order to give some bureaucrat a dollar (minus the bureaucrat's share in salary) to give to the charitable organization of the government's choice.

The tax system offers a better approach. Economic research shows that charitable giving is very sensitive to its tax treatment. Every 1 percent reduction in the after-tax cost of charitable giving produces an additional 1.2 percent to 1.3 percent in donations. Stated differently, every $1 the government spends in *increased* tax incentives produces an additional $1.20 to $1.30 for charities.[4]

Some cynics claim that people give to charity just for the deductions. If that were true, it would be very foolish behavior. Under current law for example, a top-bracket donor who contributes $1,000 to a charity gets a tax break of only $280. The donor is still out of pocket $720. Even when tax rates were much higher, donors still were net losers. People who give to charity want to do good. The deduction just encourages them to do a bit more. Part of it seems to be that people prefer to do good through a charity of their own choice rather than through the government. This may be why the deduction encourages additional contributions above and beyond what they would have given. In short, people will give up some of their own consumption if it means that government will have less to spend and charities will have more at their disposal.

This represents a marked vote of "no confidence" in government social services. But government leaders who are genuinely concerned with meeting social needs can use this attitude to meet their goals. Spending government funds on tax subsidies for private philanthropy will provide more funds to these efficient providers of social services than direct appropriations.

I have made this argument numerous times in meetings with congressional staff and have met with very little success. The Congress does not quarrel with the numbers, but with the idea that individuals should decide which charities receive the money. To members of Congress and their aides that seems undemocratic. The democratic way to allocate public money is through the legislative process, of which they are a key part. Though it is easy to be cynical about their motives, most of these people have been drawn to work on Capitol Hill by an idealistic view of the role of government. But their faith in the omniscience of the state inflicts a high price on the country's needy.

Direct federal spending on social needs is not as democratic as one might suppose. Consider for example the National Endowment for the Arts and the National Science Foundation. Each doles out money to those who have mastered an application process, a skill commentators label "grantsmanship." The decision who to fund is not made by a majority vote in the Congress but by bureaucrats in these agencies, who also conduct surveys of leading academics from the relevant fields in a process known as peer review. There is no "democratic allocation" of funds. The choice is made by individuals. The question is whether millions of people across the country should decide who will receive the money they personally contribute, or whether a handful of bureaucrats will decide for us. Private charitable contributions provide money not only more efficiently than direct government appropriations but in a more diverse manner. Generous tax treatment of individual donor decisions can fund projects that the Congress and the bureaucrats have never even heard of. And because these donors have their own money at stake the national commitment to charitable causes will also increase.

What do I mean by "generous treatment"? Simple tax deductibility, as we now have it, does not make the grade. A straight deduction does not subsidize giving. It merely prevents the government from taxing donors on money they give away. Without a deduction, the government would send me a tax bill for 28 percent of my income even if I gave away every dollar I earned. A straight deduction simply makes the tax system neutral for contributors. Generous tax treatment means going above and beyond deductibility, but it need not mean that we provide a special bonus for every dollar contributed. After all, most individuals would give something regardless of the tax consequences. Instead, generous tax treatment should be used to help establish a new social standard of generosity, and to reward those people who meet or exceed that standard. The standard should be well above the average contribution rate, which is between 1 and 2 percent of income. My personal choice for such a standard is 5 percent of income. Taxpayers giving more than 5 percent of their income should receive an extra deduction or extra tax credit for all funds contributed over the threshold amount.

Consider briefly an example of how such a system might work. We might allow an additional 15 percent credit for every dollar given over 5 percent of income. A family earning $50,000 that contributed $4,000 to charity would receive an ordinary deduction for the first $2,500 it contributed and the ordinary deduction plus an extra 15 percent credit for the remaining $1,500 of its contribution. Their extra tax benefit over and above current law would be $225. Families with the same income who gave less than $2,500 would only receive the ordinary deduction for their gifts. Thus, the entire extra incentive to give is focused on gifts well in excess of what the typical taxpayer might contribute.

Such a threshold or floor gives people a goal to shoot for. Economic studies suggest that a threshold is even more efficient than the ordinary tax deduction and may prompt people to give significantly more than the usual $1.30 for each additional $1.00 of tax benefits. A tax incentive with a floor, such as the 5 percent threshold, will produce as much as $1.50 to $1.70 in *extra* charitable giving for every dollar the government expends on such a program.[5] I know of no other government program, enacted or prospective, that even claims to do a $1.50 worth of good for every $1.00 it costs the taxpayers.

A standard objection to such a plan is that its tax benefits would go primarily to the rich. This is not true. Charitable giving is roughly proportional to family income, after controlling for the age and size of the family. The benefits of such a program would be distributed in proportion to income. Most benefits would go to the middle class. A 5 percent floor would require the rich to give quite a bit of money before qualifying.

Nonetheless, I think society would be better off if the rich did become the primary beneficiaries of this extra charitable incentive. It would be far better if the great fortunes of the country were spent on meeting social needs rather than on conspicuous consumption or building dynastic fortunes. I would much rather see a multimillion dollar fortune funding the owner's alma mater than funding a life of luxury for his grandchildren.

Giving wealthy people a tax incentive to do good seems much more sensible than most government expenditures. The purpose of the 5 percent threshold is not merely to establish a financial incentive, but a social standard. Before the days of the welfare state, the social and religious standard of giving was the tithe, a tenth of one's income. Perhaps it was honored more in the breach than the observance, but the existence of a standard gave people something by which to measure their own behavior. They might not always live up to the standard, but they almost certainly did better for having it.

In these days of welfare entitlements, it is very hard to convince people to tithe. "That's what taxes are for," they say and give 1 or 2 percent. With the program outlined here, plus a bit of leadership from Capitol and Cathedral, we should be able to establish a new standard, the half-tithe, or 5 percent. The government might even send those taxpayers who donate at least 5 percent a certificate. Those who enjoy that sort of thing could have the certificates framed and set on their wall for the Joneses to see. A bit tacky, perhaps, but it seems much better to have a nation of neighbors competing for the poor than for the Porsche.

There is a long tradition of naming parks, hospitals, and other public buildings after the donor who paid for them. The nation's small towns are littered with Carnegie libraries. On a smaller scale, churches name pews after donors to the church's building fund. My alma mater, along with most other private colleges, has different donor clubs named after famous alumni: Hawthorne, Longfellow, etc. The more you give, the more select a donor club you are admitted to. Critics of private philanthropy point to these practices and say that giving is just a form of self-aggrandizement, unworthy of favorable tax treatment. Such criticism misses the point. The philanthropists memorialized in hospitals and museums around the country, people who gave to help others, are the kind of role models the country needs more of. They are models not only of economic success, but of civic virtue. A century from now young children visiting the local library will ask, who was Andrew Carnegie? The story they will hear will teach a lot more about brotherhood than vanity.

For all the critics talk of pride, their criticism of such displays is really a form of envy. No one will ever name a library, or a church pew, after the critics of philanthropy. Neither pride nor envy are attractive qualities, but they can be channeled into usefulness. If the pride and the envy which abides in each of us could be appeased with public recognition of philanthropic activity, America would be a richer place.

Do we really need the tax system to make us do the good we should do anyway? It would be nice if we did not. But we know that tax incentives work, and that private charities outperform many public programs. A public reward for private virtue will help America to do her best at doing good.

Chapter 16

Fairness for Families

"The root of the state is in the family."
—MENEIUS (372–289 B.C.)

One of the key challenges of tax policy is to keep the tax system in tune with changes in society. In the United States, no change is more dramatic than the rapid entry of women into the labor force. Just twenty-five years ago, there were twice as many men working as women. Today, 45 percent of the people employed in the United States are women. One family in six is headed by a single female, compared with one family in ten as recently as the 1960s. More than two-thirds of these single parent families are self-supporting, with incomes in excess of the poverty level. In 58 percent of married couples under age sixty-five, both spouses work. Although many women still work part-time, the wife provides at least 30 percent of the household's earnings for two-earner couples 42 percent of the time.[1]

The changing shape of families and the growing role of women as wage earners is a challenge for the tax system. Married women entering the labor force face quite high effective tax rates. One of the important changes in the 1981 tax bill was the Two Earner Deduction, which reduced the marriage penalty and thus reduced the marginal tax rates of married women. Women responded powerfully to these tax changes, increasing their paid work time and reducing the revenue cost of the 1981 tax bill. Nevertheless, married working women still face the most punitive effective tax rates of any major group in our society.[2]

High tax rates on married women's work are a remnant of the

days when women's paid work was considered optional or even self-indulgent. Yet today the overwhelmingly majority of wives or mothers who work do so primarily for economic reasons rather than simply for a sense of fulfillment. Punitive taxation of these women punishes the American families who can afford it least. Moreover, women who do stay home to raise their families, thus providing a great unpaid service to the society as well as their children, often find that as result their families are hard pressed financially. We must not only end the punitive taxation of married working women but also lighten the tax burden of all families during those expensive child-rearing years. One of the key tax challenges of the 1990s will be to curb the tax burden on married women and mothers because when we do that we curb the tax burden on families.

The tax code particularly penalizes women in three roles: as the spouses traditionally responsible for child care, as single mothers, and as married women who feel they must work outside the home as well as in it. The tax system should not explicitly encourage or discourage a woman from filling any of these roles, but aid her in whichever she choices. The tax code should enable each woman to make the right choice for herself and her family without having to worry about tax consequences. This book has documented the gains to the economy of freeing individual decisions from overweening tax distortions. Both the economy and American families will gain from guaranteeing married women and single mothers the same freedom.

Though supply-siders heretofore have concentrated much of their energy on eliminating the barriers to work, saving, and investment faced by upper-bracket taxpayers, the greatest barriers to increased production are no longer faced by high-income Americans, but by low- and moderate-income parents of small children. One important reason is the high cost of day care. Consider, for example, the hypothetical case of Beth and Fred, a married couple with one young child. Fred earns $15,000 per year as a maintenance man in a local school. His income keeps the family above the poverty line of $10,300 per year, but can't support a middle-class standard of living. As a result, Beth is considering taking a $10,000 per year job as a receptionist. In their town, the cost of formal day care for their two-year-old child is $3,000. If Beth works, she will pay $1,500 in federal income taxes, $750 in Social Security taxes, and $500 in state income taxes. Without help from the tax code in the form of a credit or deduction for child-care expenses, the $3,000 cost of child care would raise the cost of working to $5,750, or more than 57 percent of her salary. After expenses, she would take home just $2.13 an hour, well below the minimum wage. The tax code does provide some help now, but not much and not very efficiently.

The situation is far worse for a single mother for whom the only alternative to working is welfare. With welfare, a single mother of one might receive $7,000 per year, tax free. Say she considered a job as a secretary at $14,000 per year, twice as much as her welfare payments. Under current law, she would not pay any federal income tax, but would still be liable for $1,000 in Social Security tax and $500 in state income tax. After paying $3,000 in child care expenses, she would take home $9,500, just $2,500 more than she makes on welfare. In effect, her tax rate on the $14,000 is 82 percent. Her net income is increased by just 18 percent of her $14,000 salary when she goes to work.

The best way to think about the tax treatment of working mothers is to regard child care as "a cost of doing business." A business is not taxed on the total amount of money it takes in, but on how much is left after costs. For parents going to work, child care is an unavoidable cost of "doing business," which is why the Congress in recent years has made some allowances in the tax code for day care. Not all expenses involved in producing income are considered costs for tax purposes. For example, you are not allowed to deduct the costs of commuting to work. Your decision to live in the next county rather than next door to your job is considered a personal convenience, not a business necessity. Similarly, child care expenses were once considered personal, because parents were considered to have chosen to have children.

The Congress changed this in the Revenue Act of 1954. The debate was intense. Many members of Congress feared that if women were encouraged to work outside the home their children would grow up wild. Congressman Mason argued

> I know of dozens of instances in my own little town where the mother learned she could earn money during World War II and now insists upon doing it while the children are running loose and becoming a nuisance in the town. I would not want to give that kind of mother any exemption for whomever she hires . . . Our problem, sir, is to draw a line between those women who have to work, are compelled to work because their husbands do not earn enough, or because they are unable or incapable of earning it, and those women who want to work to earn extra money to buy things they want that their husbands cannot buy for them.[3]

Congress agreed to a deduction for paid child care expenses up to $600, the equivalent of about $2,700 in 1987, but insisted that it be limited to families who absolutely needed the mother's paycheck. Only families with incomes under $4,500 (roughly $20,000 in 1987) were eligible for the full deduction. Families earning over $5,100 ($22,800 in 1987) were excluded entirely.

This method of allowing for child care expenses established two important principles. First, the allowance should be based on need. Second, child care expenses should be treated like the expenses incurred in running a business: They should be deducted from the worker's total income to arrive at the net income received from working.

As time passed, the principle of need broke down. In 1976 the deduction was changed into a flat 20 percent tax credit for child care expenses up to $2,000, regardless of a family's income or tax rate. The Economic Recovery Tax Act of 1981 (ERTA) somewhat restored the focus on need by increasing the credit to 30 percent for families with incomes of $10,000 or less. Under ERTA the credit declined by one percentage point for every $2,000 of income over $10,000. Thus a family with $14,000 in income would receive a 28 percent credit. Taxpayers with incomes over $28,000 received a flat 20 percent credit. In addition, ERTA raised the amount of the child care expenses eligible for the credit to $2,400 for a single child and $4,800 for two or more children.

By 1985 8.5 million families were claiming the child care credit. In total $3.2 billion in tax credits was awarded to families, an increase of 574 percent from the inception of the credit in 1976. Despite the ERTA reforms, the credit's benefits still go mostly to middle- and upper-income families. In 1988 roughly 43 percent of the credit went to families making over $50,000 while only 23 percent went to families making under $20,000, even though the latter group is more numerous. In 1985 single parent households with incomes under $20,000 received an average credit of $361 while couples earning $100,000 to $200,000 received an average credit of $405.

The current tax treatment of child care has strayed far from its original purpose of helping families in which both parents must work outside the home. To get back on track we must keep four objectives in mind.

First, any benefits for paid day care should focus on those who need it the most. This means providing special support for both single parents and low-income married couples.

Second, the program should allow parents to choose how their children are cared for. At present, only about one-fourth of the nation's children who receive non-parental care go to a formal day care center. Most day care is provided by relatives and neighbors, and parents seem to like it that way. The government must recognize that parents are usually the best judges of their children's needs and refrain from using the program to herd children into commercial day care against their parents' wishes.

Third, the program should be cost effective. The days of

throwing money at a problem just to make ourselves feel good are over. A well-designed child care program might be largely self-financing, as it would reduce welfare payments and increase revenues from two-earner families.

Fourth, not all parents should be expected to work as a matter of national policy. In some cases, the family, the federal treasury, and society would all clearly be better off if at least one parent stayed home. It would make little economic sense for a married woman with two or more children to work at a minimum wage job while the government picked up the check for child care. This is especially true for infants, who often cost more to care for than older children and particularly need a mother's attention. Because keeping a parent at home often is the right thing to do, we should ease the tax burden on all families with children regardless of whether both parents work.

The existing child care credit provides a useful starting point, but needs a number of modifications. First, it should be made refundable. Under current law, taxpayers can only use the child care credit if they have an income tax liability. Lower-income taxpayers, who owe little or nothing, receive little or no benefit from the credit. In order to concentrate assistance on those who need it most, taxpayers must be able to get a credit even if they owe no tax. (This is known as refundability, and is a characteristic of another low-income tax program, the earned income tax credit.) Making the child care credit refundable under current law would cost $360 million in 1988. Of this sum, 77 percent would go to single-parent households and 91 percent would benefit households with incomes below $20,000.

A second change should be to increase dramatically the amount of the credit, particularly for low- and moderate-income families. Under current law, the maximum credit rate is 30 percent, declining to 20 percent for families making over $28,000. The credit should start at 50 percent for families making $10,000 or less, and decline to 20 percent for families making $40,000 or more. This change would cost $810 million in

1988, of which 84 percent would go to families earning under $30,000.

The third major change in the tax credit should be to establish a special credit for single parents, for whom government help with child care expenses may be the only alternative to welfare. An additional 15 percent credit could be added to the usual credit for all single-parent families at a total cost of $510 million.

The combined costs of these adjustments would be about $2.4 billion. The money would be targeted to those who truly need it. Families earning under $30,000 would receive 88 percent and single-parent families would receive 76 percent of these additional funds. There is simply no way that a direct government spending program (such as government-funded day care centers), with monstrous administrative overhead and complex regulations, could match these support levels or the degree of distributional equity for anything like that cost.

The program could be made more equitable and slightly less expensive by one more change. Presently, parents are eligible for a credit on expenses up to the full amount of the earnings of the lower-earning spouse. Thus the mostly well-to-do married women with exceptionally well-paying part-time jobs can get a government subsidy for forty or fifty hours of child care a week, though they may be working only twenty. This inequity could be substantially redressed by limiting the amount of child care expenses eligible for the credit to one-third of the wages of the lower-earning spouse. This would save $400 million a year and make the credit distributionally more equitable. With this change, 93 percent of the additional benefits of the program would go to families earning under $30,000.

These four changes in the child care credit are designed to help mothers who work. Because we know how important maternal care is for infants, the government should also help women who decide to leave work while their children are very young. There should be an Infant Care Credit for women who forgo their regular child care tax credit by quitting work to take care of newborn children. This Infant Care Credit might provide up to one-third of the former earnings, up to $10,000, of a mother with children under age two. The amount of the credit should be geared to the remaining earnings of the family. Families with incomes under $10,000 should be eligible for the full credit; at higher income levels the credit should be reduced and gradually phased out. If implemented in 1990, this program would cost a total of $1.9 billion. It would provide an alternative to child care for families of low and moderate incomes.

Finally, we must aid all families with children regardless of how many parents are working. In the past, the law fully recognized the special contributions to society of all families with children, and the special burdens they face, by allowing generous deductions for every child supported by a household's income. This is only basic fairness and common sense. A household consisting of a single person earning $40,000 has a per capita income of $40,000. A family of four with a total income of $40,000 has a per capita income of $10,000. Surely they should not be paying the same in taxes.

The income tax historically took this difference into account by allowing hefty personal exemptions for each family member. Just after the World War II the personal exemption stood at $600. Accounting for subsequent inflation and the rise in real income, the exemption would have to be $6,000 today to provide comparable relief. Instead, it is only $2,000. Families are overdue for a raise.

To make an increase in the personal exemption as cost effective as possible, it should be targeted to families with young children, since they are the most expensive to support. Form 2000, the model income tax presented in chapter 17 raises the ordinary exemption for children and other dependents to $3,000 and then provides an extra $2,000 for each dependent under the age of four. This change would remove millions of families from the income tax roles altogether in 1990 and would substantially reduce the tax burdens of millions more.

Changing times require changes in the tax law. These changes

Fairness for Families

in the tax treatment of child care would help today's families carry their financial burdens as well as preserving new-found freedoms for women. It is quite likely that much of the cost of the child care provisions of these programs would be recouped by lower welfare payments and in higher income taxes from women who would otherwise would not work for pay. There should be a long-term return as well: the better the job we do now of raising our children the healthier, happier, and wealthier will be the country in the next century.

Several other inequities in the way the tax code treats working women must also be addressed. For instance, the tax code currently includes a penalty on working single mothers. Although the official language of the tax code is gender neutral, working women are the primary victims because they head most single-parent families.

The tax code provides three filing statuses for taxpayers: single, married, and head of household. This latter category is designed for single parents. To file as a head of household you must be unmarried but supporting a child under age 18. The tax rates applied are roughly midway between those applied to single filers (which are higher) and those applied to married couples (which are lower).

This compromise makes no sense. Single-parent families have nothing in common with single people and everything in common with other families. Nearly one family in five is headed by a single parent and more than a quarter of all the children in the United States live in single-parent households. A majority will live in single-parent families at one time or another. Nevertheless, head-of-household (HoH) taxpayers pay more income tax than married couples with the same number of family members. Table 16.1 illustrates the situation for families with three members; in the case of the head-of-household return, the taxpayer is typically a mother with two children, while the married couple typically has a single child.

The "single-parent tax" is most important at the bottom of the income scale and at the top. It could be eliminated at rela-

TABLE 16.1

Income Taxes for Three-Person Families

Income	Married Taxpayers	Heads of Households	Difference
$15,000	$422	$512	21%
$25,000	2,122	2,212	4
$35,000	3,622	3,823	6
$50,000	7,094	8,023	13
$75,000	14,094	15,178	8

tively little cost, $900 million per year, by making the head-of-household rate schedule the same as the married rate schedule. Such a change would primarily benefit low- and moderate-income taxpayers. Of the total savings, 38 percent, or $340 million, would benefit taxpayers earning less than $20,000 per year. More than 91 percent of the benefit from such a change would benefit taxpayers earning under $50,000 per year.

The old phrase "You're damned if you do and you're damned if you don't" applies well to working women and taxes. While single mothers must pay the single-parent tax described above, married working women pay another: the marriage penalty, partly eliminated by ERTA but restored by the 1986 tax reform.

Consider, for example, the case of a newly married couple, John and Mary. John is a construction foreman earning $30,000 per year while Mary earns $30,000 as a head nurse at the local hospital. Before they married, each paid $4,693 in federal income taxes, for a combined total of $9,386. As a married couple, they now pay $10,440, $1,054 more than when they were single. The reason for this $1,054 "marriage tax" is that the couple is now treated as a single taxpaying unit. When they are forced to combine their incomes by the tax law, a greater percentage of their income is taxed at a higher tax bracket, so their taxes go up.

The marriage penalty is particularly severe on women like Mary who wish to pursue a career. In contrast, consider the tax consequences faced by Bill and Betty, high-school sweethearts who decided to marry when Bill finished law school and joined a prestigious law firm. In his job, Bill earns $57,000, and as a single taxpayer would pay $12,698 in federal income taxes. Betty, who lived with her parents until she married, earns $3,000 doing occasional work for a temp agency. She paid no federal income tax. After marriage they will pay income tax of $10,440 on $60,000, the same as John and Mary, but $2,298 less than Bill would pay in taxes as a single taxpayer. In short, Bill and Betty receive a "marriage bonus" of $2,298.

As discussed earlier, ERTA's Two Earner Deduction made a good attempt at limiting the marriage tax. That provision allowed married couples an extra deduction equal to 10 percent of the earnings of the lower-earning spouse. The Two Earner Deduction was well designed. John and Mary, who paid a large marriage tax, were allowed a big deduction, $3,000, while Bill and Betty who actually got a marriage bonus, got a deduction of only $300. The provision targeted married taxpayers who were most burdened by the marriage penalty.

The Tax Reform Act of 1986 eliminated the Two Earner Deduction. The *General Explanation* of the bill, prepared by the staff of the Joint Committee on Taxation, argued that "the adjustments of the standard deduction and the rate schedule make it possible to minimize the marriage penalty while repealing the two-earner deduction."[4] Yet for the 85 percent of American two-earner couples who earn less than $60,000 a year the 1986 bill increased the tax consequences of marriage. As a rule, couples like John and Mary in which the wives' earnings are comparable to the husbands' paid a significantly larger marriage penalty after the 1986 act. And couples like Bill and Betty in which the husband makes much more than the wife got a bigger marriage bonus. (Again, the tax code is explicitly gender neutral, but in practice few American women earn more than their husbands.)

On the other hand, for the 15 percent of two-earner couples making more than $60,000, the Tax Reform Act did tend to reduce the tax consequences of marriage. This was mostly the result of the sharp reduction in the top tax rates: Top rates now peak at 33 percent instead of 50 percent, and there are fewer tax brackets, so the chances of being boosted into a higher bracket by your spouse's salary are small. Equity requires we also eliminate the marriage penalty for moderate- and low-income families, many of whom still pay marriage penalties of hundreds or thousands of dollars. The increase in the marriage penalty for moderate-income families not only discriminates against women, it is also bad economics. Economic studies clearly indicate that women's decision to work is quite sensitive to their after-tax wage. High taxes on working women are very detrimental to labor supply.

We should restore a version of the Two Earner Deduction. Since the marriage penalty is greatest when the lower-earning spouse earns the most, the relief offered by the deduction should also be greatest in those cases. A new Two Earner Deduction, which would allow the couple to deduct 10 percent of the lower-earning spouse's earnings over $5,000, would cost the treasury only $6 billion in lost income tax revenue, and significantly increase the after-tax wages of married women. Limiting the deduction to the first $30,000 of income would make the program more equitable and even cheaper. Alternatively, we could move our tax system toward a flat rate schedule on which all taxpayers pay the same tax rate regardless of their marital status. Such a change is considered in the next chapter. Regardless of how the change is made, we need to bring the tax treatment of women out of the 1950s and into the 1990s. Tax penalties on women for working, marrying, or having children have no place in a society dedicated to individual choice. Women, families, and society as a whole will be much better served by a tax system that lets us all choose our own paths.

Chapter 17

A Tax Code for
the Future

"If Patrick Henry thought that taxation without represen-
tation was bad, he should see how bad it is with represen-
tation."

—*Farmers Almanac*, 1966

Why do we need another round of tax reform? During the
1980s, we had a new tax bill almost every year. Hasn't there
been enough tinkering? Things are going pretty well with inflation down and the economy up. Why not leave well enough
alone?

We need another round of reform because with all we
have learned we can do better, and so can our competitors
around the world. The experiments of the 1980s have taught
us a set of lessons about what works. Those lessons were
hard learned and a lot of political blood has been spilled in
their behalf. It would be wrong to waste them. No country
yet has taken all the lessons of the 1980s to their logical
conclusions, reaping their full benefits. We can and should.
We've earned it.

Punitive taxation is dead, in theory. Only a few vestigial
redistributionists cling rhetorically to the notion that we should
soak the rich. Yet the United States still imposes punitive tax
rates. Because the government continues to tax the illusory
profits of inflation, which remains at 3–6 percent, the effective

tax rate on real interest income is well over 50 percent. It approaches 100 percent for taxpayers who keep their money in traditional savings accounts.

We still levy a hefty marriage penalty tax, in the thousands of dollars, on two-income families. The effective tax rate on a welfare mother seeking to join the labor force and establish a decent life for herself and her children often exceeds 100 percent. Entrepreneurs, and the people who back them in risky ventures also face punitive tax rates. The government will share richly in their success, but not their failure. Punitive tax rates are still levied on those Americans who do the most to help our economy work harder and work smarter.

Ordinary taxpayers face tax rates that are still too high, although lower than they were a decade ago. Middle-class families earning roughly $50,000 face marginal tax rates of roughly 40 percent: 28 percent federal, 7.5 percent for Social Security, and 5 percent for state taxes. For most of history a 40 percent rate on the middle class would have been considered an unconscionable tyranny.

The 28 percent federal rate alone is a hefty burden. Consider that 28 percent means that 11.2 hours in a tax payer's 40 hour work week, all day Monday plus Tuesday until lunch are devoted to work for the federal government. For someone who goes to work just out of college, at age twenty-two, and retires at age sixty-five, it means working purely for the federal government for a bit over twelve years, say from age twenty-two to age thirty-four or from age fifty-three to age sixty-five. It means that to buy a $15,000 car a taxpayer must earn $20,800. To pay $750 rent one must earn $1,040. All this just to cover federal income tax.

If it were impossible for us to do better and still raise enough revenue to pay for the legitimate functions of government, we would have an excuse for these burdensome and damaging levies. But tax rates can be cut further during the 1990s, and dramatically. To stop now and rest on our laurels would be to disregard the fundamental lessons of the 1980s.

We have learned that well-designed savings plans can help increase national saving. The IRA program of the early 1980s was a tremendous success in promoting long-term savings. Sharply restricting it, as we did after 1986, was a serious mistake. The program should rather be broadened and made more efficient, so that all Americans can take part. The true revenue consequences of such a plan are much lower than the apparent up-front revenue costs.

We have learned that the 28 percent capital gains tax rate is too high. It loses revenue, hampers entrepreneurship, and blunts national competitiveness. It is punitive in the true sense of the word, kept high out of envy and demagoguery, and it punishes everyone: the taxpayer, the government, and the economy.

We have learned that ever increased spending on government social programs has had very little effect, and that private philanthropy might do a better job. The tax system offers a way of increasing private social spending by much more than $1 for every $1 forgone in tax revenue. The charitable deduction can be an efficient means of providing funds to the most efficient providers of public services.

We have learned that any tax increase will collect less revenue than it purports to, because it distorts individual behavior and reduces economic activity. Conversely, we have learned that almost any tax cut will reduce revenue by less than static-revenue assumptions suggest. Equally important, we have learned that other nations have learned the same lessons. They are applying those lessons to streamlining their economies to make themselves more competitive during the 1990s.

It would be a shame not to benefit from our education. The risks of applying our knowledge are extremely low: We are not gambling with new ideas as we were in the eighties. The risks of standing pat are much greater. We risk squandering all that we have learned, even as our competitors take advantage of our experience. By applying the lessons of the 1980s in another round of tax reform, further reducing rates, increasing incentives, and ending tax distortions that reduce efficiency and waste resources, we can keep our role as the leader of the world economy.

To see how much further we can go in reducing tax rates and tax distortions, consider the following tax reform package. Though we will not play out all the calculations here (they would fill a small book), it happens to produce as much revenue with roughly the same distribution of tax payments as the current income tax even without a behavioral response by taxpayers. The one important exception is that this suggested reform substantially reduces the tax burden on low- and moderate-income families with children. The new tax code would:

· Levy a single flat tax rate of 19 percent on all taxable income (including capital gains), substantially increasing the rewards of work, saving, and investment.
· Raise the basic zero-tax threshold much higher than current law:
    * $12,000 for married couples
    * $6,000 for single individuals
  PLUS: a $5,000 exemption for each dependent under age three.
  a $3,000 exemption for each dependent over age three.
  AND: a substantially liberalized child care credit. These increased exemptions and credits will ease the presently onerous tax burdens on families with children. Besides broadening options for families, better child care should provide long-term benefits to the economy.
· Give low- and moderate-income taxpayers effective use of homeowner and other deductions now effectively available only to upper-income taxpayers.
· Index all interest and capital gains income for inflation, restraining the government from taxing illusory profits and encouraging entrepreneurship and investment.
· Allow all taxpayers a deduction for charitable contributions, with a double deduction for contributions over 5 percent of income, establishing a new social standard—the half-tithe—for all Americans to strive for.
· Establish an Individual Savings Account program with deductible contributions of up to $5,000 for each worker in the family, raising the national savings rate, helping finance business investment, and helping Americans provide for retirement, education, and health expenses.

So far we have been reducing tax obligations. For the most part these reductions will be net revenue losers, though in practice there would be some revenue feedbacks from the demand, supply, and pecuniary effects of rate reductions. We have ignored such effects here because the positive revenue effects of cutting the top rate from 33 to 19 would be very small compared to the positive effects of cutting the top rate from 70 to 50 or even from 50 to 33. We would pay for these reductions by a series of changes that recover the lost revenue while eliminating burdensome inefficiencies in the old tax code, reducing the excess burden of achieving our revenue goals. These additional changes would:

- Establish a cash flow corporate income tax. Allow immediate expensing of all new business investment in a cash flow business income tax, offset this with an elimination of the interest deduction, restoring powerful and balanced incentives for genuinely productive new business investment without subsidizing marginal or even wasteful investments as ACRS sometimes did. Expensing should be a long-term boom to American businesses and the workers who work for them, at no cost to the government. Eliminating interest deductibility would end the incentives for debt finance in the current income tax. After an appropriate revision of the corporate tax rates, expensing will be officially revenue neutral, though its long-term economic benefits should provide modest long-term revenue gains.
- Expand the tax base to include all forms of labor compensation, including fringe benefits. This single change will bring in enough revenue to offset nearly two-thirds of the losses above, yet the net burden on workers will be minimal because of the dramatic reduction in tax rates. Moreover, as this change prompts labor contracts to offer more cash and fewer benefits workers will benefit from the efficiency of being paid in cash and shopping for their own benefits. The cost of some benefits should drop as providers are exposed to stiffer, tax-neutral competition for workers' dollars.
- Place limits on the deductibility of certain items, such as state taxes, limiting use to taxpayers in need and ending abuse by upper-income taxpayers.
- Limit the homeownership deduction to $10,000 of real interest payments and property taxes for a married couple and $5,000 for a

single taxpayer, ending tax subsidies for mansions and reducing housing inflation.

- Eliminate the standard deduction, superfluous under this plan because of the vast increase in personal and dependent exemptions and because all taxpayers will have full access to itemized deductions.
- Include all transfer payments in the tax base.
- Limit personal and dependent exemptions and most personal deductions to earned and transfer income, a change that together with the limits on the deductions for state taxes and homeownership will make up most of the additional lost revenue.

If you are like most taxpayers, you want to know what this means for you. Do not count on any big tax cut. This tax system raises just as much revenue as the current code. Except for low- and moderate-income families with children, just about everyone will have to pay just about as much tax as now in absolute terms. A few taxpayers, particularly singles, will pay a bit more. Still, to see the effect on your tax liability, pull out last year's 1040 tax form and use it to help you fill in the new Form 2000 you will find at the end of this chapter. The lines on the new form have been matched to the line numbers on the old 1040 to make things easier.

This system changes not total tax bills but the incentives people face. It lightens the burdens the tax system places on productive activity. Form 2000 takes the lessons of supply-side economics learned through the Kennedy and Reagan tax cuts and applies them to all taxpayers, middle- and working-class as well as well-to-do. Even after the tax cuts of the 1980s, under the current system the government takes a substantial part of every additional dollar we earn (thus discouraging all the productive activities by which people earn dollars) and then through deductions gives it back as the government sees fit (which may not be how we want it). Under the reform proposed here, the government says, in effect, work as hard as you will, we won't penalize you. Then choose for yourselves how much health care or housing you wish to buy. Taxpayers will probably get a better deal on both. Without government guaranteeing the cash flow to home builders and health care providers, those businesses will have to cut consumers a better deal. Under the new 19 percent rate we will start working for ourselves by quitting time Monday, rather than lunch on Tuesday.

A quick glance at the tax form at the end of the chapter raises one obvious objection: it doesn't seem "simple." In fact, this revision of the Long Form, 1040, actually combines that form with the current Schedule A, Itemized Deductions. It is substantially shorter than the current version of those two forms combined. Taxpayers who only receive wage income, or only moderate amounts of income could use a short form even shorter than the current short form. Simplicity is anyway overrated. It deprives the tax code of subtlety and taxpayers of vital deductions and the IRS of details it needs to verify returns. Depriving the IRS of too much detail would mean more audits, a far worse fate than filling out a longish return.

While simplification is not without its costs, complexities can bring benefits. The complexities introduced in Form 2000 have a twofold purpose: reducing tax rates and curbing inefficient tax shelters that waste precious resources of labor and capital as well as losing revenue. The two go hand in hand. The evidence from the early 1980s shows that simply reducing the tax rate lures income and capital out of hiding, and may actually enhance tax revenue. But this happens most dramatically when rates are cut from very high levels. At the current 33 or 28 percent rates, a lot of money has already come out of the closet. A reduction to 19 percent will not coax out much more or produce big revenue feedbacks. So in addition to reducing rates we must explicitly limit or even abolish some tax shelters in order to get both enough revenue and greater efficiency for the economy. Form 2000 does just that: It trades off lower rates for limits on tax shelters.

The first big trade-off is that we sharply reduce the effective tax rate on capital income, but make it nearly impossible for taxpayers who receive net capital income to avoid paying taxes.

As previously noted, the effective tax rates on capital income are far higher than the statutory 28 or 33 percent maximum rates, because the tax code taxes nominal capital income, not real capital income. Form 2000 both cuts the rate to 19 percent and limits taxation to real interest and real capital gains income. In return, the personal exemptions and most personal deductions are limited to earned income and transfer income. Taxpayers with net capital income must therefore pay taxes. In effect, we encourage investors and entrepreneurs, who generally come from the ranks of the well-off, to do their best for themselves and the economy, but deny their capital income tax benefits designed for working people.

In chapter 13 we recommended that the current tax code should allow investors in new businesses that go bust a full deduction against ordinary income, a deduction largely eliminated by the 1986 reform. However, since Form 2000 provides both lower rates and indexing, we do not restore the full deduction here. Likewise the special exemption for capital gains from new businesses or stock shares, also suggested in chapter 13, is left out on the assumption that the difference between a 19 percent rate and a 15 percent rate, both indexed, would not substantially change investor behavior.

The second trade-off is in the area of itemized deductions. First, we limit the amount of income that can be sheltered by borrowing for a house. Under current law taxpayers can deduct their mortgage interest on home loans up to $1,000,000. This generous deduction shifts capital away from business investments and towards luxury housing. It also raises the cost of housing by bidding up demand, and then effectively reduces those costs for upper-income taxpayers. While homeownership is important in a democratic society, there is no reason for the tax system to subsidize mansions. Form 2000 limits the deduction for homeownership costs, real mortgage interest and property taxes, to $10,000 for a married couple and $5,000 for a single individual.

Additionally, the deduction for state and local taxes is limited to that portion of the state and local tax bill that exceeds 6 percent of the taxpayer's income, on the principle that the individuals who pay their state and local taxes receive a return in the services that those taxes finance. In affluent suburbs today, state and particularly local taxes can serve as a type of tax shelter. Well-to-do taxpayers can vote for lavish city services, from heated swimming pools in high schools that might as well be private, to lush municipal golf courses that substitute for country clubs, and then deduct the cost from their federal taxes.

Under Form 2000 these services would no longer be subsidized, since even with such lavish services high-income taxpayers rarely pay more than 6 percent of their income in state and local taxes. In fact, in very high-income communities, the deduction would probably be limited to the few poorer families who likely voted against the golf course. Of course, most ordinary citizens whose communities provide sensible services would also lose their present tax deduction. But because Form 2000 cuts tax rates for all, and especially for families with children, the financial impact would be small. The federal government should not be subsidizing decisions to buy services just because we call the purchase "taxation."

Combined, the limitation on the homeownership deduction and on the state and local tax deduction produce more than $60 billion in revenue, allowing the effective tax rate on taxable income to be reduced by three percentage points, a very attractive trade off.

The worldwide move to more or less free markets has just begun. Tax reform, and particularly tax rate reduction, has been integral to that liberating process—probably the most important part of it. It too will continue worldwide. As with any revolution in technique, however, the easiest gains come first. The tremendous reduction in the top marginal tax rate in the United States, from 70 percent at the start of the decade to 33 percent at the decade's close has exploited most of the potential for improving incentives by rate cuts alone. Nor can there be much more revenue feedback from rate cuts alone. Except for some specific taxes, such as capital gains, the American tax system is today clearly on the correct side of the revenue maximization curve.

The Kennedy tax cuts, which reduced the top rate from 91 percent to 70 percent, were universally hailed as a success and Reagan's reductions, while not as universally acclaimed, were clearly successful. But there are no further improvements to be had by taking a meat axe to the existing rate structure. Future tax reform will require more skill and more attention to detail. We have gained the skill and learned the details. What we need now is the political courage and perseverance to create a tax system that liberates economic energy, not enervating envy; a tax system that puts people before political pandering; a tax system that will keep America great in the 1990s and beyond.

FORM 2000—AN INCOME TAX FOR THE FUTURE[1]

Part I. Labor Income

(1) Cash compensation (Form 1040 Line 7.) _____

(2) Fringe benefits (See note for estimate.)* _____

(3) Business income (Form 1040 Line 12; if less than zero enter 0.) _____

(4) Farm income (Form 1040 Line 19; if less than zero, enter 0.) _____

(5) Other labor income (Schedule E if earned income; if less than zero, enter 0.) _____

(6) Total labor income Add Lines 1 Through 5 _____

Part II. Retirement Income and Transfers

(7) Alimony received (Form 1040 Line 11.) _____

(8) IRA or Keogh distributions (Form 1040 Line 16.) _____

(9) Pension income (Form 1040 Line 17.) _____

(10) Unemployment compensation (Total received.) _____

(11) Social Security Benefits (Total received.) _____

(12) Other Transfer Payments (Total received.) _____

(13) Total Transfer Payments Add Lines 7 Through 12 _____

Part III. Capital Income

(14) Taxable interest income (Form 1040 Line 8a.) _____

(15) Tax-exempt interest (Form 1040 Line 8b.) _____

(16) Dividend income (Form 1040 Line 9.) _____

(17) Capital gains (Form 1040 Lines 13, 14, and 15; if less than zero, enter 0.) _____

(18) Other investment income (Form 1040 Lines 18 and 22; if less than zero, enter 0.) _____

(19) Total capital income Add Lines 14 Through 18 _____

*A good estimate of your fringe benefits is 25 percent of the amount your salary exceeds $10,000. So, someone with a $30,000 salary receives about $5,000 in fringe benefits.

FORM 2000—AN INCOME TAX FOR THE FUTURE *(continued)*

Part IV. *Total Income*

(19) Enter line 6a

(20) Enter line 6b

(21) Enter line 13

(22) Enter line 19

(23) Total Income Add Lines 19 Through 22

Part V. *Deductions*

A. Deductions from Labor Income

(24) a. Taxpayer ISA contribution (Enter lesser of amount contributed, $5,000, or Line 6a.)

 b. Spousal ISA contribution (Enter lesser of amount contributed, $5,000, or Line 6b.)

 c. Deduction limitation (Enter one-half of line 19.)

 d. Deductible ISA contribution (Add Lines 24a and 24b, subtract line 24c.)

(25) Standard child care deduction (If Line 23 is less than $20,000, see Child Care Credit Form.)

 a. Enter lesser of Line 6a or Line 6b

 b. If Line 6a is entered, enter 24a

 If Line 6b is entered, enter 24b

 c. Subtract Line 25b from Line 25a

 d. Divide Line 25c by 2

 e. Enter child care expenses up to $3,000 per child under age 12

 f. Child care deduction (Lesser of Line 25d or 25e.)

(26) Farm or business losses (Enter amount lost.)

 a. Business loss (1040 Line 12.)

 b. Farm loss (1040 Line 19.)

 c. Other loss from employment

 d. Add Lines 26a, b, and c

(27) Total labor deductions (Add Lines 24d, 25e, and 26d.)

FORM 2000—AN INCOME TAX FOR THE FUTURE (continued)

B. Labor or Transfer Deductions

(28) Home ownership incentive

   a. Mortgage interest (Schedule A Lines 9a, 9b, and 10.) _____

   b. Property taxes (Schedule A Line 6.) _____

   c. Add Lines 28a and 28b _____

   d. Enter $5,000 if single, $10,000 if married. _____

   e. Enter lesser of 28c or 28d _____

(29) Excess state and local taxes

   a. State income tax paid (Schedule A Line 5 less Form 1040 Line 10) _____

   b. State sales taxes paid (See note below for estimate.)* _____

   c. Other state taxes paid except for property taxes. (Schedule A Line 7.) _____

   d. Total state taxes (Add Lines 29a, b, and c.) _____

   e. Multiply Line 23 by 0.06 _____

   f. Total tax deduction (Subtract Line 29e from Line 29d; if less than zero enter 0.) _____

(30) Excess medical expenses (Schedule A Line 4.) _____

(31) Charitable contributions (Schedule A Line 17.) _____

(32) General deductions

   a. Enter $6,000 if filing singly, $12,000 if married filing jointly _____

   b. Multiply number of dependents (Form 1040 Line 6c.) by $3,000. _____

   c. Multiply number of dependents under age 3 by $2,000 _____

   d. Add Lines 32a, 32b, and 32c _____

(33) Total labor or transfer deductions (Add Lines 28e, 29f, 30, 31, and 32d.) _____

C. Deductions from Capital Income

(34) Losses on investments _____

*You can estimate your sales tax by looking at your 1986 tax return, the last year it was a deduction. Otherwise put down 1 percent of your income if your state has a sales tax in the 4-5 percent range.

FORM 2000—AN INCOME TAX FOR THE FUTURE *(continued)*

(35) Tax-exempt interest

(36) Inflation adjustment to interest (Enter one-half of Line 14.)

(37) Total deductions from capital income (Add Lines 34, 35, and 36.)

Part V. *Tax Computation*

(38) Labor income. (Add Lines 6a and 6b.)

(39) Deductions from labor income. (Enter Line 27.)

(40) Subtract Line 39 from Line 38 (If less than zero, enter 0.)

(41) Transfer income (Enter Line 13.)

(42) Total labor and transfer income (Add Lines 40 and 41.)

(43) Labor and transfer deductions (Enter Line 33.)

(44) Subtract Line 43 from Line 42; if less than zero, enter 0.

(45) Capital income (Enter Line 19.)

(46) Deductions from capital income (Enter Line 37.)

(47) Net capital income (Subtract Line 46 from Line 45.)

(48) Taxable income (Add Lines 44 and 47.)

(49) Tax (Multiply Line 48 by 0.19)

Notes

Chapter 1

1. The Consumer Price Index is compiled by the Bureau of Labor Statistics, U.S. Department of Labor. Although there is some question about the precision of the index, it is easily the most commonly used measure of inflation and is used for adjusting Social Security payments, income tax brackets, and numerous labor contracts for inflation.

2. This figure is calculated by including the compounding of inflation for twelve months. Mathematically it is equal to $(1.014)^{12} - 1$. Multiplying 1.4 by 12 will understate the annual inflation resulting from 1.4 percent monthly increases.

3. *Economic Report of the President, 1981* (Washington, D.C.: Government Printing Office, 1981), 32.

4. This means that prices in December 1980 were 12.5 percent higher than they were in December 1979. On average in all of 1980, prices were 13.5 percent higher than they averaged in 1979.

5. Fortunately, this decline only lasted one quarter. During the Great Depression, the economy shrank 30 percent over four years, or at an 8.4 percent average annual rate.

6. After declining in the first few months of 1980, the M1 money supply expanded at a 16 percent annual rate between May and October.

7. Unemployment data is collected by the Bureau of Labor Statistics, U.S. Department of Labor.

8. The Misery Index is now tracked for a number of countries by the *Economist* magazine.

9. The Prime Interest Rate is set by the credit market. It is a base rate charged by banks to business customers. The quote of the rate is usually based on the prime charged by large New York banks. It rose to 21.5 percent in January 1981.

10. The average weekly earnings in private non-agricultural industry is the index used. It is compiled by the Bureau of Labor Statistics, U.S. Department of Labor. It represents before tax earnings adjusted for inflation of production on non-supervisory workers.

11. Measured by employees on non-agricultural payrolls. This data is collected from establishments by the Bureau of Labor Statistics. It differs from the usual unemployment measure which surveys households.

12. To understand this reasoning, the reader should refer to any major introductory economics text. Texts such as Stanley Fischer, Rudoger Dornbusch, and Richard Schmalensee, *Economics,* 2d Edition (New York: McGraw-Hill, 1988) and R. Lipsey, P. Steiner, and D. Purvis, *Economics,* 8th Edition (New York: Harper and Row, 1987) are quite good.

13. Success and failure are always in the eye of the beholder. This author is struck by those commentators who talk about the "failed" policies of the 1980s, a decade which seems remarkably successful. As supporting evidence note that the unemployment rate rose from 5.9 percent in 1971 to 7.1 percent in 1980 while the inflation rate rose from 3.3 percent to 12.5 percent over the same

period. By contrast, unemployment fell from 7.6 in 1981 to 5.3 percent as of this writing, while inflation fell from 8.9 percent in 1981 to under 5 percent.

14. The creator of the term is unknown, though it is obviously a combination of stagnation and inflation.

15. Keynes's quip was given in *A Tract on Monetary Reform* (London: MacMillan, 1923) 80.

16. *U.S. News and World Report,* 4 August 1980, 40.

17. Walter Heller, "The Kemp-Roth-Laffer Free Lunch," *Wall Street Journal,* 12 July 1978, 20.

18. Some may say I'm being too easy a grader—on both schools. Here, I'm grading based on results, not on comparison to what the various schools promised. Some polemicists who called themselves supply-siders clearly oversold their goods. But their Keynesian critics should remember that they too oversold their product. Keynesian "Fine Tuning" promised to repeal the business cycle, according to many in the 1960s, and usher in continued low unemployment and low inflation.

19. Paraphrased from *Keynes' General Theory of Employment and Money* (New York: Harcourt, Brace, and World, 1935), preface.

20. See a discussion of this in the 1981 *Economic Report of the President,* 57–68.

21. The period is 1982 to 1986. As later discussion will show, the first real reduction in taxes didn't occur until July 1982. Nineteen eighty-six was the last year in which ERTA, the 1981 tax bill, was in effect.

22. The impatient reader might skip forward to chapter 8. Or, he might choose to read Martin Feldstein and Douglas Elmendorf, "Budget Deficits, Tax Incentives, and Inflation: A Surprising Lesson from the 1983–84 Recovery" in *Tax Policy and the Economy,* vol. 3, ed. Lawrence H. Summers (Cambridge: MIT Press, 1988).

23. The author gratefully acknowledges the help provided by the National Bureau of Economic Research TAXSIM model. A detailed description of this model and some of the author's contributions to the methodological study of the effect of taxes can be found in Lindsey, *Simulating the Effect of Tax Changes on Taxpayer Behavior,* unpublished Doctoral Dissertation at Harvard University, 1985. That dissertation won the Outstanding Doctoral Dissertation award from the National Tax Association. The thesis is obtainable from University Microfilm, Ann Arbor, Michigan, phone 313-761-4700. Theses are available in hardcover, softcover, microfiche, or microfilm.

Chapter 2

1. This observation was first clearly demonstrated in Martin Feldstein and Charles Clotfelter, "Tax Incentives for Charitable Contributions in the United States," *Journal of Public Economics* 5 (1976):1–26.

2. For a survey by the Gallup organization, see *The Independent Sector, Giving and Volunteering in the United States: Findings from a National Survey* (Washington, D.C.: Independent sector, 1988).

3. *McCulloch v. Maryland,* 17 U.S. (4 Wheat.) 316, 4 L.Ed. 579 (1819). The actual tax varied with the size of the banknote, but averaged about 2 percent.

4. The concept of excess burden, also known as deadweight loss, is a very important one in microeconomic analysis. The reader interested in more detail

with some background in economics might choose a good public finance text such as Harvey Rosen, *Public Finance,* Chapter 12.

A more detailed description of the problems in measuring excess burden appears in Alan Auerbach and Harvey Rosen, "Will the Real Excess Burden Stand Up?" (National Bureau of Economic Research Working Paper No. 495, 1980). Readers not interested in technical details should think of excess burden as economic costs in excess of the tax revenue collected.

5. Richard Musgrave and Peggy Musgrave, *Public Finance in Theory and Practice* (New York: McGraw Hill, 1973), 457–58.

6. For a sophisticated model of the sensitivity of the tax base see Don Fullerton, "On the Possibility of an Inverse Relationship Between Tax Rates and Government Revenues," *Journal of Public Economics* 19 (October 1982):3–22. Fullerton does not, however, incorporate into his model all the factors that affect the income tax base.

7. According to data compiled by the U.S. Chamber of Commerce Research Center the fringe share of compensation has risen continuously, along with marginal tax rates, over most of the past thirty years. Their study, *Employee Benefits,* is available from the Economic Policy Division, U.S. Chamber of Commerce, 1615 H St. N.W., Washington, D.C. 20067. The National Income and Products Accounts mirror this, indicating a sharp rise in non-wage labor compensation.

8. For historical data on the income tax, see *Historical Statistics of the United States, Colonial Times to 1970,* U.S. Department of Commerce, Bureau of the Census, 1975. The *Statistics of Income* (Washington, D.C.: U.S. Government Printing Office) series by the Internal Revenue Service is excellent and provides detailed breakdowns of income and taxes paid by income class. The 1943 *Statistics of Income* provides detailed data for the early income tax.

9. To preserve a family's relative position in the income distribution, its income must rise in real terms as well as with inflation. Real family incomes have roughly tripled since 1913 on top of the tenfold rise in prices.

10. Most taxpayers earning over $100,000 saw their rates rise from 7 or 8 percent to 64 or 68 percent. The very top rate rose fivefold from 15 percent to 77 percent.

11. Calvin Coolidge, State of the Union, December 3, 1924.

12. The personal exemption for both married couples and single individuals dropped by roughly one-third while personal income dropped 30 percent between 1931 and 1933. Thus, the decline in the exemption maintained the relative position of the threshold at which taxpayers owed tax.

13. The tax collected from taxpayers earning more than $100,000 dropped from $239 million in 1930 to $137 million in 1933, in spite of the 150 percent rise in tax rates.

Chapter 3

1. The difficulties turned out to be more apparent than real. While periodicals such as *Business Week* and *Time* mentioned slowdowns, the economy actually did quite nicely. Still, the stock market was scared. It plunged 27 percent during the first half of 1962.

2. *Business Week,* 9 February 1963, 120.

3. Data reported in the *Historical Tables of the Budget of the United States Government* (Washington, D.C.: U.S. Government Printing Office, 1989).

4. Kennedy proposed a $13.5 billion tax rate reduction in his state of the union address, *Newsweek,* 21 January 1963. GNP that year was $606 billion.

5. *Business Week,* 2 February 1963, 25.

6. *Business Week,* 9 February 1963, 25.

7. Wilbur Mills, Democratic Chairman of Ways and Means, said, "The function of taxation is to raise revenue—I do not go along with economists who think of taxation primarily as an instrument for manipulating the economy," *Newsweek,* 14 January 1963, 15. Democratic Senator Harry Byrd, Chairman of the Senate Finance Committee denounced Kennedy as "the first President to deliberately ask for a tax reduction that would add to the deficit" (*Newsweek,* 24 December 1962).

8. *Newsweek,* 2 March 1964, 61.

9. Walter Heller, "The Kemp-Roth-Laffer Free Lunch," *Wall Street Journal,* 12 July 1978, 20.

10. These figures are all expressed in 1965 dollars. Real GNP in 1963 was 633.1. So, normal growth accounted for $44 billion of the $72 billion increase, or 61 percent was due to normal growth. We will attribute the residual to the tax cuts.

11. Budget outlays fell from $102.8 billion in FY64 to $101.7 billion in FY65. Spending growth averaged 6 percent between FY60 and FY64. Had the trend continued, spending would have been $109 billion, or $7.3 billion more than what Congress actually spent.

12. Donald W. Kiefer, "An Economic Analysis of the Kemp-Roth Tax Cut Bill, H.R. 8333: A Description and Examination of its Rationale and Estimates of its Economic Effects," *Congressional Record* (2 August 1978):H777-H7778; also in *The Economics of the Tax Revolt: A Reader,* ed. Arthur Laffer and Jan P. Seymour (New York: Harcourt Brace Jovanovich, 1979), 13–27. Kiefer, who is an excellent analyst, would probably consider himself more of a Keynesian than a supply-sider. But, like most modern economists, he has a philosophy that combines aspects of both schools of thought.

13. See the *Statistics of Income* series compiled by the IRS, which provides detailed tables of the composition of income in these years by income bracket and type of income. The data used here are from the 1963, 1964, and 1965 *Statistics of Income* tabulated by the Internal Revenue Service (Washington, D.C.: U.S. Government Printing Office).

14. These assumptions stack the analysis against the supply-side claim since they presume that the entire rise in income was due to demand-side effects.

15. There was a brief pause in 1966 which some considered a recession. However, data revisions have removed this slowdown from the list of recessions. In any event, the 1966 slowdown was due to a sharp upward spike in interest rates deliberately caused by the Federal Reserve in order to slow down a booming economy.

16. This was non-partisan. Richard Nixon followed this course of policy with a vengeance. More than any president in memory, he perfected Keynesian fine-tuning to produce a glowing economic situation for the 1972 elections. The looming inflation was temporarily held in check by wage and price controls. When lifted, a rapid inflation followed by a deep recession quickly ensued.

17. *Economic Report of the President 1980* (Washington, D.C.: Government Printing Office, 1980), 68.

18. *General Explanation of the Economic Recovery Tax Act of 1981* (Washington, D.C.: U.S. Government Printing Office), 382–401.

19. Strictly speaking, the marriage penalty overtaxed the earnings of the lower-earning spouse, regardless of sex, in a two-earner family, but only a minority of American wives earn more than their husbands.

20. *General Explanation of the Economic Recovery Tax Act of 1981* (Washington, D.C.: Government Printing Office), 38.

21. Between 1977 and 1981 personal tax receipts rose 76 percent while personal income grew just 57 percent. Furthermore, as note 17 indicated, it was the intention of the Carter Administration to continue to use bracket creep to balance the budget.

22. As early as April 1981, Democrats had signed on to a cut in the top rate to 50 percent, *Business Week,* 13 April 1981, 135.

Chapter 4

1. This analysis was first presented in Lawrence Lindsey, "Simulating the Response of Taxpayers to Changes in Tax Rates" (Ph.D. diss., Harvard University, 1985), which won the Outstanding Doctoral Dissertation Award from the National Tax Association. It is available through the University of Michigan but, like most doctoral dissertations, should be resorted to only by the inordinately dedicated. For a more readable though still technical analysis see Lawrence Lindsey, "Estimating the Behavioral Responses of Taxpayers to Changes in Tax Rates: 1982–1984. With Implications for the Revenue-Maximizing Tax Rate," *Journal of Public Economics* (July 1987): 173–206. For those interested in a complete account of the analysis as applied in this chapter, using the numbers that were current when this chapter was written, see Manhattan Institute Associates, *Decomposing the Revenue Effects of a Tax Cut* (New York: Manhattan Institute, 1989). It is available from the Manhattan Institute, 42 East 71 Street, New York, NY 10021.

2. Both the Treasury Department and the Joint Committee on Taxation usually incorporate demand-side effects in their revenue estimates, but the process is constrained by official forecasts. Technically all treasury estimates assume both that the administration's economic forecast is accurate and that the president's program will be adopted. The committee relies on an alternative forecast, usually that of the Congressional Budget Office. Neither agency explicitly separates demand-side effects from its overall revenue estimates.

3. Economists hedge this answer: Someone who gets a raise may choose to work less, as he is now richer he'll need to work fewer hours to enjoy the same level of consumption. Most evidence suggests, however, that over the range under discussion most people would work more.

4. There might be some additional labor supply, because workers might feel they were better off overall under the new deal. But that would be a supply-side response and any additional revenue that resulted would properly be part of a supply-side effect.

5. See Lawrence Lindsey, "Estimating the Behavioral Responses of Taxpayers to Changes in Tax Rates: 1982–1984. With Implications for the Revenue-Maximizing Tax Rate," *Journal of Public Economics* (July 1987):173–206. A brief summary is in order here: Each income item in each of the 34,000 tax returns is increased by the growth in that item, per tax return, in the overall economy.

For example, if the per-return level of wages rose 20 percent, then the reported wages on each return are increased 20 percent. The same procedure is repeated for wages, interest, dividends, capital gains, business income, farm income, unemployment compensation, and partnership income. A similar procedure is performed for itemized deductions in order to sort out changes in the income distribution caused by a rise in interest rates or unemployment, as distinct from tax-induced changes in taxpayer behavior. Each tax return is given a "sample weight" reflecting how many of the roughly 95 million total returns it represents. These sample weights are adjusted to reflect changes in the number of returns filed. Similar sample weight adjustments are made to returns receiving unemployment compensation in order to reflect changes in the unemployment rate. The extrapolation thus resembles as closely as possible the changes in macroeconomic conditions between the year of the sample (1979) and the years simulated (1981–85).

6. Otto Eckstein, *The DRI Model of the U.S. Economy* (New York: McGraw Hill, 1983), xx, 37.

7. See Gary Burtlass and Jerry Hausman, "The Effect of Taxation on Labor Supply: Evaluating the Gary Negative Income Tax Experiment," *Journal of Political Economy* 6 (December 1986):1103–30; Michael Boskin, "The Economics of Labor Supply," and Robert Hall, "Wages, Income, and Hours of the U.S. Labor Force," in *Income Maintenance and Labor Supply*, ed. G. Cain and H. Watts (Chicago: Markham, 1973), 101–162; M. Kosters, "Effects of an Income Tax on Labor Supply," in *The Taxation of Income From Capital*, ed. Arnold Harberger and Michael Bailey (Washington, D.C.: The Brookings Institution, 1967), 301–324; Harvey Rosen, "Taxes in a Labor Supply Model With Joint Wages-Hours Determination," *Econometric* 44, no.3 (May 1976): 485ff.; Jerry Hausman, "Stochastic Problems in the Simulation of Labor Supply," in *Behavioral Simulation Methods in Tax Policy Analysis*, ed. Martin Feldstein (Chicago: University of Chicago Press, 1983), 47–82.

8. For a complete description of this test of the behavioral responses, see Lawrence Lindsey, "Did ERTA Raise the Share of Taxes Paid by Upper-Income Taxpayers? Will TRA86 Be a Repeat?" in *Tax Policy and the Economy*, ed. Lawrence H. Summers (Cambridge: MIT Press, 1988), 131–160.

9. Robert W. Turner, *The Effect of Taxes on Fringe Share of Compensation*, Colgate University Department of Economics Discussion Paper 88-05. Turner also wrote "Are Taxes Responsible for the Growth of Fringe Benefits?" *National Tax Journal* 40 (June 1987): 205–220.

10. The pecuniary effect has been the focus of some research. Lindsey's *Journal of Public Economics* article, as well as a series of pieces in *Tax Notes* (March 17, 1986; October 13, 1986; and May 4, 1987) all focus on the pecuniary effect: "Estimating the Behavioral Response of Taxpayers to Changes in Tax Rates: 1982–84 With Implications for the Revenue Maximizing Rate," *Journal of Public Economics*, (July 1987): 173–206; "Criticizing the CBO Analysis of ERTA's Effect on the Distribution of Income and Taxes" *Tax Notes* (4 May 1987): 491–496; "Revenue Response to the 1982 Personal Tax Cuts—A Reply," *Tax Notes* (13 October 1986): 197–200; "Revenue Response to the 1982 Tax Cuts," *Tax Notes* (17 March 1986): 1157–1161.

11. This number may seem high as a figure for real returns but is consistent with current estimates; return on business investment by definition must be somewhat higher than the real rate on corporate bonds.

Chapter 5

1. The definition of "rich," like so much else, is in the eye of the beholder. According to income tax data in 1981 the top 1 percent made $85,000 or more. The top 10 percent made $38,000 or more. While "rich" on a relative basis, much of this latter group probably considered itself decidedly middle class. Since the entire rich and poor argument is a matter of appearances rather than fact, this discussion shall leave the concept of "rich" to the definition of the reader unless an explicit fact is being stated.

2. The poverty rate is the percent of the population living in families earning less than the poverty level. It is an admittedly imperfect measure. It is based on an index established by a federal interagency committee and is updated annually based on the consumer price index. Details can be found in the Commerce Department's Current Population Reports, (Washington, D.C.: U.S. Government Printing Office) series P-60, no. 160. Since the poverty rate is the statistic most often used by Reagan critics, it is examined in further detail here.

3. Congressional Budget Office, "CBO Replies to Lindsey," *Tax Notes* (May 1987):501. The CBO analysis focused only on the pecuniary effect and ignored the demand-side and supply-side effects discussed here.

4. The tax rate increase from 28 percent to 33 percent lowers the after-tax share received by taxpayers from 72 cents to 67 cents for each dollar earned. Lindsey, *Journal of Public Economics,* July 1987, found that a 7 percent cut in after-tax shares could easily cause a 10 percent shrinkage of the base.

Chapter 6

1. *Newsweek,* 2 March 1981, 24.

2. *Newsweek,* 2 March 1981, 34.

3. These data are for calendar years as compiled by the Bureau of Economic Analysis, U.S. Department of Commerce. They reflect National Income and Product Account accounting, not budgetary accounting, though these differences are relatively minor.

4. Here, unlike the previous chapters, there is no "counterfactual" to worry about. We are looking at what actually occurred and comparing those events with history. Shares of GNP are used in order to make the historical comparisons meaningful. Not only does this avoid the problem that all numbers tend to go up over time, but percent of GNP is the standard measure of the amount of fiscal stimulus that a tax cut or spending increase involves.

5. In 1944, at the height of World War II, federal taxes still took only 19.4 percent of GNP. The only higher year was 1969 when federal receipts took 20.7 percent of GNP.

6. The Vietnam War had contributed only modestly to this figure; in the Kennedy years prior to Vietnam, defense spending already averaged 8.9 percent of GNP.

7. The author does not claim expertise in judging the efficacy of such expenditures. However, recent events around the world suggest that the money invested in defense has paid big dividends in advancing the cause of liberty.

8. These figures were calculated by taking the change in the deficit caused by these factors in each year and paying interest on them at the six-month T-bill rate.

9. *America's New Beginning: A Program for Economic Recovery* (Washington, D.C.: U.S. Government Printing Office, 18 February 1981) includes a presidential address to the Congress and a detailed set of budget proposals.

10. *1983 Budget of the United States* (Washington, D.C.: U.S. Government Printing Office, 1983) 3–6.

11. Reagan had called for total non-defense spending of 14.3 percent of GNP and 6.1 percent for defense. In fact, defense ended at 6.3 percent and non-defense at 18.2 percent. A small part of the reason for the higher shares of GNP was the recession of 1982 which produced a lower GNP in FY 1983.

Chapter 7

1. Both World War II and Korea involved single years of double digit consumer price inflation, measured either year over year or December to December. The 1974 inflation similarly was in double digits only for a single year. The Carter inflation was in double digits for two years on a December-to-December basis and three years on a year-over-year basis.

2. *U. S. News and World Report,* 4 August 1980, 40.

3. Walter Heller, "The Kemp-Roth-Laffer Free Lunch," *Wall Street Journal,* 12 July 1978, 20.

4. *U.S. News and World Report,* 7 July 1980, 23.

5. We select this period as it represents the years that ERTA was in effect.

6. This equation is also expressed as $MV = PT$ where T represents transactions.

7. The very astute reader might note that many checking accounts—called NOW accounts—do pay interest. There is some indication that the advent of NOW accounts changed the relationship between money and interest. In fact, the definition of M1 was changed to reflect this. That is one of the reasons we use M2 in this exposition.

8. For example, between the end of 1982 and the end of 1986, the ratio of cash and checking account balances to money market fund balances rose from 1.67 to 1.91. The same period was one of sharply falling interest rates.

9. Over the same period, 1982–1986, non-financial corporate businesses doubled their cash and checking deposits while the money market balances remained unchanged.

10. Federal Reserve Board, *Balance Sheets of the U.S. Economy.* It is summarized in the *Economic Report of the President 1989,* table B.29.

11. See also Mankiw-Summers, "Money Demand and the Effects of Fiscal Policy," *Journal of Money Credit and Banking* (November 1986): 415–429.

12. This fact is certainly contrary to the conventional wisdom that the Reagan recovery was financed by massive consumer borrowing. The net borrowing by individuals in 1983, the first year of the recovery, was only 10.5 percent of personal income. In 1979 it was 13.6 percent of personal income. The "red ink" hypothesis will be discussed more in chapter 8.

13. The price of imports actually fell 8 percent between 1981 and 1986. The reason that the price didn't fall 64 percent was that foreign inflation pushed up production costs. The fact is the dollar's rise exceeded this foreign inflation, thereby causing a reduction in the dollar cost of imports.

14. The figure is obtained by multiplying the 11 percent share of imports by the 64 percent appreciation of the dollar. This is of course an oversimplification.

Had the dollar not risen, both our GNP and our level of imports would have been different. However, it is unclear which direction the oversimplification biases the result. The import share in 1980, with a lower dollar, was actually higher than in 1985.

15. This is the proper period to analyze: 1973 and 1981 were both business cycle peaks. It is too early to tell whether or not 1989 was also a business cycle peak.

Chapter 8

1. Martin Feldstein and Douglas Elmendorf, "Budget Deficits, Tax Incentive, and Inflation: A Surprising Lesson from the 1983–84 Recovery," in *Tax Policy and the Economy*, vol. 3, ed. Lawrence H. Summers (Cambridge: MIT Press, 1988). This careful comparative study is the source of many of the facts presented here.

2. The economic literature on this problem is quite extensive. Particular academic attention was paid to this issue during the late 1970s and early 1980s when inflation was so high. Alan Auerbach and Dale Jorgenson wrote a very interesting and quite readable article, "Inflation-Proof Depreciation of Assets," *Harvard Business Review* 58 (1980):113–18. The early analysis of this issue is provided by Robert Hall and Dale Jorgenson in "Tax Policy and Investment Behavior," *American Economic Review*, 57 (June 1967):391–414.

3. For some critical detail on this issue some good sources are Jane Gravelle's "Effects of the 1981 Depreciation Revisions on the Taxation of Income from Business Capital," *National Tax Journal* 35 (March 1982):1–20; Don Fullerton and Yolanda Henderson's "Investment Effects of Taxes on Income from Capital: Alternative Policies in the 1980s" in *The Legacy of Reaganomics: Prospects for Long-Term Growth*, ed. Charles Hulten and Thomas Sawhill (Washington D.C.: Urban Institute Press, 1984).

The best summary volume is Mervyn King and Don Fullerton, eds., *The Taxation of Income from Capital* (Chicago: University of Chicago Press, 1984).

4. This data comes from the 1982 *Economic Report of the President*, pp. 122–125. Table 5.3 provides the real after-tax return needed to make a 4 percent real hurdle. The hurdle rate presented here is obtained by adding the inflation rate to this real hurdle rate.

5. Feldstein and Elmendorf, "Budget Deficits," 12.

6. Some economists overlook this because they use figures that are not adjusted for inflation. For a wide variety of reasons the price of investment goods actually declined in the early 1980s while the price of most other goods continued to rise.

7. Steven F. Venti and David A. Wise, "The Determinants of IRA Contributions and the Effects of Limit Changes," in *Pensions and the U.S. Economy*, ed. Zvi Bodie, John Shoven, and David Wise (Chicago: University of Chicago Press, 1988).

8. Popular belief is that the effect was horrible, so it isn't too hard for the facts to indicate a better result. Our purpose here is not to argue that Americans should save more. Rather, it is to point out that the doomsayers are quite wide of the mark.

9. Much of the gain in the value of the house is due to inflation. The individual is not richer to the extent of the inflation. What we do here is to take

the inflationary gains into account by reducing the value of the house, and other assets, by the rise in the Consumer Price Index. This captures the real increase in the individual's wealth without counting the inflation.

10. *Balance Sheets for the U.S. Economy* are obtainable from the Board of Governors of the Federal Reserve System, Washington, D.C. 20551.

11. This data was computed by taking the nominal net worth of households at the end of each year as calculated by the Fed and dividing by the Consumer Price Index to get real net worth. Changes in real net worth represent the real saving of the household sector. This divided by real personal income provides the saving rate.

12. Internally generated funds as calculated by the Federal Reserve.

Chapter 9

1. *Wall Street Journal,* 17 March 1988.

2. Data compiled by the British Treasury is available from the Adam Smith Institute, 23 Great Smith Street, London SW1P 3BL.

3. *The Economist,* 18 March 1989, 14.

4. Much of this discussion appeared in an article by your author in "Socialism and the Supply Side in Sweden," *The Wall Street Journal,* 6 June 1988, European edition.

5. The expert on this subject is Alan Reynolds of Polyconomics, Morristown, New Jersey 07960, who has written numerous articles on this subject.

6. "U.S. Tax Cuts Go Global," *Fortune,* 29 November 1986, 131.

Chapter 10

1. *U.S. News and World Report,* 3 March 1986, 50.

2. See Martin Feldstein, ed., *The Effects of Taxation on Capital Accumulation* (Chicago: University of Chicago Press, 1989); one of the best compendiums of serious research in this area, it is a compilation of papers given at a conference sponsored by the National Bureau of Economic Research in the midst of the debate over tax reform, February 1986.

3. *The Tax Reform Act of 1986* P.L. 99-514, 22 Oct. 1986, 2687.

4. Ibid., 2687.

5. The 33 percent bracket was created to raise the average tax rate on the rich to the level of the top marginal rate of 28 percent. To do this, zero rated and low rated income had to be taxed at higher rates. To do this, the "tax savings" from having part of one's income in the 15 percent bracket and the personal exemptions that taxpayers get for themselves and their children were eliminated. Taxpayers lost these features at a 5 percent rate, thus adding 5 points on top of the existing 28 percent rate, making it 33 percent. After the tax tables have taken away everything taxed at low rates, the regular 28 percent rate again applies. Amazingly, some congressmen have proposed eliminating the perceived unfairness of this 5 percent phase out by raising the top rate to 33 percent directly.

6. Congressional Budget Office, *How Capital Gains Rates Affect Revenue: The Historical Evidence* (Washington, D.C.: United States Congressional Budget Office, March 1988).

7. Roger H. Gordon, James R. Hines, and Lawrence H. Summers, "Notes on the Tax Treatment of Structures," in *The Effects of Taxation on Capital Accumulation*, ed. Martin Feldstein (Chicago: University of Chicago Press, 1989).

Chapter 11

1. The following explanation of excess burden is intentionally simplified to provide the non-economist with a flavor of what is involved. Those wishing a more detailed explanation might select a good public finance textbook such as Harvey Rosen's *Public Finance* (Irwin: Homewood Illinois, 1985): 275–299. A classic work on excess burden and income taxation is provided by Michael Boskin, "The Efficiency Aspects of the Differential Tax Treatment of Market and Household Economic Activities," *Journal of Public Economics* 4 (1975):1–25.

2. Jude Wanniski, "Tax Revenues and the Laffer Curve," *The Public Interest*, (Winter 1978): 4–5.

3. An exception might be a case in which the government wanted a certain tax base to shrink. Thus concern about cancer might justify a severe tax on cigarette sales, as an attempt to make that particular tax base shrink. But the tax would raise less revenue than the present lower rate. The government would still have to make the implicit decision that the loss in revenue was "worth it" in order to reduce shrinking.

4. A more technical explanation of taxpayer behavior is given by the Theory of Demand. The demand curve provides the number of units people will buy at a given price. When a tax is imposed, the price rises and individuals choose to buy fewer goods. The excess burden provides the value, to the consumer, in excess of price paid, absent the tax, of the goods not purchased. Note in figures 11.1 and 11.2, taxpayers would have been willing to pay *some* tax on the goods not purchased. The tax that they would have been willing to pay had the rate been lower is a measure of how much excess burden (or forgone value) the higher rate imposes.

5. See Anthony Atkinson, *The Economics of Inequality* (Oxford: Oxford University Press, 1975), for a very thorough explanation of the competing theories.

6. A classic work by John Stuart Mill is *Principles of Political Economy*, ed. W. J. Ashley (London: Langmans', 1921).

7. Though this prescription may sound statist, Mill was very much an individualist. His fundamental concept was that total social welfare was the sum of the welfare enjoyed by each individual in society. Utilitarianism, Mill's underlying philosophy, is an important underpinning of free market thinking.

8. James McCullough, cited in Dan T. Smith, *Federal Tax Reform* (New York: McGraw Hill, 1961), 16.

Chapter 12

1. *The New Republic*, 17 October 1983, 4.

2. The estimate for FY89 as this book was going to press was $161 billion.

3. See for example Richard and Peggy Musgrave's *Public Finance in Theory and Practice* (New York: McGraw Hill, 1973), 551.

4. Consider, for example, the period 1965 to 1969 which saw a constant set of corporate tax rules (although a rate surcharge was imposed). While the

economy grew 36.7 percent, corporate tax receipts, adjusted downward for the surcharge, grew 64.3 percent on a NIPA basis. That would imply an elasticity of roughly 1.6, not 1.4. In the 1982–85 expansion (where the law was constant) corporate taxes grew 55.7 percent while the economy grew 26.8 percent, implying an elasticity of almost 1.9. The 1.4 elasticity shown here is an extrapolation for a longer run expansion.

5. This was the average rate of interest paid on outstanding publicly held debt during 1989 according to the 1990 Federal Budget.

Chapter 13

1. An excellent description of a cash flow corporation income tax is provided by Mervyn King in "The Cash Flow Corporate Income Tax" in *The Effects of Taxation on Capital Accumulation,* ed. Martin Feldstein (Chicago: University of Chicago Press, 1987).

2. See Jane Gravelle and Lawrence Lindsey's "Capital Gains" *Tax Notes* (25 January 1988), for a detailed discussion of the problems with this.

3. This issue was discussed by Lindsey in "Capital Gains Taxes Under Various Assumptions" in the *National Tax Journal* (September 1987, XL:3): 489–504.

Chapter 14

1. Excellent discussions of taxes and housing include Mervyn King's "An Econometric Model of Tenure Choice and the Demand for Housing as a Joint Decision," *Journal of Public Economics* 14 (1980):137–159, Patrick Henderschott's "Tax Changes and Capital Allocation in the 1980s" in *The Effects of Taxation on Capital Accumulation,* ed. Martin Feldstein (Chicago: University of Chicago Press, 1987), and Frank de Leeuw and Larry Ozannes's "Housing" in *How Taxes Affect Economic Behavior,* ed. Henry Aaron and Joseph Pechman (Washington: The Brookings Institution).

2. These assumptions are discussed in Lindsey's "Managing the Variability of the Social Security System With the Personal Income Tax" (Washington, D.C.: American Enterprise Institute, January 1989).

3. These are the actuarial assumptions used by the Social Security Administration.

Chapter 15

1. "Wealth," *North American Review,* June 1889.

2. *Historical Tables: Budget of the United States Government FY1990* (Washington, D.C.: U.S. Government Printing Office, 1989), 70–71.

3. Rudney, G. "Toward a Quantitative Profile of the Non-profit Sector" in *Program on Non-Profit Organizations* (New Haven: Yale University, 1981), 3.

4. An excellent review of this literature is given by Charles Clotfelter and Eugene Steuerle, "Charitable Contributions" in *How Taxes Affect Economic Behavior,* ed. Henry Aaron and Joseph Pechman (Washington, D.C.: The Brookings Institution, 1981), 403–446. Also highly recommended is Charles Clotfelter's *Federal*

Tax Policy and Charitable Giving (Cambridge: National Bureau of Economic Research; Chicago: University of Chicago Press, 1985).

5. Martin Feldstein and Lawrence Lindsey, "Simulating Nonlinear Tax Rules and Nonstandard Behavior: An Application to the Tax Treatment of Charitable Contributions" in *Behavioral Simulation Methods in the Policy Analysis,* ed. M. Feldstein (Chicago: University of Chicago Press, 1983).

Chapter 16

1. 1985 Individual Tax Model File Public Use Sample available from the Internal Revenue Service and the NBER TAXSIM model.

2. An excellent early study of this issue was Harvey Rosen's "Is It Time to Abandon Joint Filing?" *National Tax Journal,* 30 (December 1977):423–428.

3. U.S. Congress, House of Representatives, Committee on Ways and Means Hearing, "Forty Topics Pertaining to the General Revision of the Internal Revenue Act," (Washington, D.C.: U.S. Government Printing Office, 1953), 27.

4. *General Explanation of the Tax Reform Act of 1986* prepared by the staff of the Joint Committee on Taxation (Washington, D.C.: U.S. Government Printing Office, 1987), 19.

Chapter 17

1. Robert Hall and Alvin Rabushka proposed a 19% tax rate in the early 1980s. See for example: *Low Tax, Simple Tax, Flat Tax.* New York: McGraw Hill, 1983.

Index